IMAGES
of America

METCALFE COUNTY

I0805804

On the Cover: Logging was a way of life for many living in Metcalfe County. Four mules are pulling what is believed to be a white oak log through the Wisdom community sometime between 1890 and 1900. The store in the background is the Young-Shirley Store, which is still standing today at the intersection of US Highway 68 and Kentucky Highway 640. (Courtesy of Richard Young.)

IMAGES
of America

METCALFE COUNTY

Richard Hines and Dean Rowe

ARCADIA
PUBLISHING

ISBN 978-1-4671-0788-4

Published by Arcadia Publishing
Charleston, South Carolina

Printed in the United States of America

Library of Congress Control Number: 2021949379

For all general information, please contact Arcadia Publishing:
Telephone 843-853-2070
Fax 843-853-0044
E-mail sales@arcadiapublishing.com
For customer service and orders:
Toll-Free 1-888-313-2665

Visit us on the Internet at www.arcadiapublishing.com

To the past, present, and future residents of Metcalfe County,
let us not forget our past and share it with the future.

Contents

ACKNOWLEDGMENTS

This history of Metcalfe County would not have been possible except for the efforts and cooperation of numerous people who helped us obtain photographs and information. In one instance we found one door closed, but the result was phenomenal, as we met new friends who wanted to assure that the story of Metcalfe County would be told.

We are extremely grateful to Cora Emma Jessie, who not only opened her collection of photographs but shared her knowledge of Sulphur Well and Metcalfe County. Barry and Nora Gilley provided photographs and helped with historical fact checking. Dr. Nancy Richey (Western Kentucky University Special Collections) assisted with many aspects of the project. Many others who made the book possible by loaning material were Gaye Shaw and the Edmonton-Metcalfe Chamber of Commerce, Richard Young of the Kentucky Headhunters, Jody Curry, Willard Parnell, Stanley Harbison, Joe and Pricilla McDonald, Metcalfe County Extension Service, Gary Richardson, Carol Hurt, Doug Smith, Dawn Devore, City of Edmonton, Henry and Bonnie Froggett, Cathy Nunn, Phil Refbord, Ed Bell, Danny Froggett, Brandon Bell, Benny Lile, Freeda Reece, Johnny Thompson, Edmonton State Bank, Laurie Butler, Frankie Bell, Stephen Glass, Tom Emberton, Sharon Howard Bowles, Julian Campbell, Freddie Ray, Donnie Butler, Larry Wilson, Jeneve Crenshaw, Ricky Parnell, Cathy Nunn, Reba Gravens Norman, Marla Young, Cebie Edwards, Tudor and P.J. Martin, Edmonton *Herald-News*, Sherron Westerfield, and Sarah Dorpinghaus (Goodman-Paxton Photographic Collection, University of Kentucky Libraries Special Collections Research Center).

To our wives, Gena Rowe, who helped with the book organization throughout the project, and Pam Hines, who retyped the manuscript, helped with page organization, and kept the process going!

Throughout the research for this book, the authors accumulated a great deal of historical material and photographs, which we felt should be available for future projects. With the permission of the owners who graciously provided photographs and other material, the authors have donated high-resolution images and documents to Western Kentucky University Special Collections to assist future researchers to continue building on our findings about Metcalfe County.

Introduction

Prior to the arrival of early explorers, the area encompassing Metcalfe County was first occupied at the end of the ice age 11,000 years ago by Native Americans. At that time, the area was coniferous forests dominated by spruce and jack pine; however, as the climate began warming, forests shifted from coniferous to deciduous tree species, like today's Metcalfe County forests. Even today, scattered stands of hemlock trees that were once common in earlier forests are still present along cool, north-facing cliffs bordering the South Fork of the Little Barren River.

Today, rock tools, pottery, and projectiles are all that remain of once large numbers of Native American encampments along major streams in the area. These streams provided Native Americans with fish, mussels, and a wide range of aquatic foods, while adjacent floodplain forests supplied hickory, mulberry, and walnut. Higher ridges, particularly in the eastern portion of the county, were dominated by oak, tulip poplar, beech, and American chestnut.

Fires were set annually by Native Americans, both to drive game during hunts and to attract game. Following the fires, native grasses and forbs respond rapidly, sending up new growth and helping attract game. Over thousands of years, these annual fires created extensive grasslands devoid of trees, which settlers called barrens. Most of the barrens were covered in grasses such as little bluestem, big bluestem, and numerous wildflowers. Within the barrens were isolated groves of post oak and blackjack oak. Both of these species are relatively fire resistant due to thicker bark.

Giant cane (river cane) was prominent along stream bottoms where annual fires helped regenerate this native bamboo further, making it attractive forage for elk and bison. Settlers adapted the practice of grazing cattle on the cane.

Elk and bison frequented the edges of grasslands, feeding on acorns in adjacent woodlands and seasonally moving into heavily forested areas to forage on chestnuts. It was along these edges where hunters encountered black bear, turkey, and the red wolf. They would have seen massive flocks of passenger pigeons feeding on beech mast in forests in the eastern portion of the county, and swampy areas, still present in several sections of Metcalfe County, would have attracted migrating waterfowl and sandhill cranes.

By the 1760s, long hunters, so named because their hunts extended over a period of a year or more in the wilderness, began traveling into present-day Metcalfe County. One of the most significant features not just in this area but in Kentucky was Big Blue Spring. Noted on John Filson's map of Kentucky, Big Blue Spring was bounded by heavy timber for a mile on each side, a feature that stood out in the barrens. Big Blue Spring was an important stop and was known as a good place to harvest deer or buffalo. There is little doubt that Big Blue Spring had been important for perhaps thousands of years. During later years, Big Blue Spring was mentioned in many land patents. The spring was well known to the first settlers, who used two major Indian trails later called the Great Warriors Trail and the Lexington-Nashville Trail. Another natural feature making the area attractive to hunters were the numerous mineral licks. Across Metcalfe County, sulfur, salts, and other elements continue seeping from the ground in the same springs that once attracted elk and bison. One Metcalfe County community, Knob Lick, is named after one of these mineral licks. Because game congregated near these licks, long hunters sought out mineral licks to harvest game.

One reference to these expeditions, described by Cyrus Edwards, tells of a hunt led by Henry Skeggs in spring of 1769. Skeggs "went with a large party of explorers, hunters and trappers through the Cumberland Gap and the Cumberland and Green Rivers to the border of the barrens, (now Metcalfe County)." The long hunters remained in the area for several years. Henry Skeggs later settled in the area and is buried in northern Metcalfe County.

While the original barrens extended into far western Kentucky, many accounts show that the early barrens began along the South Fork of the Little Barren River. Some refer to this river as the "ancient fire line of the Barrens." As early settlers looked west of the South Fork, it is easy to understand why many remained near the forested lands, opting not to move farther west. There is one account in 1808 of a traveler who had expected the barrens to be a desolate land but was surprised by the abundant grass and wildflowers.

By the spring of 1791, eight years after the Revolutionary War, in what would become Metcalfe, some of the first permanent settlements had appeared in Lincoln County, Virginia, including the villages of Frederick (Center), Savoyard, and Knob Lick. In the 1790s, settlement was rapid. Land grants called military warrants, the first step in land patents, were given as payment for military service. Each allotment was determined by rank and time in service for the Revolutionary War, Indian Wars, and War of 1812, but early settlement was perilous, with numerous skirmishes between settlers and Indians. During one of these skirmishes, Stephen McKinney, who had built a station on land granted from a military warrant along the South Fork of the Little Barren, was killed during an Indian attack in 1792.

Edmund Rogers (1762–1843) came to the area in 1783 to begin surveying the Green River area with his cousin George Rogers Clark. Rogers had served in the Virginia campaign of the Revolutionary War in the battles of Green Springs and Jamestown and was also present during the surrender of Cornwallis. By 1800, Rogers had established Edmunton (original spelling) on his land. In April 1818, Rogers began advertising for people to build and establish businesses in Edmunton. A portion of that advertisement stipulated that within two years the purchasers "shall put up and complete a house of hewed logs, frame, brick or stone, not less than 20 feet square, two stories high with a brick or stone chimney." Rogers also specified that two acres would be left in the center of town for a town square.

Rogers further added that "this town combines many advantages, being high and healthy, well-watered, and in a neighborhood, of the richest timbered land in the county."

Present-day Metcalfe County was originally in the Virginia county of Kentucky, which was later divided into Lincoln County (Virginia) until 1792, when Kentucky became a state. At that time, it was part of Green County until 1793, when portions of Green County were divided into Barren and Monroe Counties.

During the mid-1800s, Kentucky continued creating new counties. One bill in 1856 proposed establishing Bibb County in what would be the present-day location of Metcalfe County. That bill failed. During the same year, additional bills in the Kentucky General Assembly proposed creating a county in honor of the 10th governor of Kentucky, Thomas Metcalfe. Two locations were proposed. The first involved splitting land from Fleming and Carter Counites, while the second recommended splitting land from Hopkins and Union Counties. Both proposals failed.

Finally, in January 1860, a bill to establish the County of Metcalfe out of parts of Barren, Monroe, Cumberland, Adair, and Green Counties passed. The act, established by the General Assembly, stated "that from the first Monday in May 1860, all the parts of Barren, Adair, Cumberland, and Monroe counties . . . stricken from said counties and erected into one county called Metcalfe."

Thomas Metcalfe, who served as governor from 1828 to 1832, was also a captain in the War of 1812, served in Congress from 1819 to 1828, and was part of the Kentucky Senate from 1834 to 1838. Metcalfe, who had been a stonemason by trade, was given the name "Old Stone Hammer."

Within a year of Metcalfe County's establishment, the Civil War erupted, and Metcalfe men answered the call. In Judge Joseph Martin's *History of Metcalfe County*, he lists over 100 men who enlisted in the Union army while fewer than a dozen Metcalfe County residents served in the Confederate army. One of these was Dr. George Washington Sandridge, who served as an army surgeon.

Metcalfe County avoided many of the larger battles that occurred across Kentucky. One skirmish occurred near Edmonton between the 5th Indiana Cavalry and the 1st Brigade of Morgan's Calvary.

Throughout the war, there were numerous examples of Metcalfe County's support for the Union, as was common for Kentucky's Republican counties. One newspaper article described Edwin Ferguson, a bugler killed in a skirmish, who was remembered by Metcalfe Countians as the person who pulled down the Confederate flag that had been raised on the square in Edmonton and raised the stars and stripes.

During a public meeting on the Edmonton Square on February 23, 1863, Metcalfe residents made it clear "that although Metcalfe Countians live in close proximity to scenes of border warfare, where guerrillas, horse thieves, and robbers' prey upon our property and seek to intimidate us, we have not forgotten our duty to our government," as reported by the Louisville *Daily Journal* on March 3, 1863. This statement demonstrates the seriousness of guerrilla fighters. Bands of guerrillas were originally comprised of military units but later in the war were primarily nonmilitary personnel or military personnel who had gone rogue—deserters, murderers, thieves, and even runaway slaves.

Throughout the war, small guerrilla raids took place, but in many cases, because Metcalfe County residents remained armed, they were able to fight off numerous attacks. In one such attack, there is an account of guerrillas attempting to fire on the storehouse of the Newman family in the Rockland Mills community, but those inside fired back and kept them away, enabling the Newmans to save their building.

In January 1864, the county began soliciting bids for the construction of a new courthouse, which was completed in 1865. However, the new courthouse did not last long. In one of the largest raids by guerrilla fighters from Tennessee in March 1865, a group of 75 riders began robbing and killing across northern Tennessee, then moved into Kentucky, where they robbed and burned the Louisville & Nashville Railroad (L&N) train near Glasgow. Following this raid, they came to Randolph (Wisdom) where "they robbed everybody they met," according to the *Courier Journal*. When they arrived in Edmonton, the guerrillas burned the courthouse and clerk's office and robbed merchants of some $5,000 of goods and money, all while killing and wounding several Metcalfe residents. The group was said to be a combination of the Smith, Bennett, and Gentry gangs from central Tennessee.

Following the raid, the courthouse was rebuilt, but burned a second time due to a chimney fire. In 1868, the courthouse was moved to the town square when the current building was constructed there.

Two distinguished sons of Metcalfe County were described in 1907, when the story was told of Dominie Hodges, who found himself in the barrens during the 1850s broke and without a job. Hodges, a Yale graduate, was promptly hired to tutor the son and nephew of a prosperous farmer in the Chicken Bristle community in mathematics, Greek, and Latin. The two boys would later become famous. William H. Newman became president of the New York Central Railroad, and Eugene Newman became a noted newspaper columnist who used the pen name "Savoyard" in his political essays published in the *Courier Journal* and dozens of other newspapers.

For many years, travel into Metcalfe was difficult. There were several efforts to establish railroads that would have traversed the county,but all failed. One railroad planned in 1885 was to pass through Summer Shade, while another line connecting Glasgow with the river port at Burkesville failed to obtain needed funding. One proposal in 1906 that showed much promise would have passed through Edmonton, connecting Stanford and Nashville.

While surrounding counties had access to rivers and later railroads, Metcalfe County did not have easy contact with outside communities. The current route of Kentucky Route 90 was originally a stagecoach route for the Keen and Baker Glasgow-Burkesville Stage line, which changed horses in Summer Shade and Beaumont before going on to the next destination. Another stage line ran between Center through the Echo community to Tompkinsville. As today's residents drive Highway 90, they can see a sign for the John Muir Trail, which marks the location of Muir's 1,000-mile walk from Indianapolis to the Gulf of Mexico in September 1867. Muir's walk took him through Summer Shade and southern Metcalfe County.

Today, two major highways connect Metcalfe with other locations, the Cumberland Parkway, which later changed its name to the Louis B. Nunn Parkway, and US Route 68. According to a Kentucky Department of Transportation map published in 1938, only three roads—Kentucky Route 80 (KY 80), Kentucky Route 90 (KY 90), and Kentucky Route 163 (KY 163)—existed at that time. It was not until 1948 that US Highway 68 was given its current alignment between Perryville and Bowling Green when it took over a section of KY 163 between Edmonton and Sulphur Well. The oldest road in Metcalfe County, originally the stagecoach line, is KY 90, which was chartered into Kentucky's highway system in 1929.

One of the most notable attractions in Metcalfe County was the Beula Villa Hotel in Sulphur Well. Built in 1903 by Catlett W. Thompson, the Beula Villa was known nationwide and provided guests with lodging, meals, and entertainment when they came to drink the mineral water believed to have medicinal value. Because of the hotel, Sulphur Well grew, and by the 1960s, the town had added a dance hall and a bowling alley. All these businesses were centered around the famous artesian well discovered by Ezekiel Neal in 1845 as he drilled for saltwater. The hotel was later taken over by King C. Crenshaw in 1920, who operated the business until 1969. Although efforts were made to reopen the hotel, it remained closed and was abandoned and later burned by an arsonist.

Numerous other communities also developed across the county. Each was possibly centered around either a church or school, but more likely near a post office and general store. These stores were the hub of the community, providing locations where residents could catch up on local and national news.

Metcalfe County has always been an important source of agriculture products, primarily tobacco, horses, and beef, followed by row crops. Although only a few trees or scattered groves of trees existed in the western portion of Metcalfe around 1800, forests grew rapidly, and along with the forests in the eastern section of the county, Metcalfe became an important lumber source supporting numerous sawmill operations from the 1800s until the present. The county also had several gristmills that milled grain for markets across Kentucky.

Oil and gas operations have been active, with leases on both being sold as early as 1865. In 1959, Metcalfe County earned notoriety when several successful shallow wells were drilled, helping Kentucky set a record in oil production.

In 1971, Metcalfe Countian Tom Emberton was the Republican candidate for governor but was defeated by Wendel Ford. Emberton was appointed to the Kentucky Court of Appeals in 1987 and served until 2004.

Over the past century, several musicians covering a wide range of genres have called Metcalfe County home, from Chic Hurt with the Prairie Ramblers and Lonzo and Oscar to the Kentucky Headhunters and Black Stone Cherry.

In 2021, Metcalfe County remains one of the larger producers of burley tobacco in the United States. The county also produces other agriculture products, including dairy, hay, and poultry, and a wide range of horticulture products such as blueberries and pumpkins.

Over the past two centuries, Edmonton and Summer Shade have supported factories in Metcalfe, including Tops, a clothing manufacture that operated from 1952 until 2020, as well as small manufacturing operations selling truck bed rails, barrel staves, and pallets. These factories have continued providing jobs into the 21st century. Today, Metcalfe Countians are employed at numerous light industries, including Sumitomo Electric Wiring Systems, Carhart, Kingsford Charcoal, KL Woodland Management, Parks Panel Processing, and numerous sawmills. In 2021, the county welcomed Pennington Stave and Cooperage, which will provide barrels for Kentucky's bourbon industry.

Over the years, Metcalfe County has retained its rural roots, outdoor atmosphere, and small-town appeal, making it an attractive destination for many.

One

Before Metcalfe County

Long hunters were attracted to Metcalfe County, and one of the earliest accounts of them is from 1788. Henry Skeggs guided a party into the barrens, where he mentioned traveling the Warrior Trail to Big Blue Spring at the head of Blue Spring Creek. The other trail was called the Lexington-Nashville Trail and went from Greensburg through Edmonton.

By 1802, Skeggs made his home in Metcalfe County where he told stories of the early days around Big Blue Spring. One told of approaching six Indians at the spring who had been part of a raiding party. After gunfire, Skeggs discovered the possessions of a settler who had been killed by the Indians. One of the Indians killed that day was known as "old Cinquo," a renegade Creek who had been expelled from his nation. Skeggs lived out the rest of his life in northwestern Metcalfe County.

A large portion of Metcalfe County was granted through military warrants. Through the Act of 1788, land patents granted free land in the public domain to soldiers and sailors of the Continental Army. The acreage of each patent was determined by rank and time in service. Enlisted personnel obtained 100 acres, while officers received from 200 to 1,100 acres. These land warrants were issued from 1789 to 1833; they also were granted to veterans of the War of 1812.

Not all soldiers wanted free land in such a desolate location. A newspaper advertisement in 1808 offered 822 acres of military patented land on the Little Barren River, either for sale or in exchange for land in Richmond, Virginia.

With all the resources at hand, times were still hard financially. In August 1827, Edmund Rogers wrote a letter to Nimrod Bailey stating that "there is little or no money in our county." Rogers was hoping the Kentucky legislature would create a new county, which he was certain would specify Edmonton as the county seat. Rogers believed this would attract more settlers, further improving economic conditions for the area. It would be another 33 years before Metcalfe became a county.

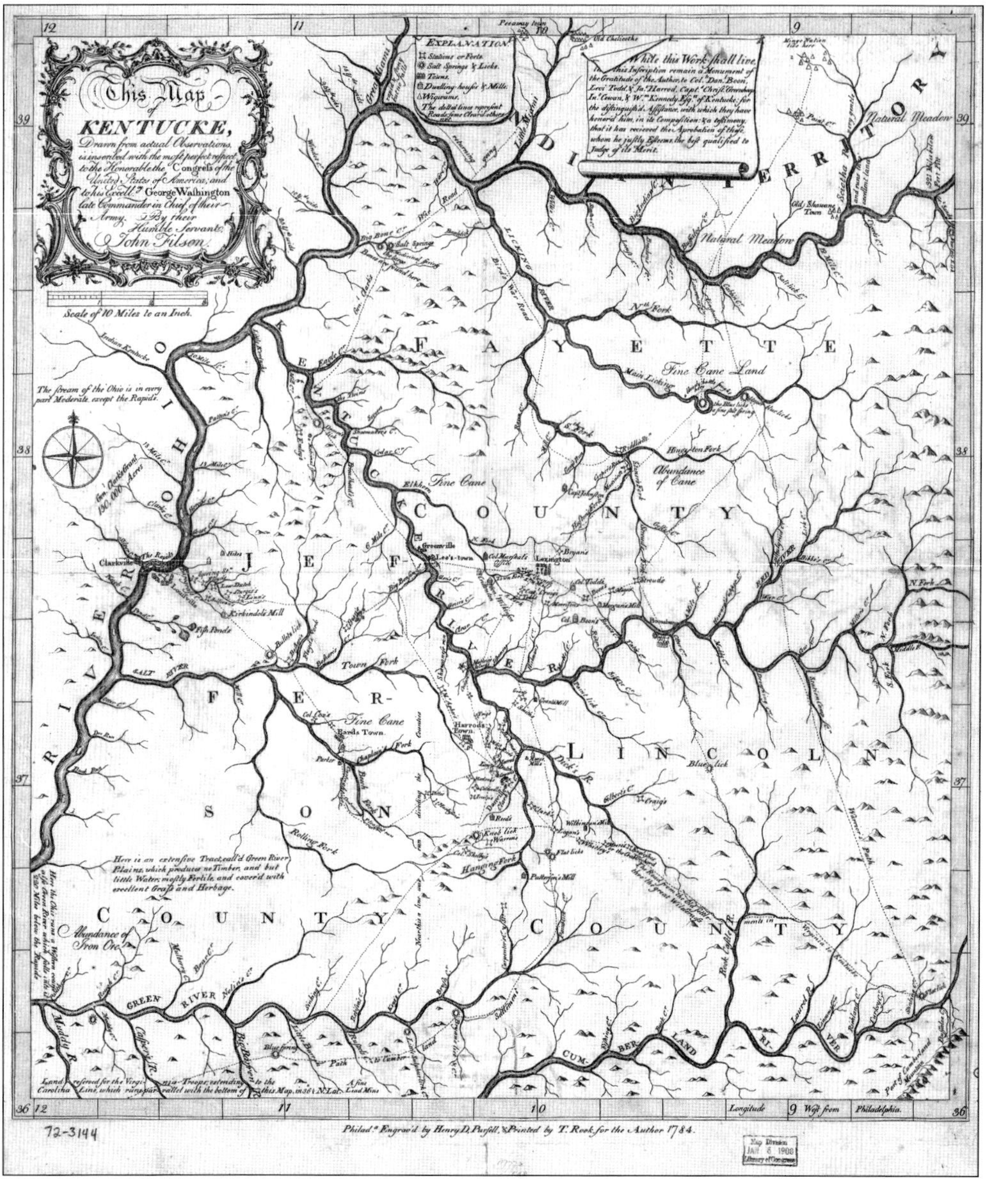

The first map of Kentucky was developed by John Filson in 1784 showing it as Fayette and Lincoln Counties. Filson's 1784 map shows the location of Blue Spring and the intersection of two major Indian trails that were later used as settler roads for those traveling west into the barrens. Filson also referred to this extensive open area as the "Green River Plains." (Courtesy of Western Kentucky University Special Collections.)

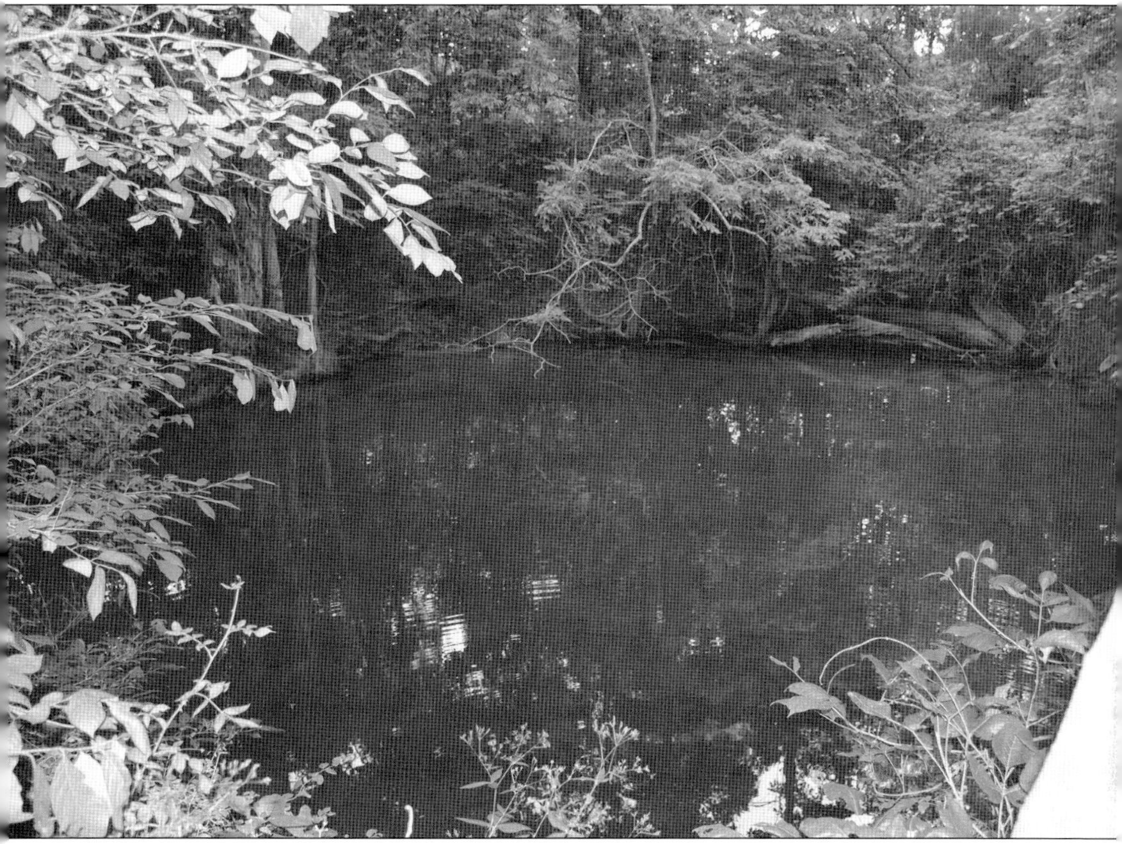

In 2021, Blue Spring, later referred to as Big Blue Spring, continues running a steady stream of water. Early accounts describe skirmishes between long hunters and Indians at the spring. While open barrens surrounded the spring, the spring and the creek were situated within a large stand of timber, 2,000 to 3,000 acres in size. The spring, in private ownership, continues being protected. (Photograph by Richard Hines.)

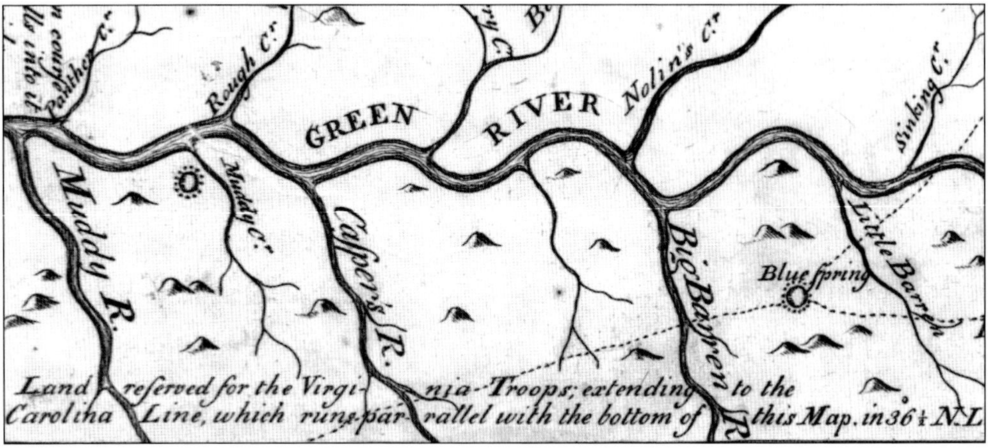

This enlargement from John Filson's 1784 map of Kentucky shows Blue Spring just west of the Little Barren River and the intersection of the Lexington-Nashville Trail and the Warriors Trail, which led from the Chattanooga, Tennessee, area to the Falls of the Ohio at today's Louisville, Kentucky. (Courtesy of Western Kentucky University Special Collections.)

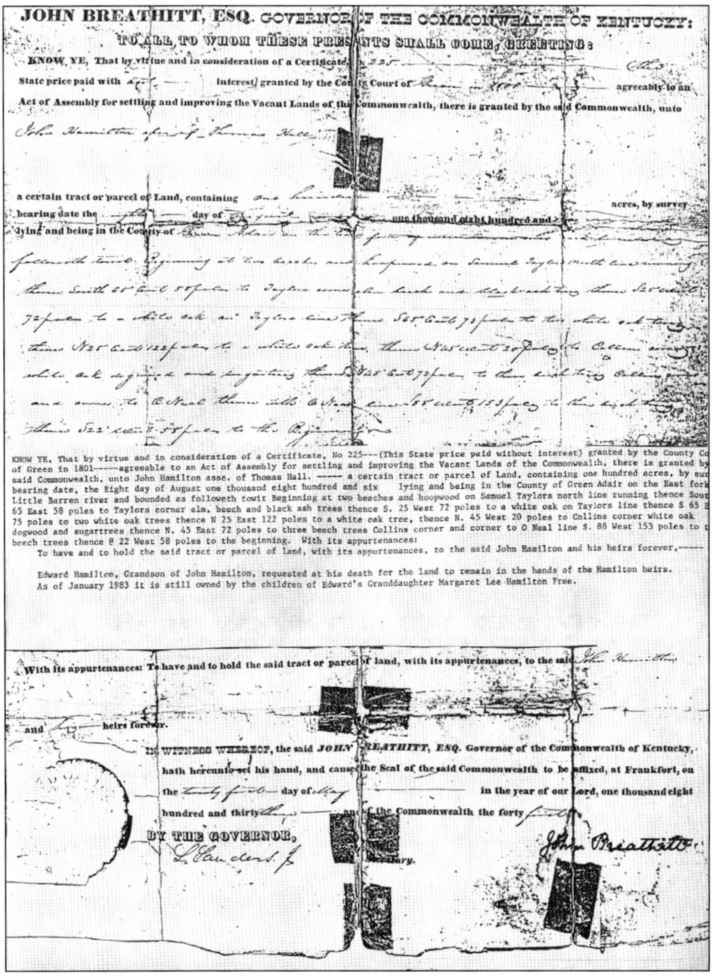

JOHN BREATHITT, ESQ. GOVERNOR OF THE COMMONWEALTH OF KENTUCKY:

TO ALL, TO WHOM THESE PRESENTS SHALL COME, GREETING:

KNOW YE, That by virtue and in consideration of a Certificate, No 225 [illegible] State price paid with [illegible] interest) granted by the County Court of [illegible] agreeably to an Act of Assembly for settling and improving the Vacant Lands of this Commonwealth, there is granted by the said Commonwealth, unto [illegible]

a certain tract or parcel of Land, containing [illegible] acres, by survey bearing date the [illegible] day of [illegible] one thousand eight hundred and [illegible] lying and being in the County of [illegible]

KNOW YE, That by virtue and in consideration of a Certificate, No 225---(This State price paid without interest) granted by the County Co of Green in 1801-----agreeable to an Act of Assembly for settling and improving the Vacant Lands of the Commonwealth, there is granted by said Commonwealth, unto John Hamilton asse. of Thomas Hall. ----- a certain tract or parcel of Land, containing one hundred acres, by sur bearing date, the Eight day of August one thousand eight hundred and six lying and being in the County of Green Adair on the East fork Little Barren river and bounded as followeth towit Beginning at two beeches and hoopwood on Samuel Taylors north line running thence Sout 65 East 58 poles to Taylors corner elm, beech and black ash trees thence S. 25 West 72 poles to a white oak on Taylors line thence S 65 E 75 poles to two white oak trees thence N 25 East 122 poles to a white oak tree, thence N. 45 West 20 poles to Collins corner white oak dogwood and sugartrees thence N. 45 East 72 poles to three beech trees Collins corner and corner to O Neal line S. 88 West 153 poles to t beech trees thence @ 22 West 58 poles to the beginning. With its appurtenances:

To have and to hold the said tract or parcel of land, with its appurtenances, to the said John Hamilton and his heirs forever,-----

Edward Hamilton, Grandson of John Hamilton, requested at his death for the land to remain in the hands of the Hamilton heirs. As of January 1983 it is still owned by the children of Edward's Granddaughter Margaret Lee Hamilton Free.

With its appurtenances: To have and to hold the said tract or parcel of land, with its appurtenances, to the said [illegible] and [illegible] heirs forever.

IN WITNESS WHEREOF, the said JOHN BREATHITT, ESQ. Governor of the Commonwealth of Kentucky, hath hereunto set his hand, and caused the Seal of the said Commonwealth to be affixed, at Frankfort, on the [illegible] day of [illegible] in the year of our Lord, one thousand eight hundred and thirty [illegible] and of the Commonwealth the forty [illegible]

BY THE GOVERNOR,

[illegible] Secretary.

John Breathitt

Soldiers and sailors who served in the Continental Army during the Revolutionary War were paid with land grants called military patents. John Hamilton, who migrated from Ireland to America, served in the 3rd Maryland Regiment as an ordnance sergeant, for which he received 100 acres on the East Fork of the Little Barren River. (Courtesy of Brookshier family.)

Edmund Pendleton Rogers, born in 1762, was only a teenager when he served as a soldier in the Continental Army. Rogers, who was in several battles, later became a dispatch carrier for George Washington. After the war, Rogers was issued military warrants by Gov. Patrick Henry of Virginia granting him the land where he settled in 1800. Rogers established Edmunton in 1818; he died there in 1843. Edmunton's name was later changed to Edmonton. Rogers and his wife are buried in the Edmonton Cemetery. (Courtesy of Freddie Ray.)

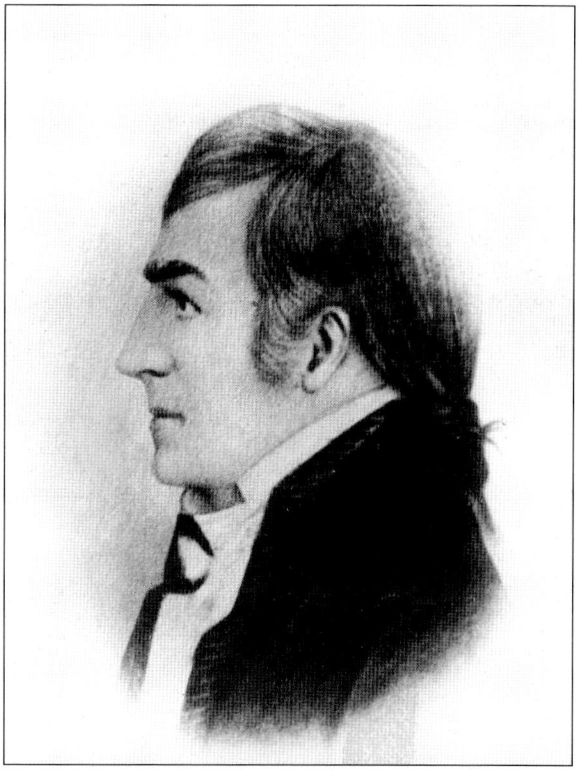

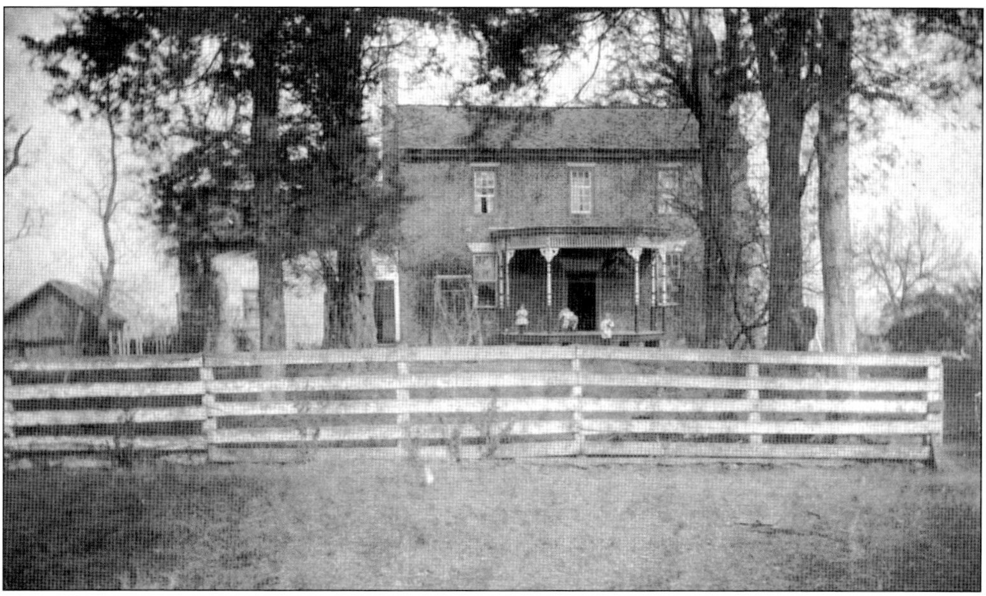

The oldest home in Metcalfe County was built in 1808 by Rev. Robert Stockton. A Revolutionary War chaplain, Stockton was captured by the British at Brandywine and held from 1777 to 1779. He later settled near Edmonton in 1799. Stockton was a pioneer Baptist preacher who helped form the Strawberry and Green River Baptist Associations and was also noted as having established Dripping Springs Baptist Church near Wisdom. This photograph of his house was taken around 1900. (Courtesy of Freddie Ray.)

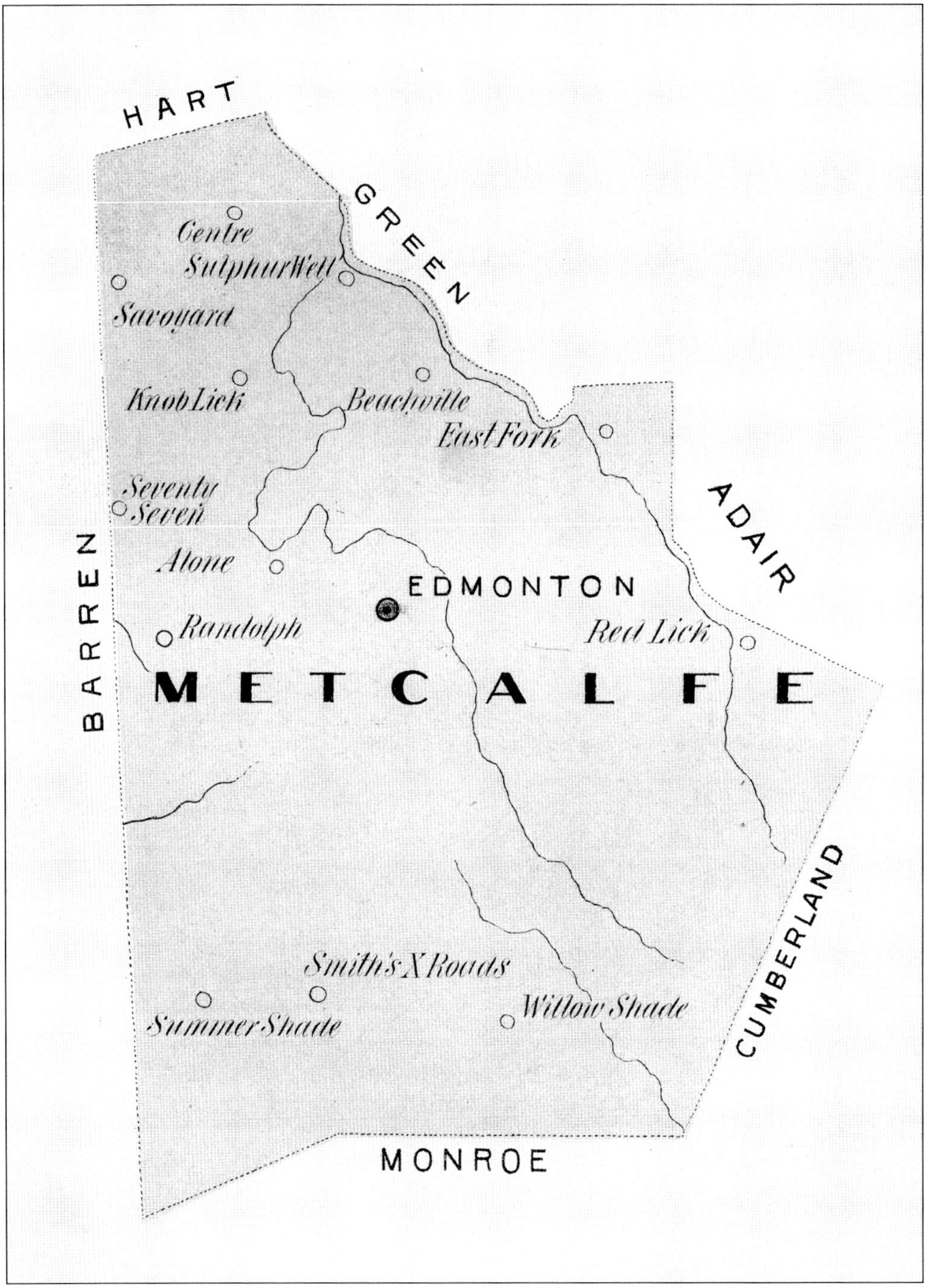

When Metcalfe County was designated by the General Assembly in 1860, the act stated, "That from and after the first Monday in May 1860, all the parts of Barren, Green, Adair, Cumberland, and Monroe Counties, lying with the designed boundary were stricken from said counties." Slight modifications were made in 1861 that added an additional 10 square miles (6,400 acres) from Adair County to better suit local property owners, with the resulting boundary lines shown here. (Courtesy of Western Kentucky University Special Collections.)

Two

EDMONTON

The city of Edmonton was named for Edmund Rogers, who settled in Barren County (now Metcalfe County) in 1800. In 1818, Rogers began advertising for persons to settle in the area, which he said, "in all probability will be a new seat of justice for a new court, should there ever be made in that section of the county." The town was carefully planned, and those settling there were given a contract in which they would have two years to "put up and complete a house of hewed logs, frame brick or stone, not less than twenty feet square, two stories high with a brick or stone chimney." People who met these requirements in two years were given the property debt-free.

Twelve years later, the first post office opened on February 18, 1830, with the original spelling of Edmunton; however, the town name was later changed to the current spelling.

When Metcalfe County was established in 1860, the population of Edmonton was around 70 residents. Today, the population of Edmonton is approximately 1,600.

Edmonton operated under city government from 1867 until 1871, when the Kentucky General Assembly passed an act incorporating the city. The present government was established in 1945, with Donnie Butler serving as the first mayor in 1964.

Throughout the early part of the 19th century and into the 1970s, the Edmonton Square was a vibrant business center, and it was said that "you could buy everything you need on the square." However, as transportation improved and chain stores began opening in nearby towns, business on the square dropped. Recently, the loss of Tops clothing manufacturing also dropped the number of visitors to the square.

Edmonton did make national news as World War II was about to begin when Metcalfe County judge W.W. Kelly was asked by the mayor of Edmonton, England, to help finance a new Spitfire fighter plane for the Royal Air Force. Three cities named Edmonton (in Alberta, England, and Kentucky) were to partner on a plane named *Edmonton*. Kelly declined to send any money and told reporters that "he couldn't spare the money to pay the costs of a cablegram to answer the Edmonton England Mayor."

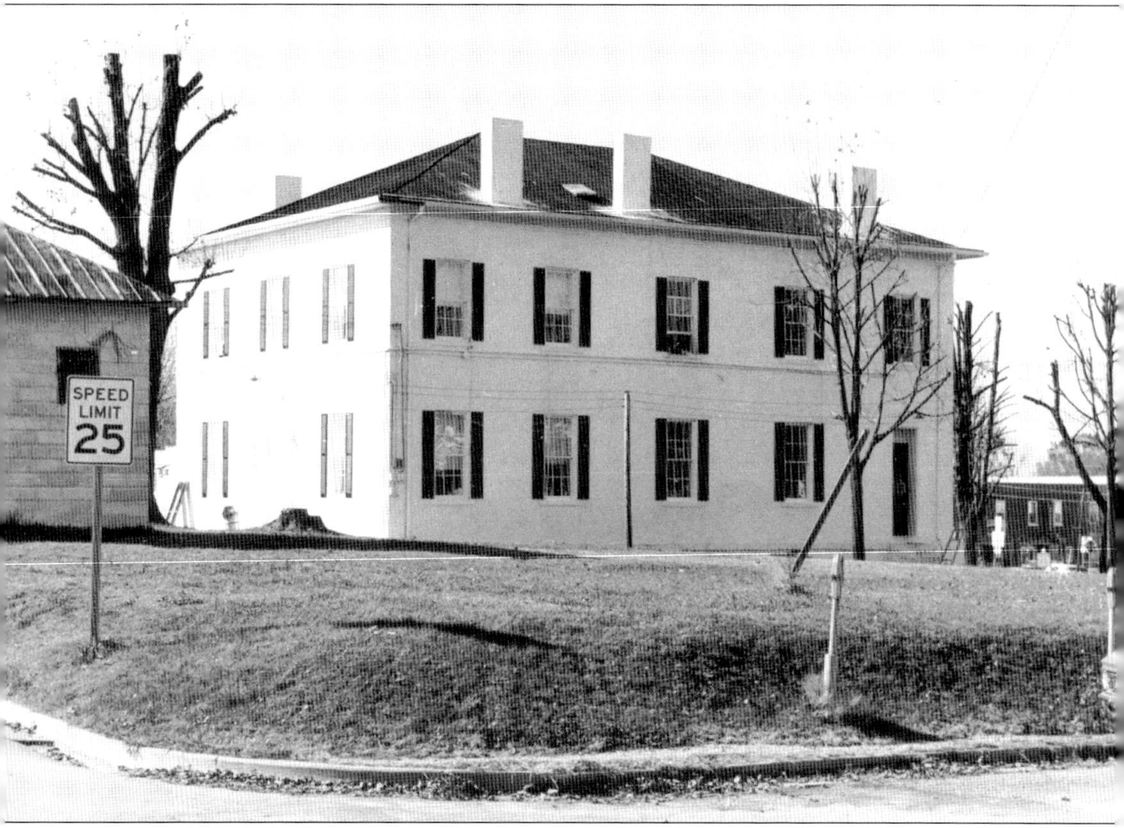

The most significant building on the Edmonton Square is the Metcalfe County Courthouse. Built in 1868, this was the third courthouse and the only one built on the square. The first courthouse was burned by guerrilla raiders in 1865, and the second was destroyed as the result of a chimney fire. This building functioned for Metcalfe County government business until a new justice center was built in 2003 and the Metcalfe County Government Center was constructed in 2018. (Courtesy of Cathy Nunn.)

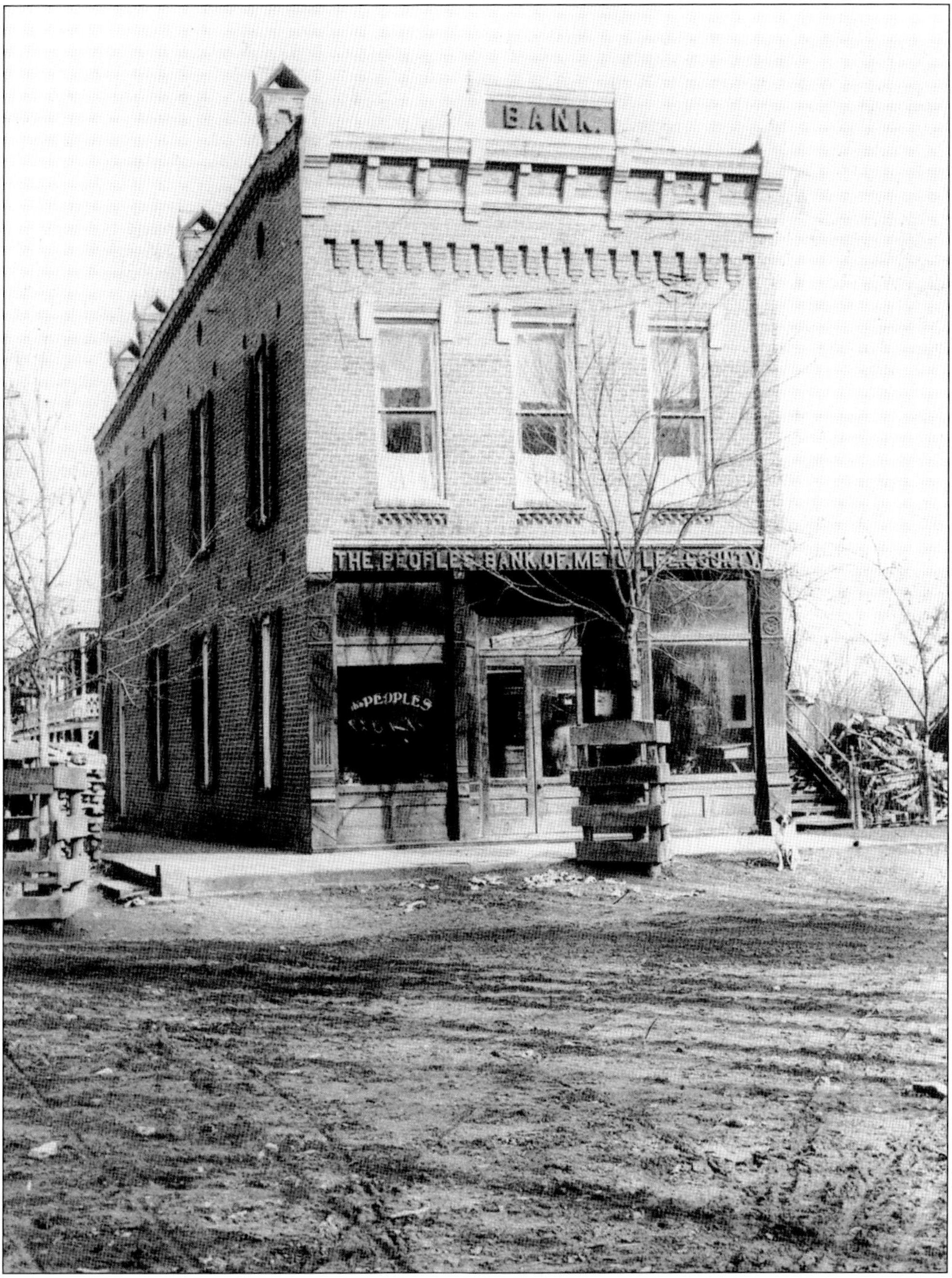

One of the first banks in Edmonton was on the square. It was originally the People's Bank of Metcalfe County, established in 1898 by C.W. Thompson, who served as bank president until his death in 1919. At this time, the square and all the streets in Edmonton were dirt. Decorative trees that had been planted along the streets had to be protected from horses, which were tied to the trees. Note the firewood stacked on each side of the bank, which was used for a wood stove, the only source of heat for the bank. (Courtesy of Edmonton State Bank.)

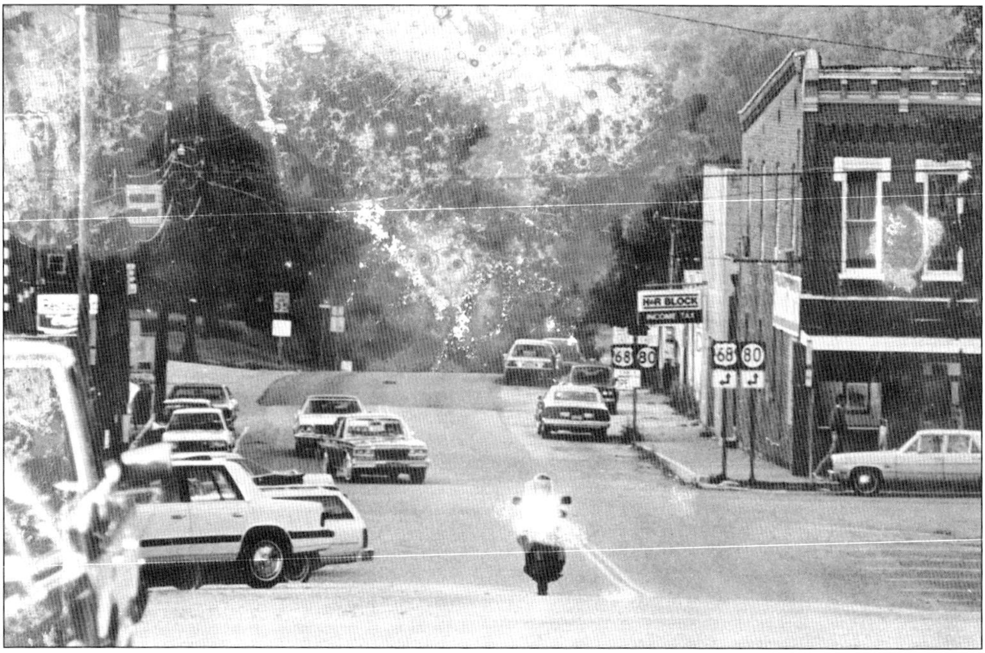

Seventy years later, the same location shows the old People's Bank at the intersections of US Highway 68/KY 80 and KY 163. This building is the current office of Metcalfe County attorney Barry Gilley. The iron steps on the east side of the building were forged by ironsmith Leroy Ford. (Courtesy of Barry Gilley.)

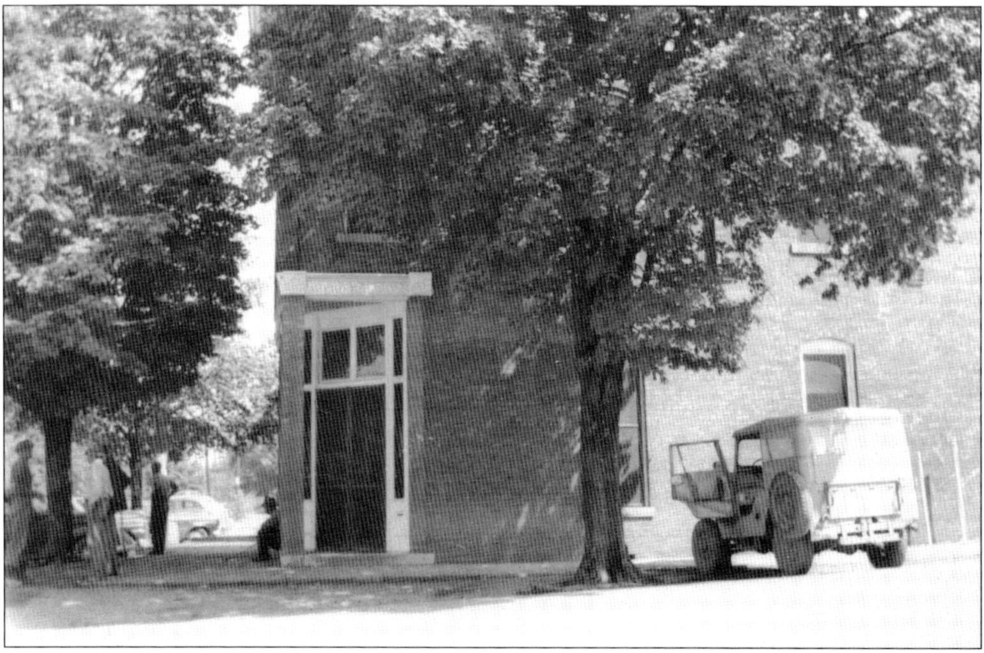

Shown here in the late 1940s, shortly after World War II, are the Farmer and Merchant Bank, built in 1908 on the south side of the square, and a Willys jeep, which were very common after the war. Even into the early 1950s, jeeps helped farmers who lived on dirt back roads get into town when those roads were previously only passable with horse and wagons. (Courtesy of Cathy Nunn.)

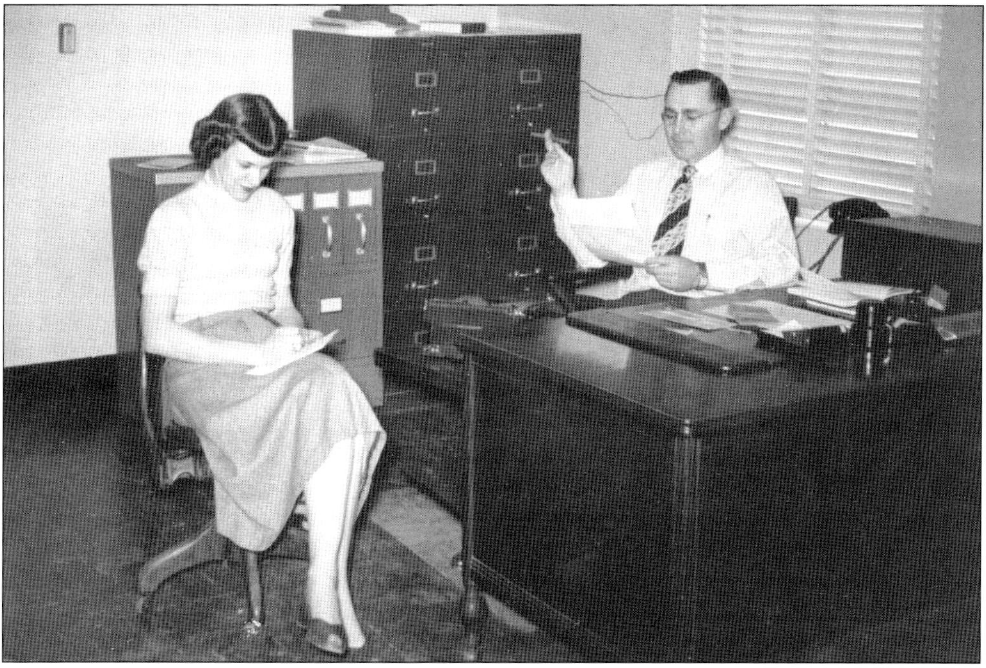

In this typical office scene in the 1950s, Edmonton State Bank president John Thompson is working with his secretary Geneva Butler on correspondence and various other daily bank duties. (Courtesy of Edmonton State Bank.)

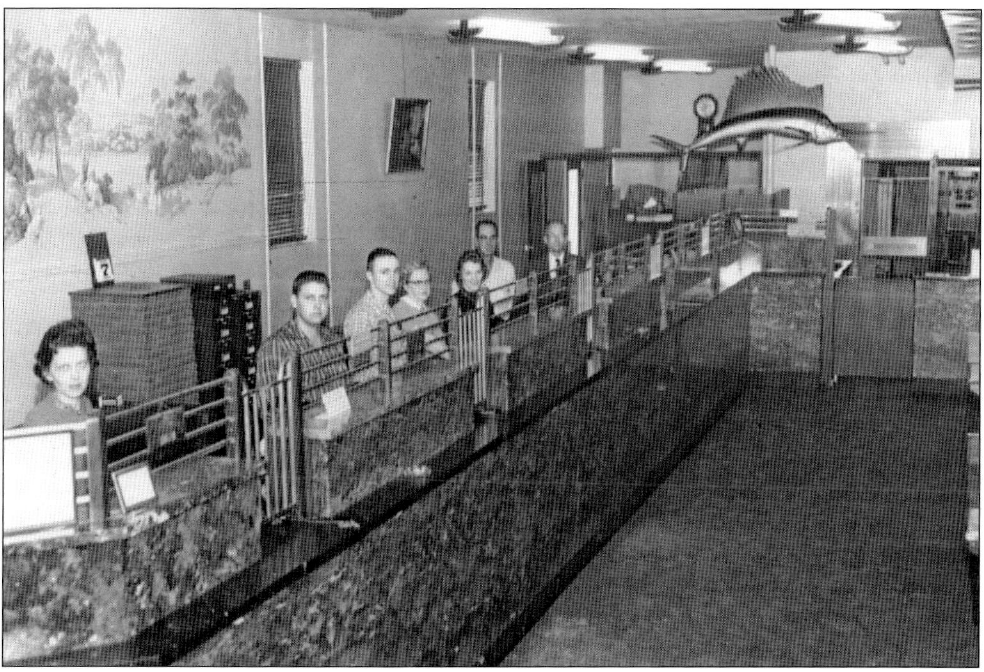

Bank customers were greeted by the staff as they entered the lobby of the Edmonton State Bank, seen here in the early 1960s. Employees that day were, from left to right, Marianne Minsey, Jerry Stevens, Richard Duncan, Clara Demumbrum, Patsy Sims, Harvey Hurt, and William Barton. (Courtesy of Edmonton State Bank.)

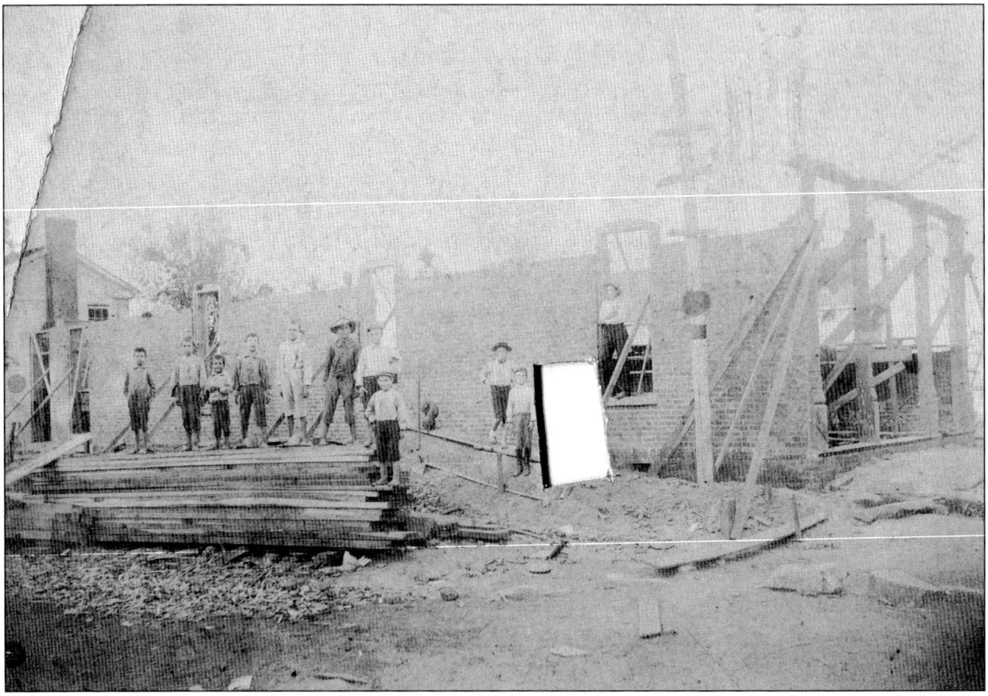

This image, taken by professional photographer G. Buell and his wife from Marrowbone, shows the construction on a new building in Edmonton. It is believed to be the start of the People's Bank. (Courtesy of Edmonton State Bank.)

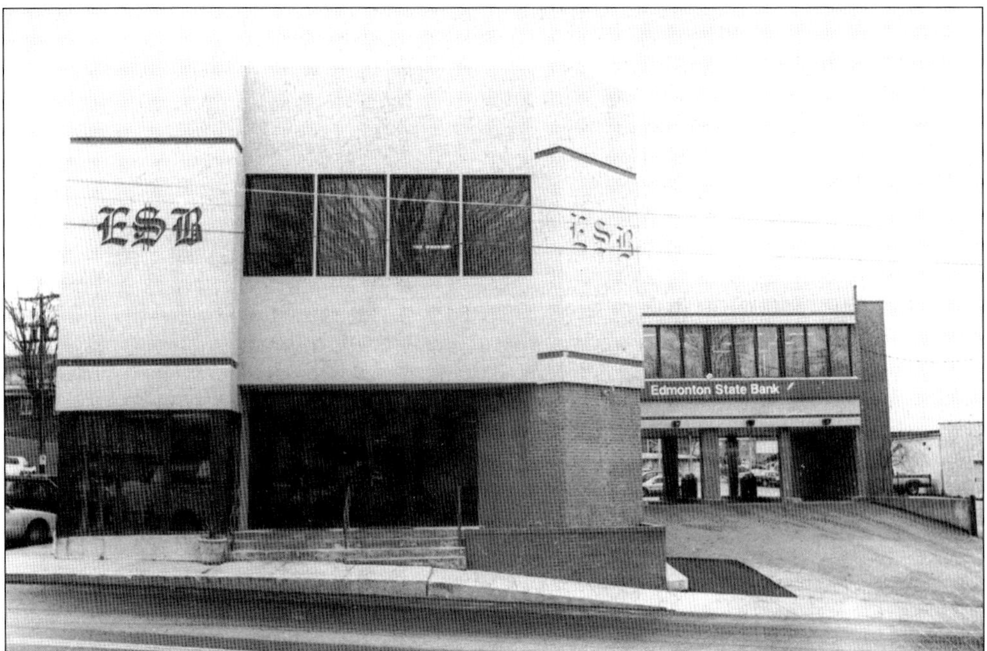

The new Edmonton State Bank had its grand opening in October 1966. At the time, the new bank was considered extremely modern because it had been built with drive-in windows and other modern design elements. (Courtesy of Edmonton State Bank.)

A centennial celebration was held on October 8, 1960. Over 5,000 people attended, coming from many counties and states. The parade was over a mile long, with buggies, wagons, trucks, and cars. Standing on top of this wagon are, from left to right, Gertie Franklin, Lucy Bowles, Bill Allen, Rudy Wallace, and Katie Lacey. (Courtesy of Sharon Howard Bowles.)

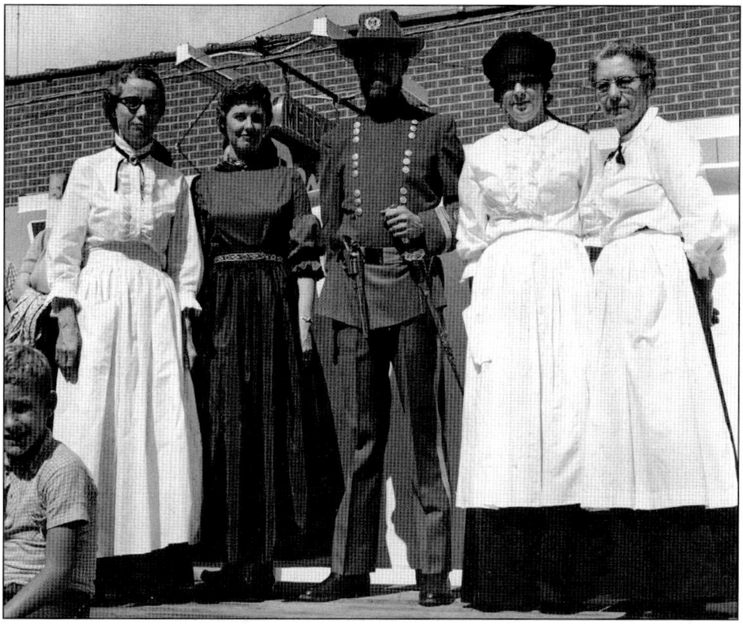

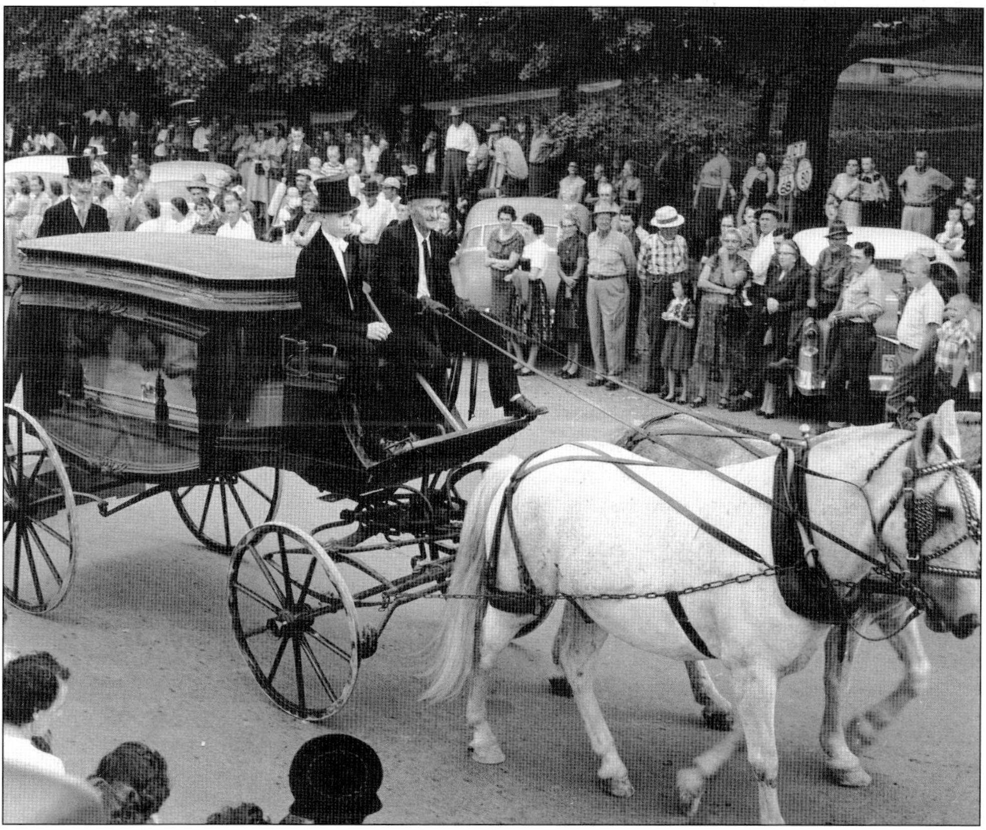

Wearing black top hats and dress coattails, Donnie Butler (left) and Arthur Martin drive the horse-drawn hearse in the centennial parade. Howard Davis rode his hose behind the hearse. (Courtesy of Donnie Butler.)

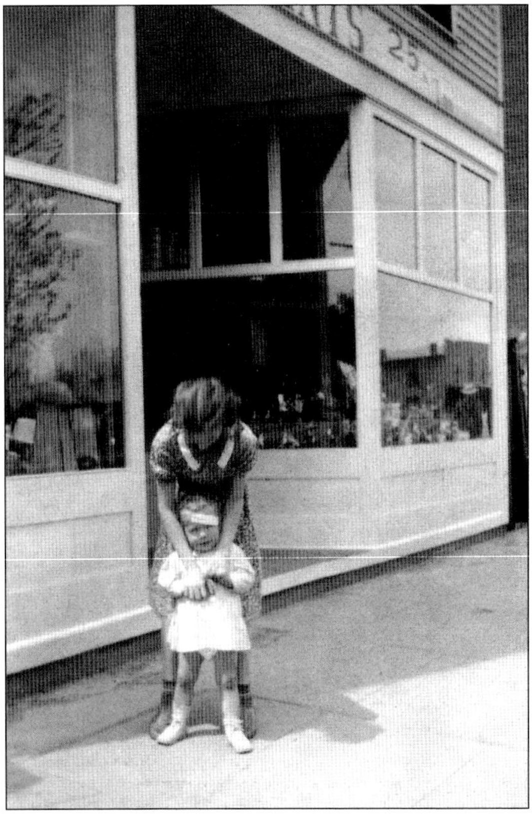

Charles "Snookum" Nunn stands in front of Nunn Drugs around 1940 with an unidentified woman. This section of the square burned in 1946, destroying several stores on the north side of the square, including the drugstore. The store was rebuilt in 1946 and is still a drugstore. (Courtesy of Cathy Nunn.)

Here is a typical scene in a small drugstore. Drugstores served families and provided everything from medicine to household needs. On the left is Winnie Nunn, the owner of Nunn Drugs in Edmonton. The original store burned in the 1940s, and this store replaced that one in 1946. (Courtesy of Cathy Nunn.)

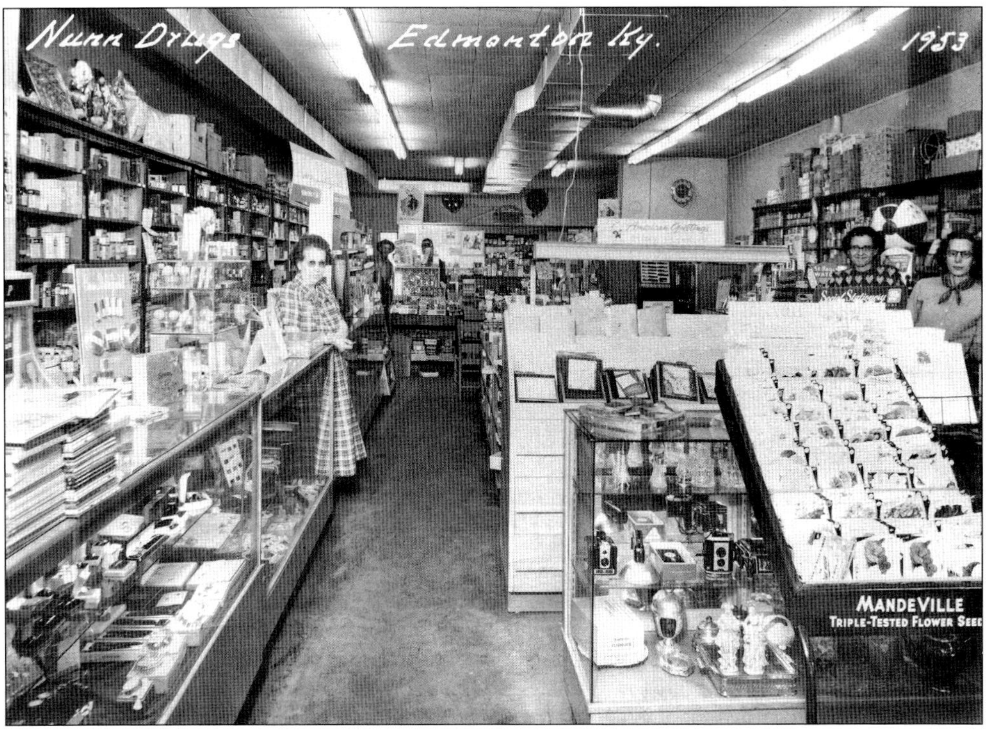

Judge Joseph Martin (1892–1973) was the author of *A Brief History of Metcalfe County 1860–1970*. Martin was admitted to the bar in 1916, served in the Army during World War I, served in the Kentucky Auditors Office from 1920 to 1924, was elected state representative from 1926 to 1930, was Metcalfe County judge executive from 1933 to 1937, and was elected Metcalfe County attorney, a position he served in for seven consecutive terms. (Courtesy of Joe McDonald.)

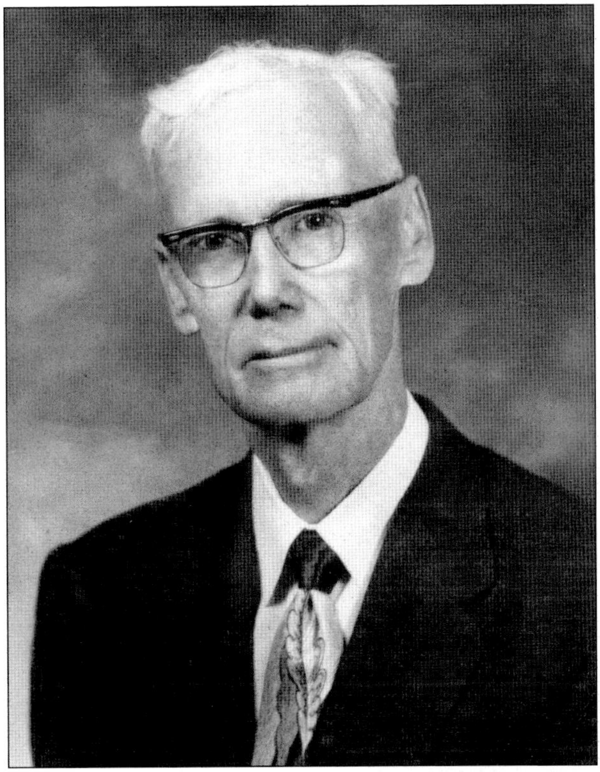

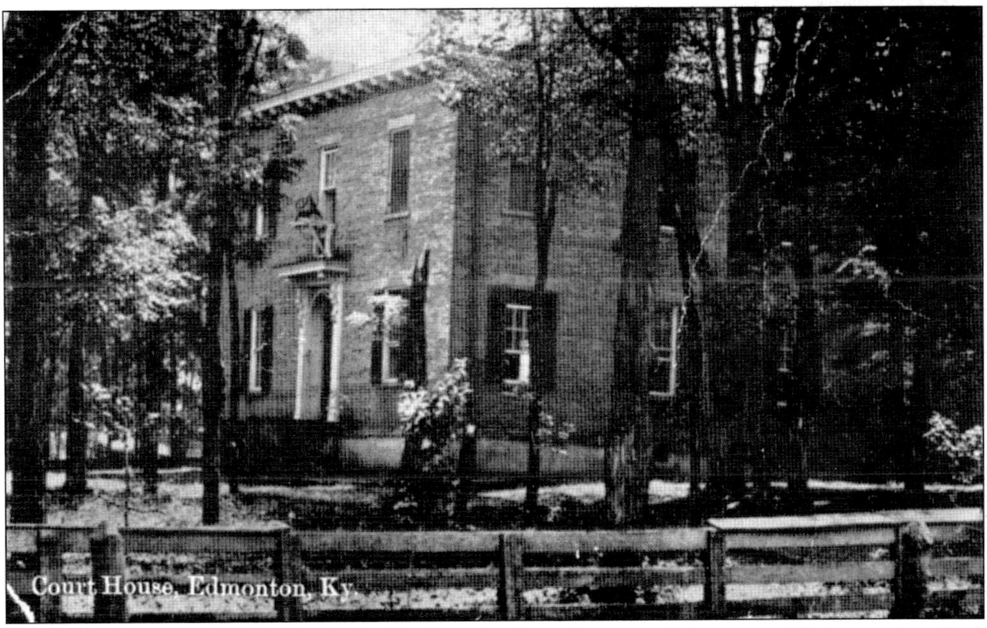

This 1909 postcard shows the Metcalfe County Courthouse in Edmonton. This was the third courthouse, built in 1869. The architect was H.P. Bradshaw, and the contractor was Henry Perry. Documents stated the courthouse was to be built in a "habitable condition." It was designed in the Italianate style with nearby stone used for the foundation and redbrick laid in a common bond pattern. The total cost of the courthouse was $14,438.48. (Courtesy of Cathy Nunn.)

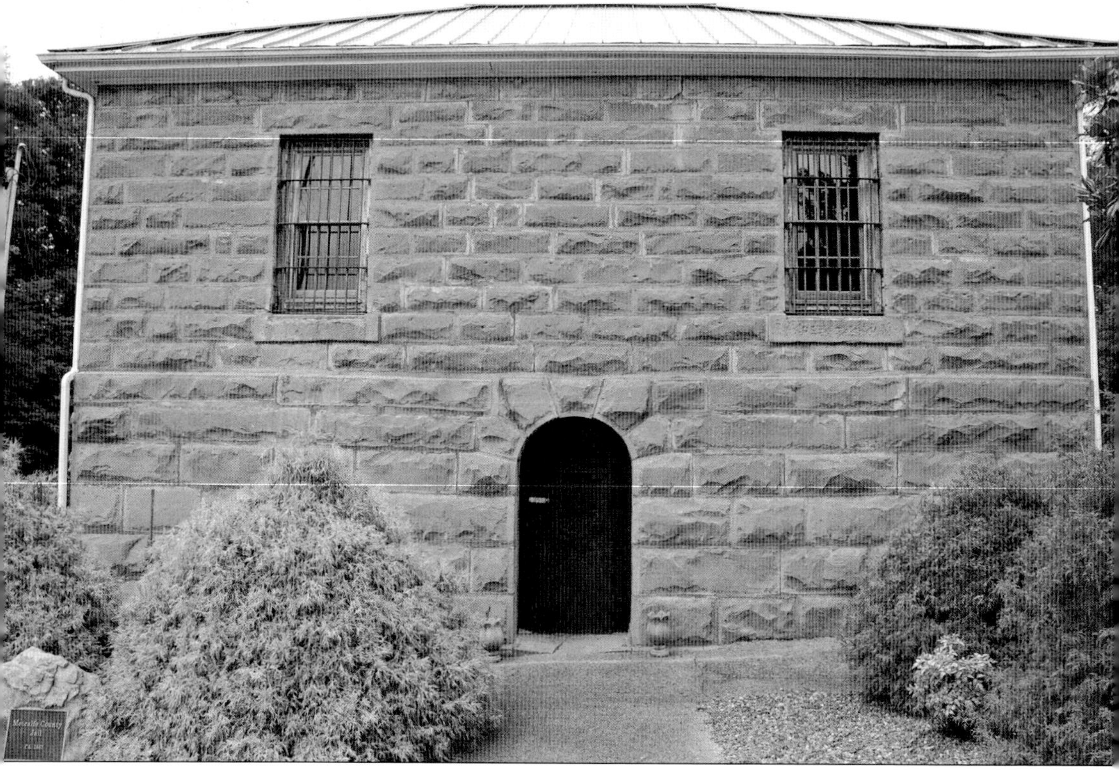

Built in 1861, the Metcalfe County Jail had an interesting history, making national news in 1896 when a group of citizens attempted to remove and lynch a prisoner and again in 1897 when three prisoners escaped after tunneling out beneath the floor. There were also successful escapes in 1971 and 1977. The jail was closed by the Kentucky Corrections Cabinet in 1983 due to safety code violations. (Photograph by Richard Hines.)

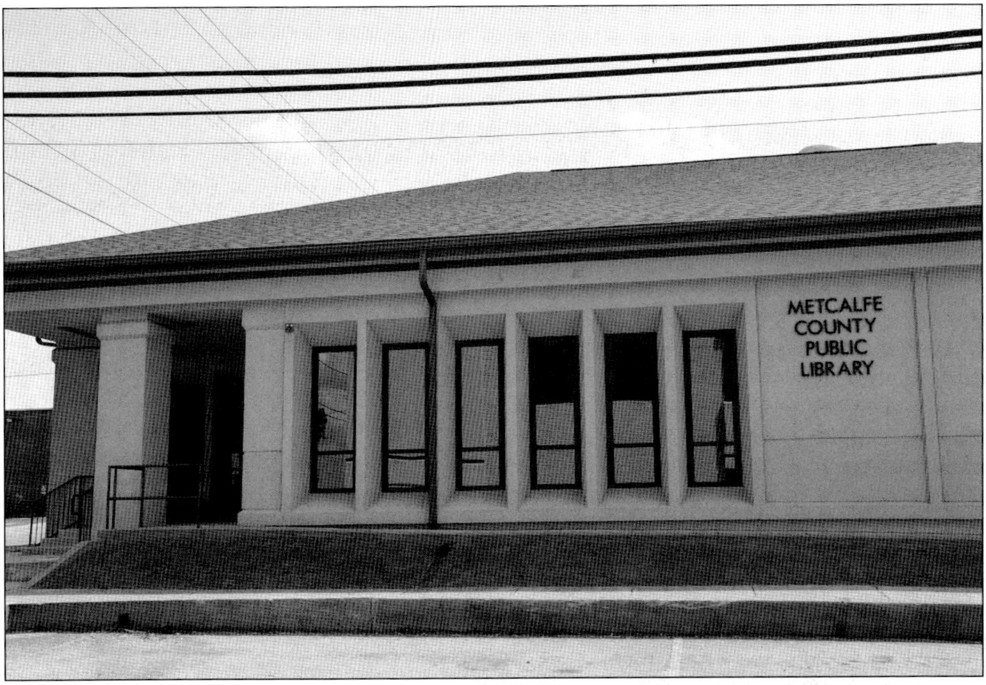

The Metcalfe County Public Library is pictured here in 2021. Lasca Martin, with help from the Jaycees, obtained a $175,000 grant to build the new library in 1970. After an exhaustive effort spanning 30 years, the new library was constructed. A 1970 *Courier Journal* article quoted Metcalfe County attorney Paul Blevins saying, "Had it not been for Lasca Martin, there would have never been a library program here." (Photograph by Richard Hines.)

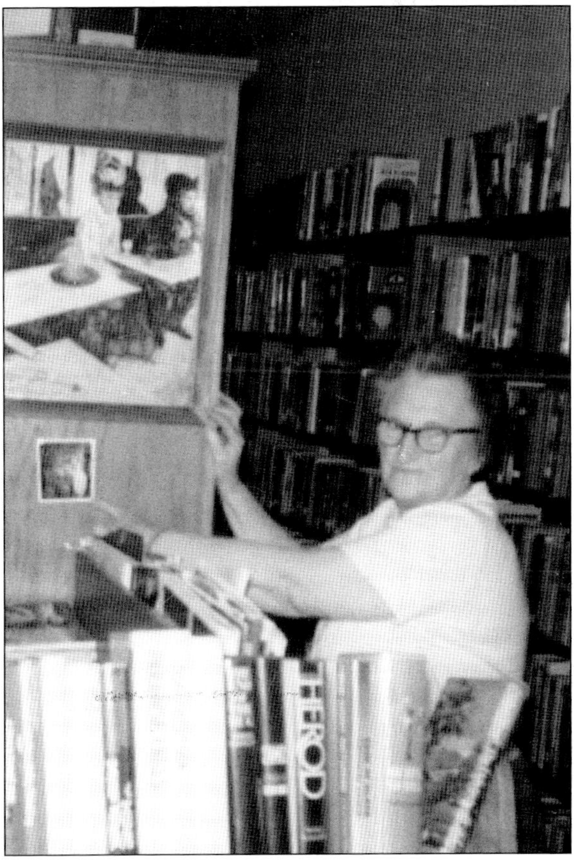

What started as a day of volunteering became a lifelong passion for Metcalfe County librarian Lasca Martin (1898–1982). The library, which began as a Works Progress Administration (WPA) project in 1935, never had a permanent home, and over a 30-year period, Martin oversaw moving the library's 18,000 volumes three times until the new library was funded in 1970. (Courtesy of Metcalfe County Public Library.)

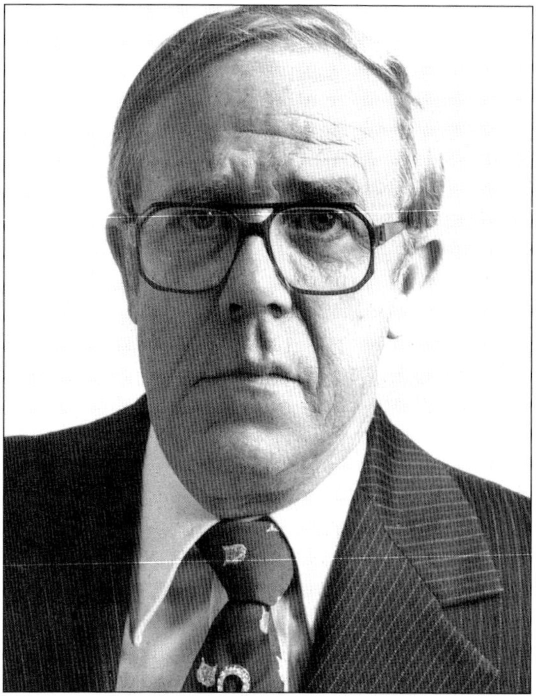

Although Edmonton was incorporated in 1860, it was not until 1964 that Don Butler became the first elected mayor of the city. Butler served in this post through 1965 and then again from 1970 to 1973. Early records indicated that Edmonton was governed by a board of trustees from the 1930s until 1964. In 1930, the chairman of the board was James Ennis. (Courtesy City of Edmonton.)

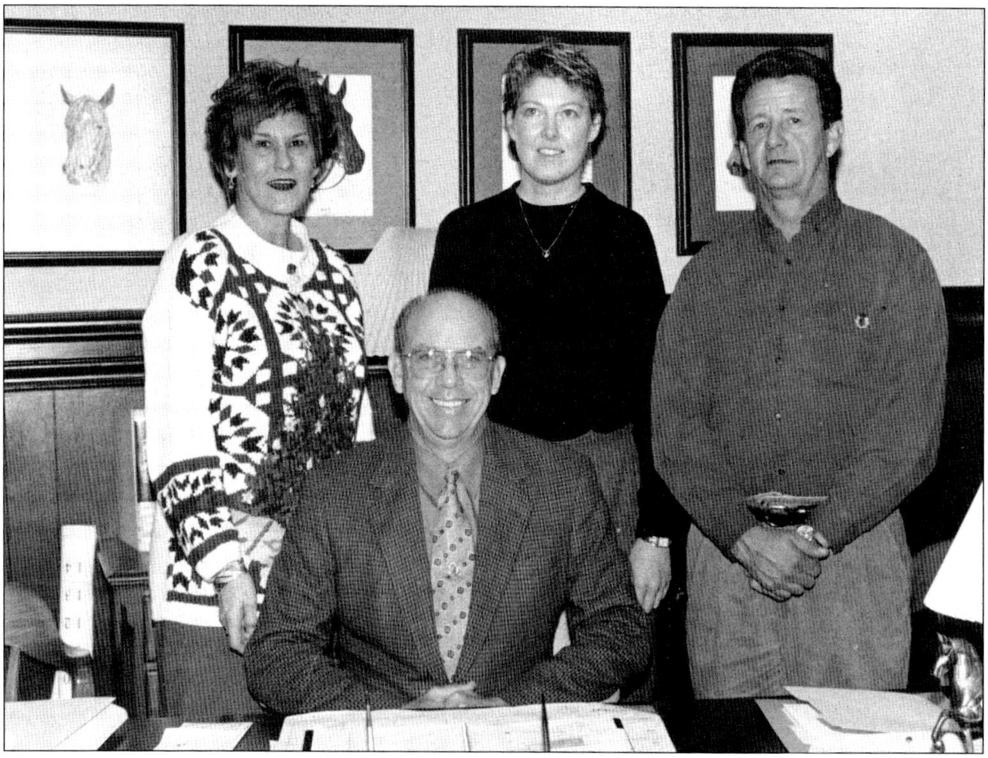

Newly elected Metcalfe County judge elect Donnie Butler (seated) is pictured with his new staff in 1999. From left to right are county treasurer Martha Richardson, secretary Tina Acre, and county road supervisor Dean Rowe. (Courtesy of Dean Rowe.)

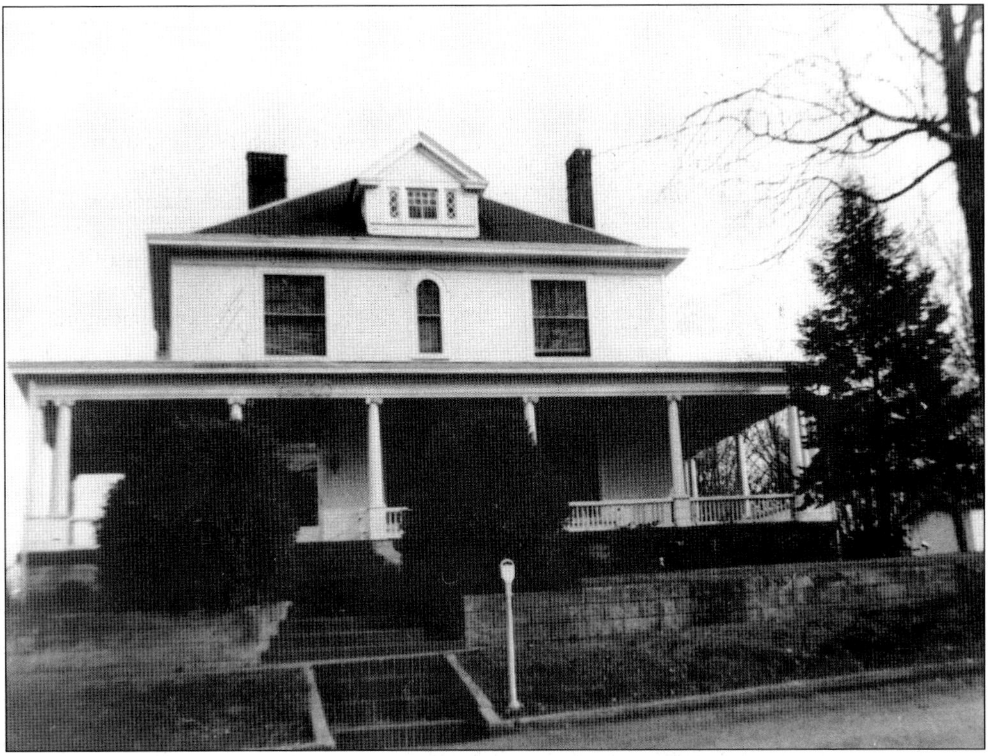

Butler's Funeral Home is pictured here in 1948. It was originally the home of Judge Kinnaird but was purchased by the Butler family in 1948 when they moved the funeral home from Center to Edmonton, where it remains in business today. (Courtesy of Donnie Butler.)

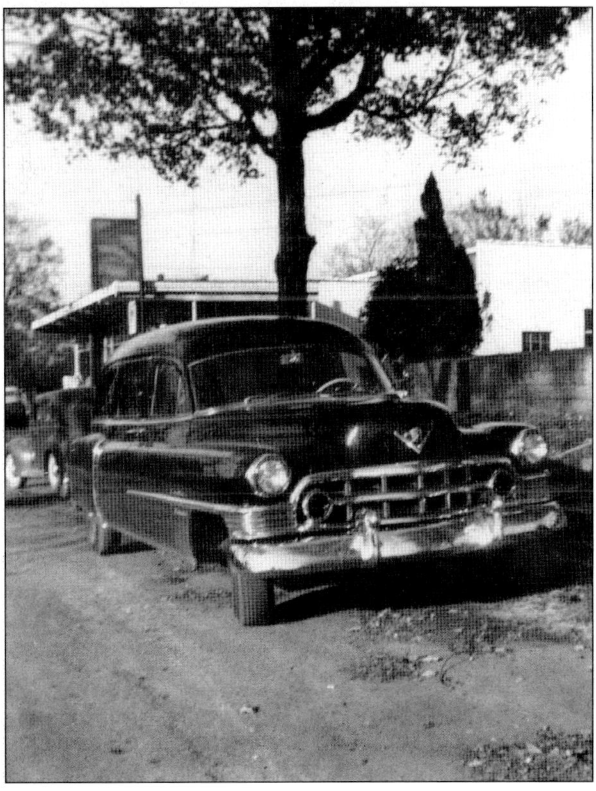

The Butler's Funeral Home hearse is shown here around 1948. As was the custom at that time, funeral homes also provided local ambulance service, and Butler's provided this service for Metcalfe County. In many cases, there was little or no training for the people who drove the ambulance, but they were expected to provide first aid to victims. Many times, 16-year-old Donnie Butler would drive the ambulance, bandaging wounds or splinting broken bones with any available material he could find at the site. (Courtesy of Donnie Butler.)

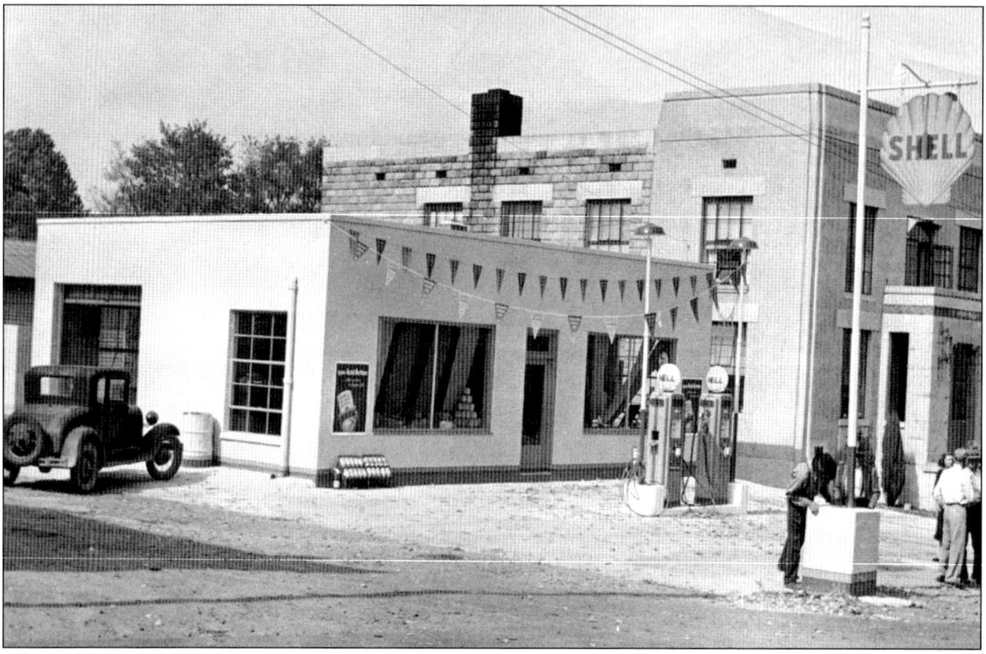

One business on Edmonton Square was this service station. Over the years, it was both a Shell station and an Ashland station. James Pedigo operated it for many years. In the background is the Metcalfe County Board of Education building, constructed by the WPA in 1940. Both buildings were torn down in 1965 to make room for the new Edmonton State Bank. (Courtesy of Edmonton State Bank.)

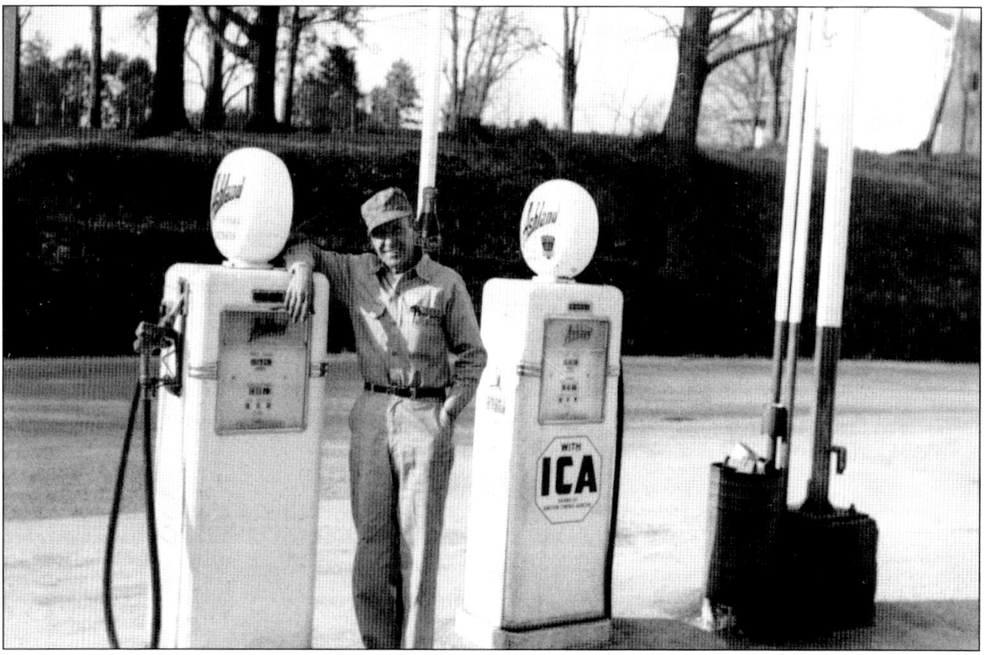

Marshall Strange is standing next to the gas pumps ready to wash windows and fill gas tanks. All service stations were full service until the early 1980s, and customers expected everything to be taken care of. (Courtesy of Richard Young.)

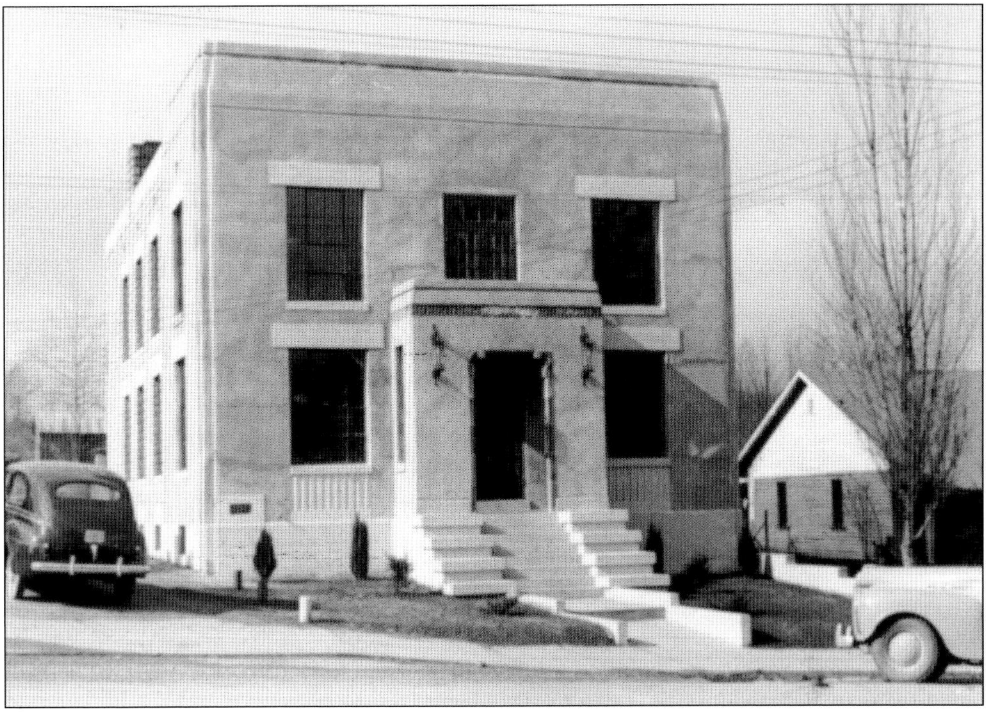

The Metcalfe County Board of Education building was constructed by the WPA in 1940. Over the years, the building served the board of education and was also the Metcalfe County Library for a short period. (Courtesy of University of Kentucky Library Special Collections, Goodman-Paxton Photographic Collection.)

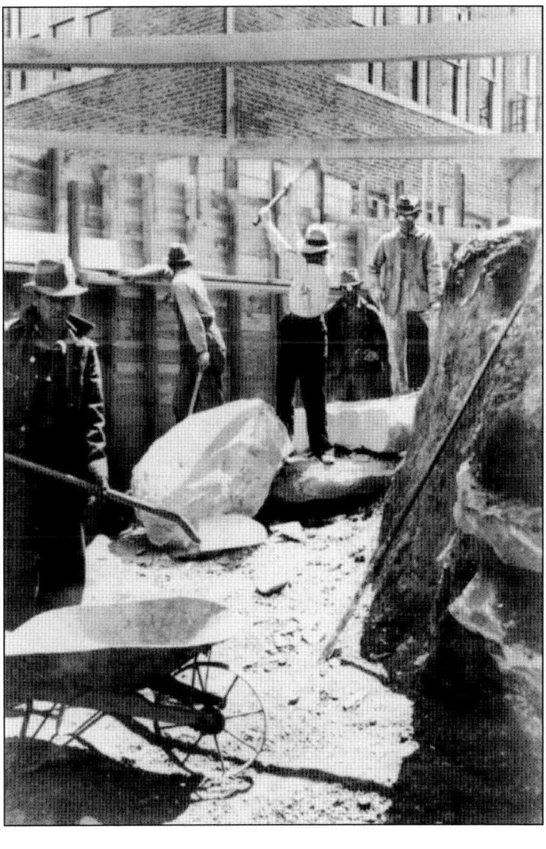

Here, WPA workers are completing work on the new high school gym in Edmonton. The WPA was one of the New Deal agencies established during the Roosevelt administration. The old high school was torn down in 2019. (Courtesy of University of Kentucky Library Special Collections, Goodman-Paxton Photographic Collection.)

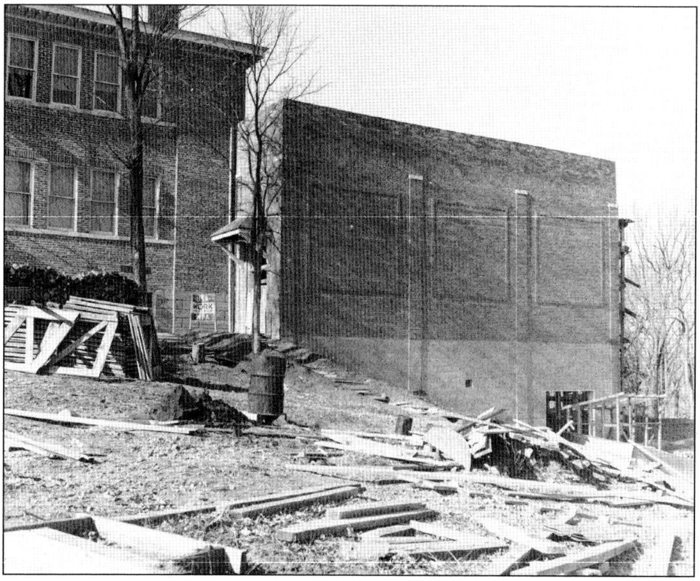

Each project the WPA worked on would display a sign out front. From 1935 to 1942, over $4.9 billion was spent nationwide. During the Roosevelt administration, Metcalfe County received several appropriations for new public buildings, bridges, and roads. (Courtesy of University of Kentucky Library Special Collections, Goodman-Paxton Photographic Collection.)

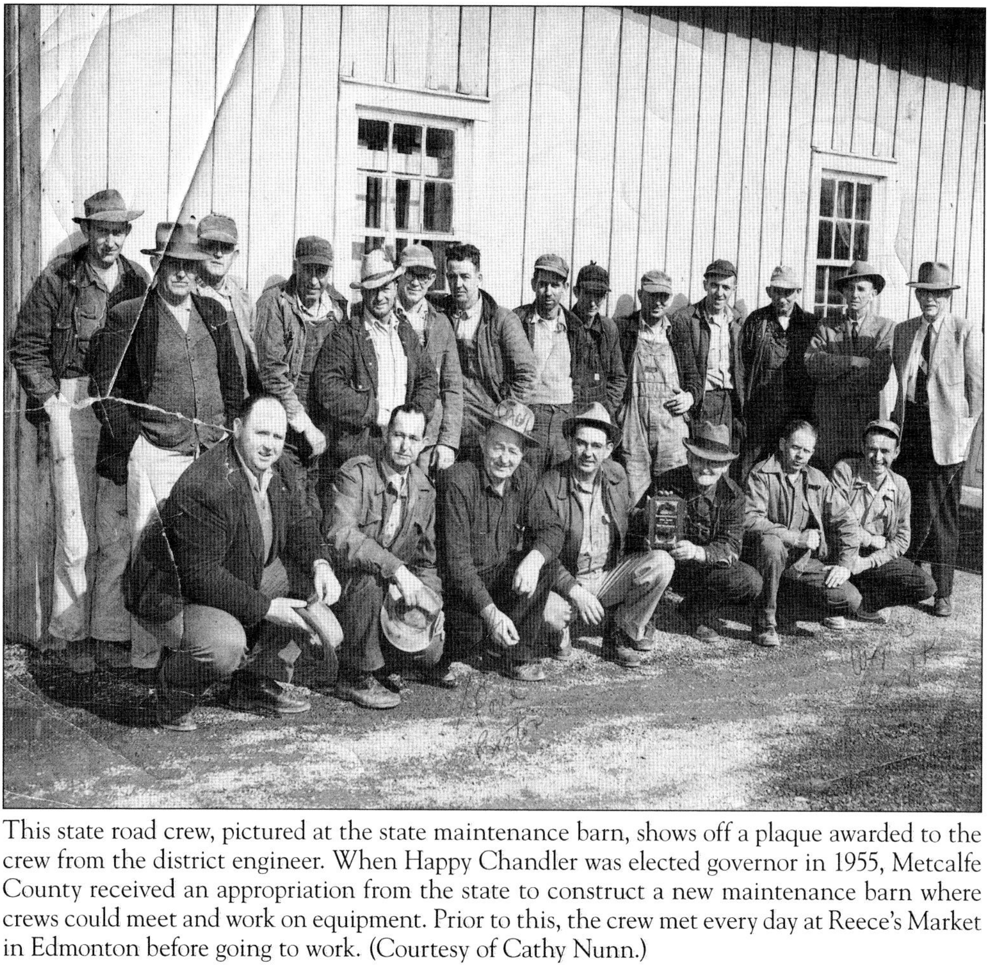

This state road crew, pictured at the state maintenance barn, shows off a plaque awarded to the crew from the district engineer. When Happy Chandler was elected governor in 1955, Metcalfe County received an appropriation from the state to construct a new maintenance barn where crews could meet and work on equipment. Prior to this, the crew met every day at Reece's Market in Edmonton before going to work. (Courtesy of Cathy Nunn.)

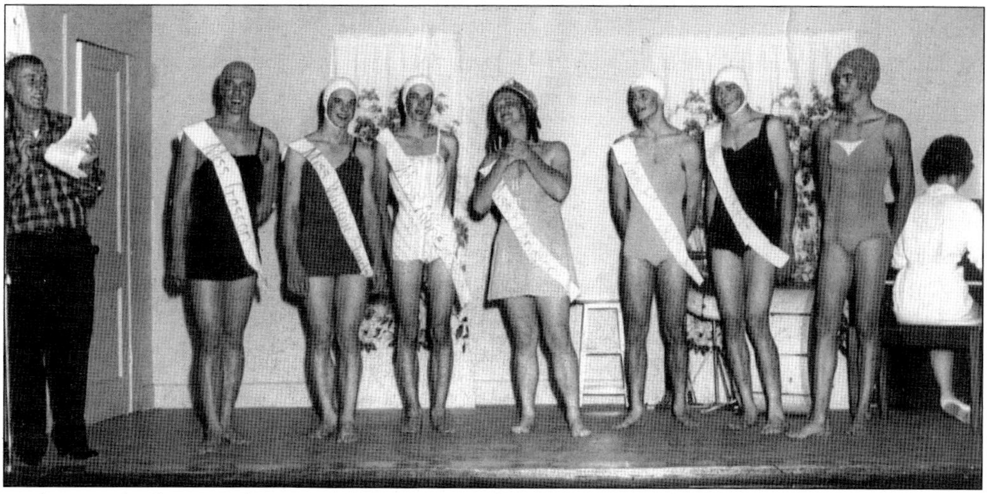

Each year, the boys in the Metcalfe County High School Beta Club would put on a womanless beauty contest for the elementary school students, which was great fun for everyone. The announcer at left is Herb Sparks, followed by contestants Rowe Harper, Gary Richardson, Rondel Watson, Jerry Irvin (winner), Jim Coleman, Doug Clemons, and Johnny Martin. (Courtesy of Gary Richardson.)

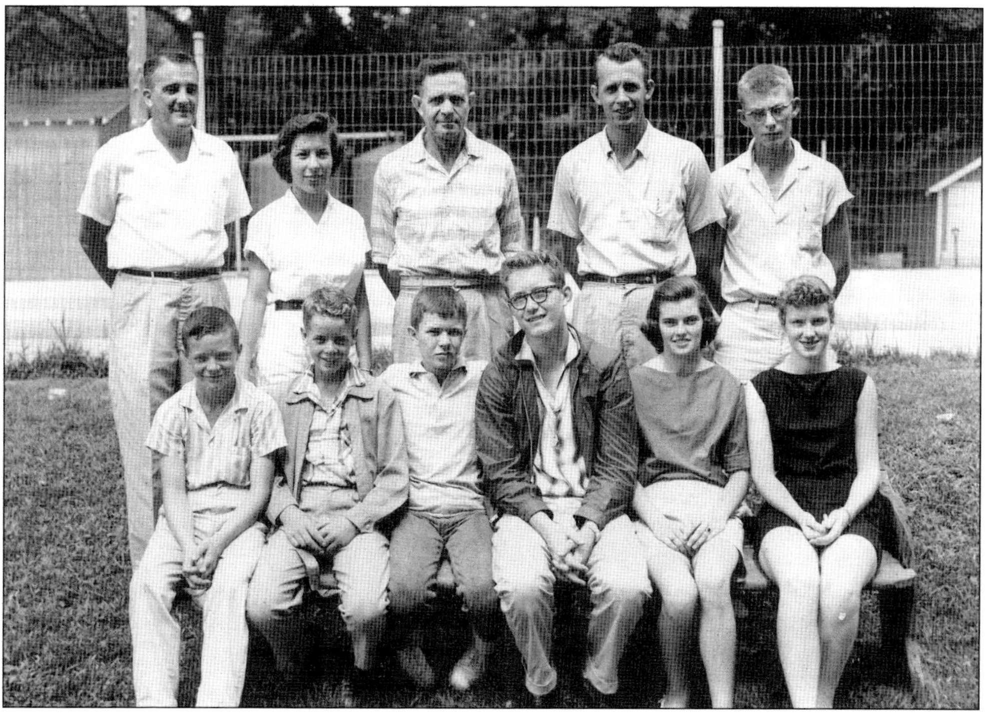

Pictured is a group of adult leaders and students who attended 4-H camp in the early 1960s. Camp was a major event each summer for youth who were involved in Metcalfe County clubs. It gave club members opportunities to learn about the natural history of the area and participate in outdoor recreation, including swimming, boating, and marksmanship. (Courtesy of Gary Richardson.)

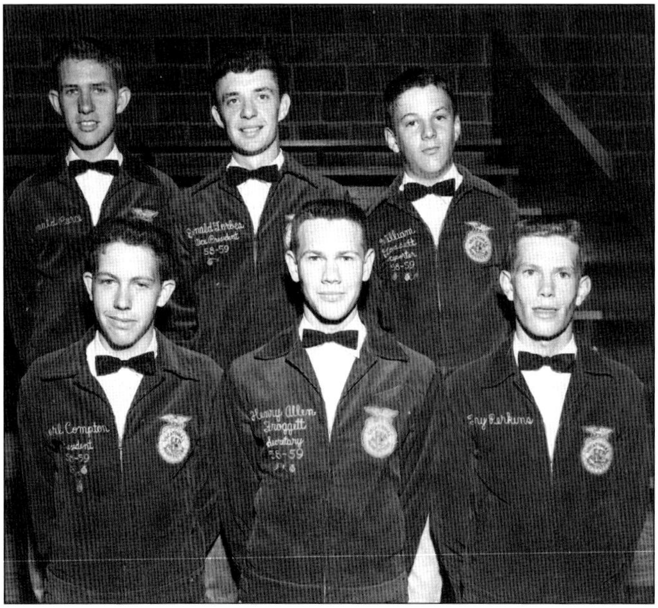

Almost every high school in Kentucky had a chapter of the Future Farmers of America (FFA). The primary goal of vocational agriculture was twofold—establishing farming knowledge in students, and developing leadership that would be used in rural communities across the United States. Pictured are, from left to right, (first row) Carl Compton, Henry Allen Froggett, and ? Perkins; (second row) Don Pierce, Don Forbes, and William Gossett. (Courtesy of Henry Froggett.)

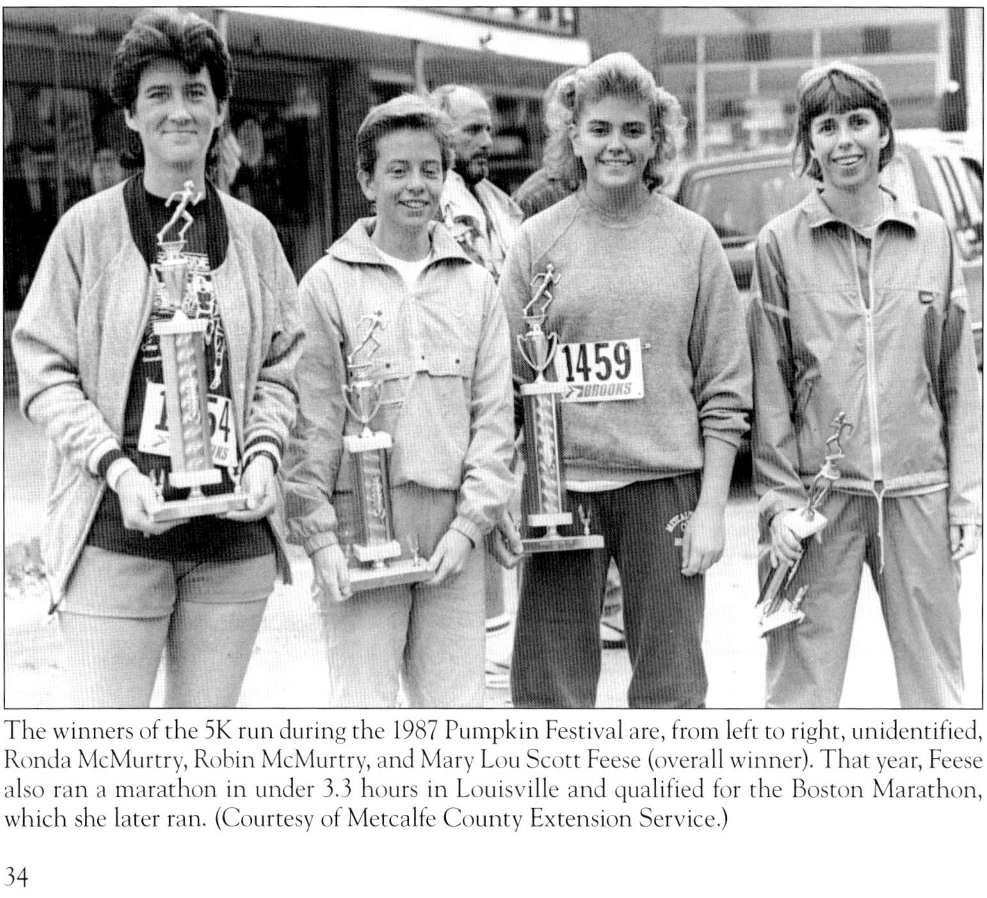

The winners of the 5K run during the 1987 Pumpkin Festival are, from left to right, unidentified, Ronda McMurtry, Robin McMurtry, and Mary Lou Scott Feese (overall winner). That year, Feese also ran a marathon in under 3.3 hours in Louisville and qualified for the Boston Marathon, which she later ran. (Courtesy of Metcalfe County Extension Service.)

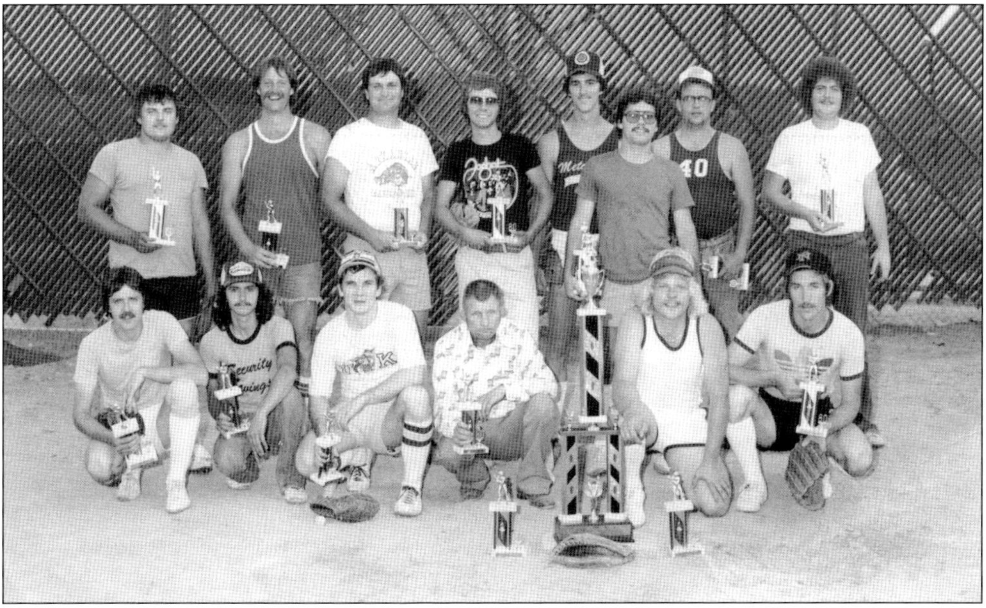

In small towns and rural areas, summer was softball season, and teams were sponsored by local businesses. Nightly games were attended by Metcalfe County residents in large numbers, and competition between teams and businesses was fierce. Two of the team members shown here, Howard Garrett (first row, third from left), and Doug Smith (second row, third from left), would later serve as mayors of Edmonton. (Courtesy of Doug Smith.)

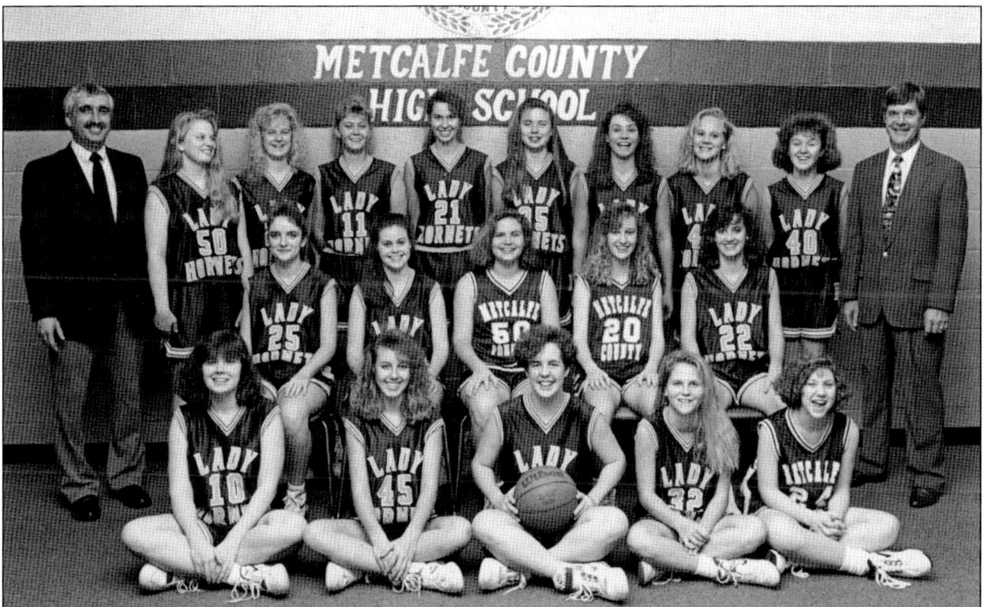

During the 1974–1975 school year, Metcalfe County organized its first girls' basketball team. The head coach was Gary Richardson, and the assistant coach was Mary Alice Yokley. One of the best seasons for the Lady Hornets was in 1992, when they were district and regional class A champions with a 29-7 record. The team also reached the final four of Kentucky's state class A championships. (Courtesy of Gary Richardson.)

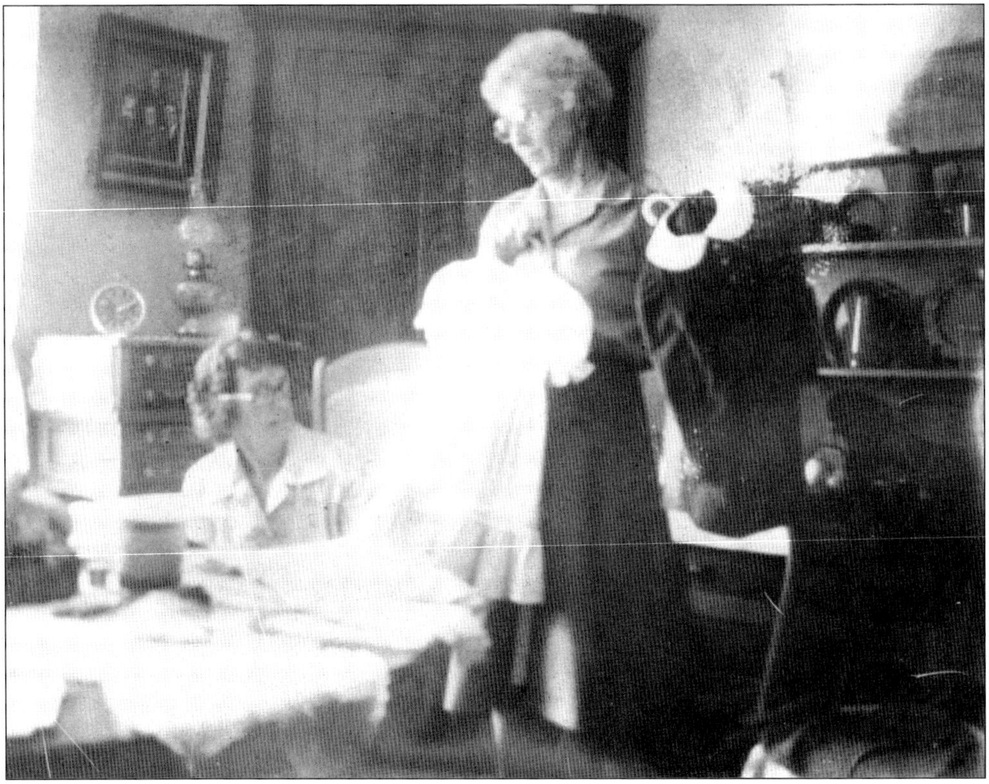

Local homemaker clubs have always been an important part of the University of Kentucky Extension Service, providing instruction on sewing, cooking, canning, and healthy living among the state's rural residents. (Courtesy of University of Kentucky Extension Service.)

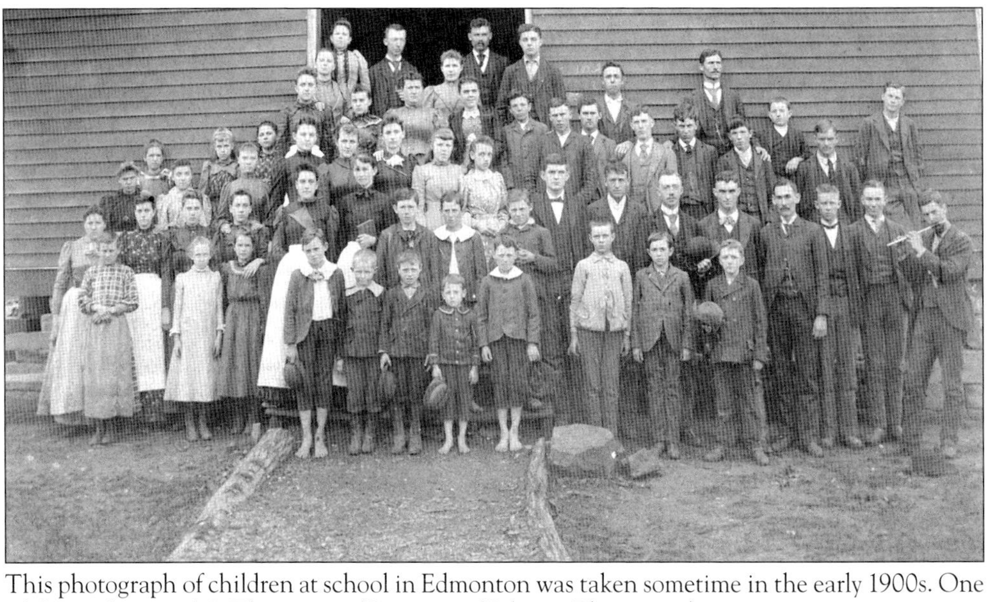

This photograph of children at school in Edmonton was taken sometime in the early 1900s. One of the students is A.J. Thompson. (Courtesy of Johnny Thompson.)

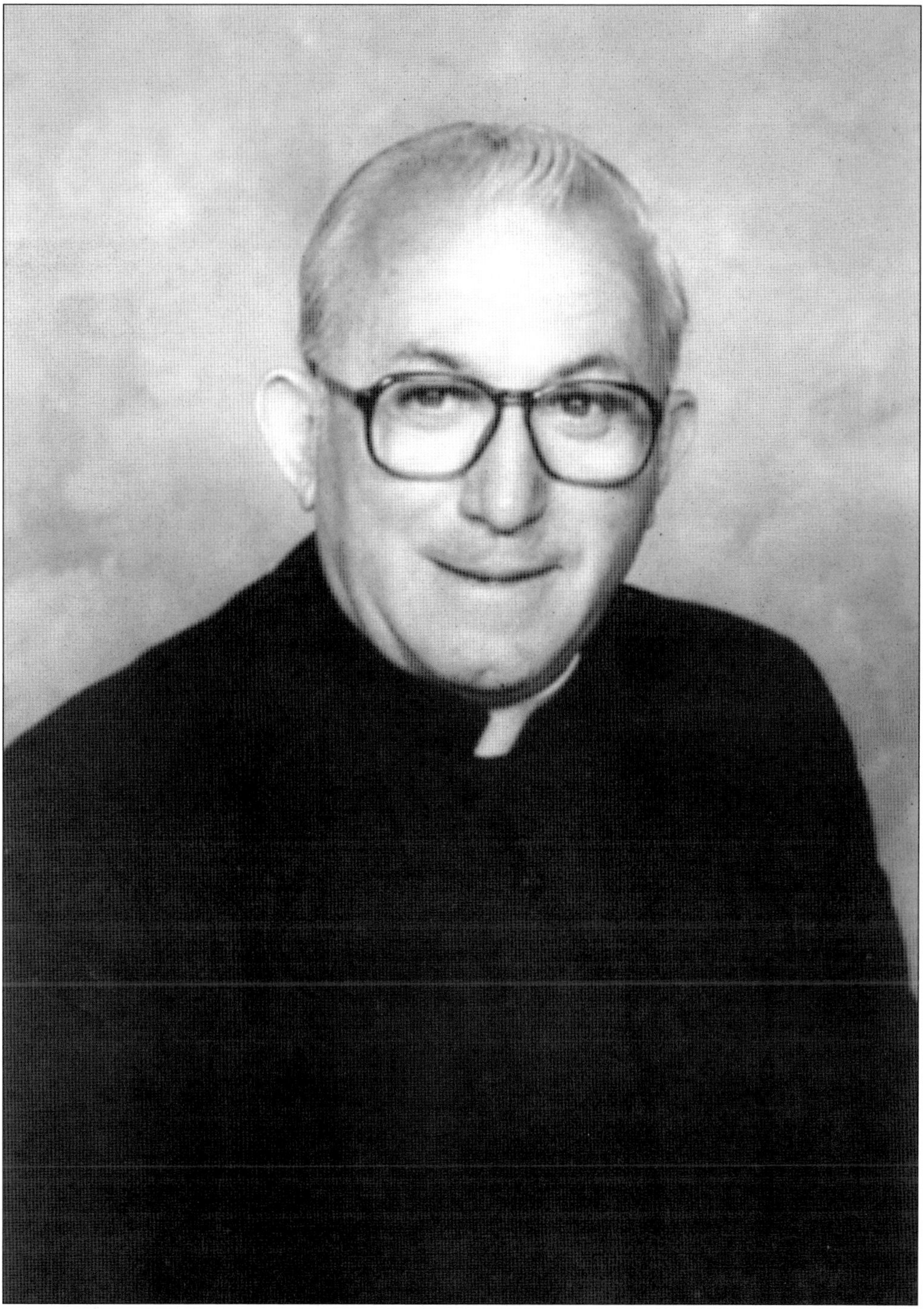

Fr. George Bowling worked in south-central Kentucky for 25 years applying the approach of "theology of recreation." After he inherited his family's farm, Bowling mortgaged it to build recreational facilities and infrastructure for a park. Today, Bowling Park, the food pantry, and other amenities are the result of Father Bowling's efforts and friendship to Metcalfe County. (Courtesy of Bowling Park.)

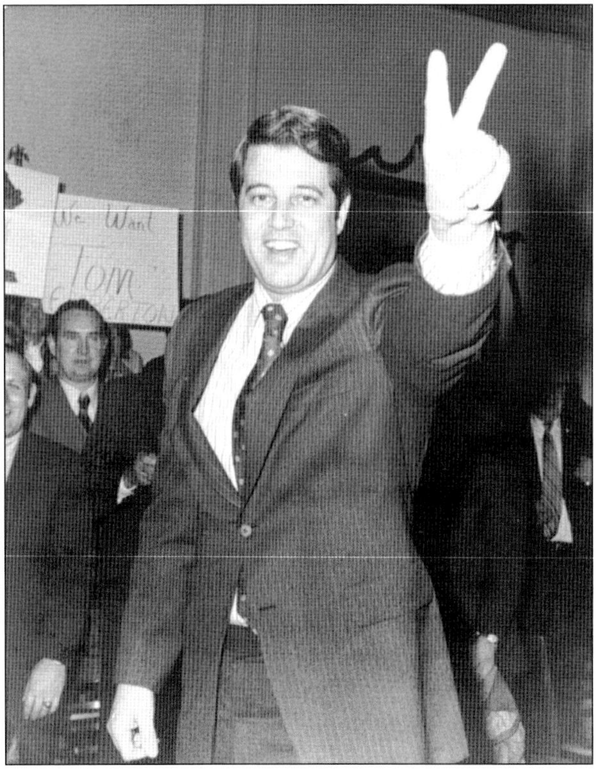

Tom Emberton began his career as an attorney, later serving under Gov. Louie Nunn. Emberton was the 1971 Republican gubernatorial candidate for Kentucky, only losing by a small margin. He was appointed to the Kentucky State Court of Appeals in 1987 and later became chief justice of the court, where he served until his retirement in 2004. Emberton said, "Serving on the court was the most rewarding experience of my life." (Courtesy of Tom Emberton.)

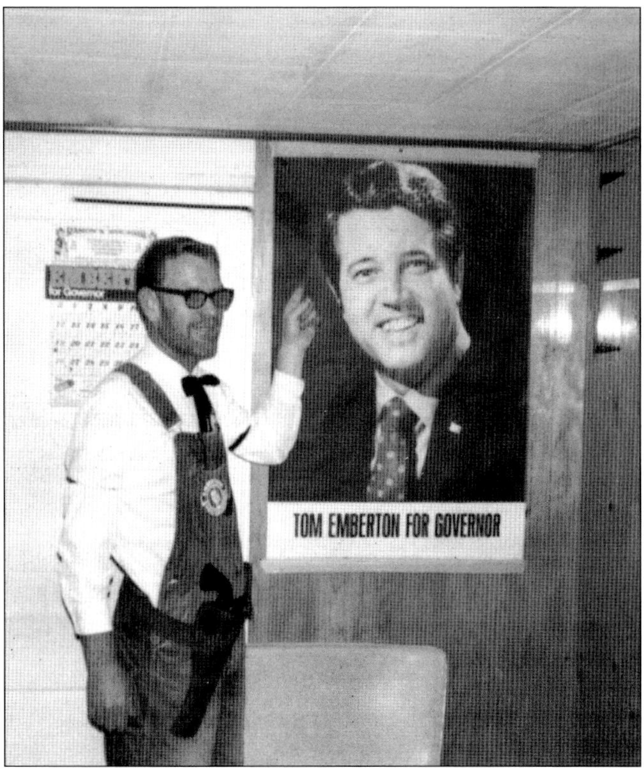

Willard Parnell shows off his beard and a political poster of Tom Emberton as he prepares for the Metcalfe County centennial celebration and parade. It was all in fun, but during the centennial, men were required to grow beards or be fined unless they had purchased a special permit. Money from the fines and permits was used during the centennial. (Courtesy of William Parnell.)

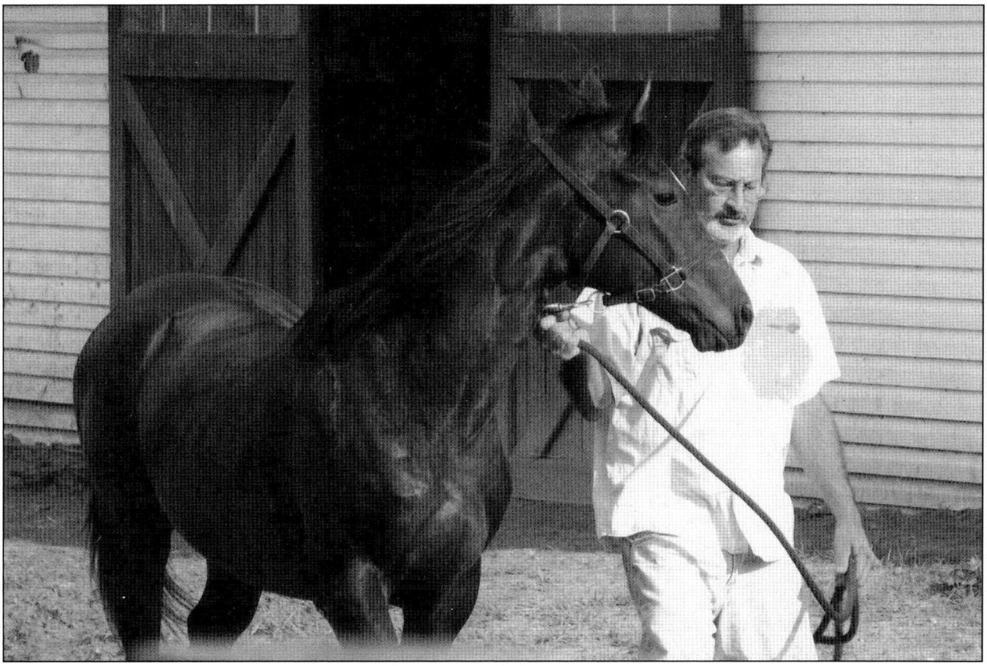

Every farming community needs a veterinarian, and Dr. David LaFever has served Metcalfe County for over 31 years. LaFever took care of every aspect of animal health, from small pets to top-quality Thoroughbred racehorses. He and his wife, Donna, were also responsible for organizing the county's first animal shelter. (Courtesy of David LaFever.)

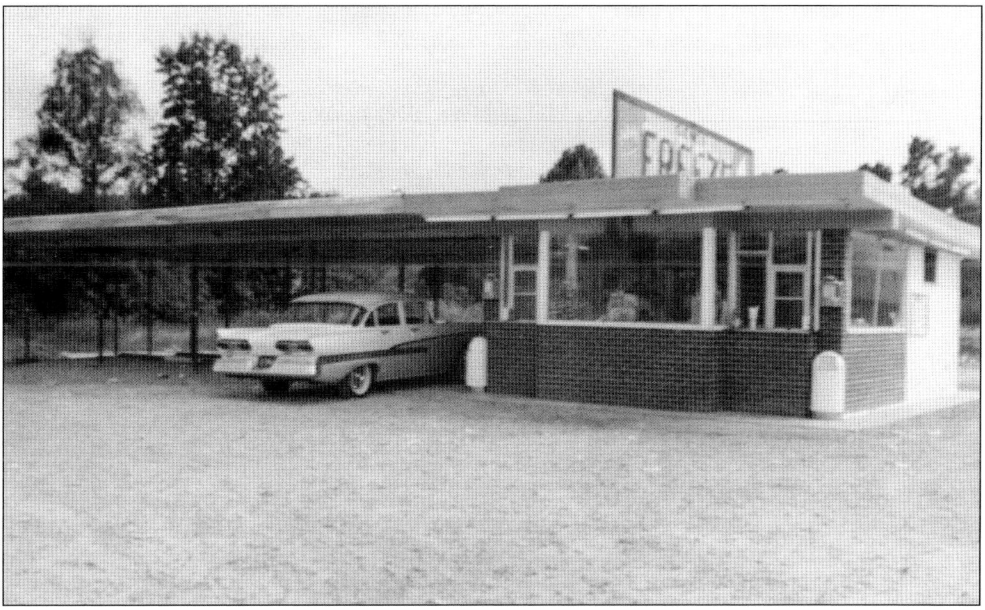

Traveling along US Highway 68 from Edmonton, Gene's Freeze was the place to stop. When Gene and Geneva Wyatt opened the restaurant in August 1958, the Freeze had carhops who waited on cars. It was also known as the "Hornets' Nest" because everyone came here to eat before or after Hornets games. The Freeze is still family owned and operated. (Courtesy of Sandy Curry, Brenda Walden, and Jeff Wyatt.)

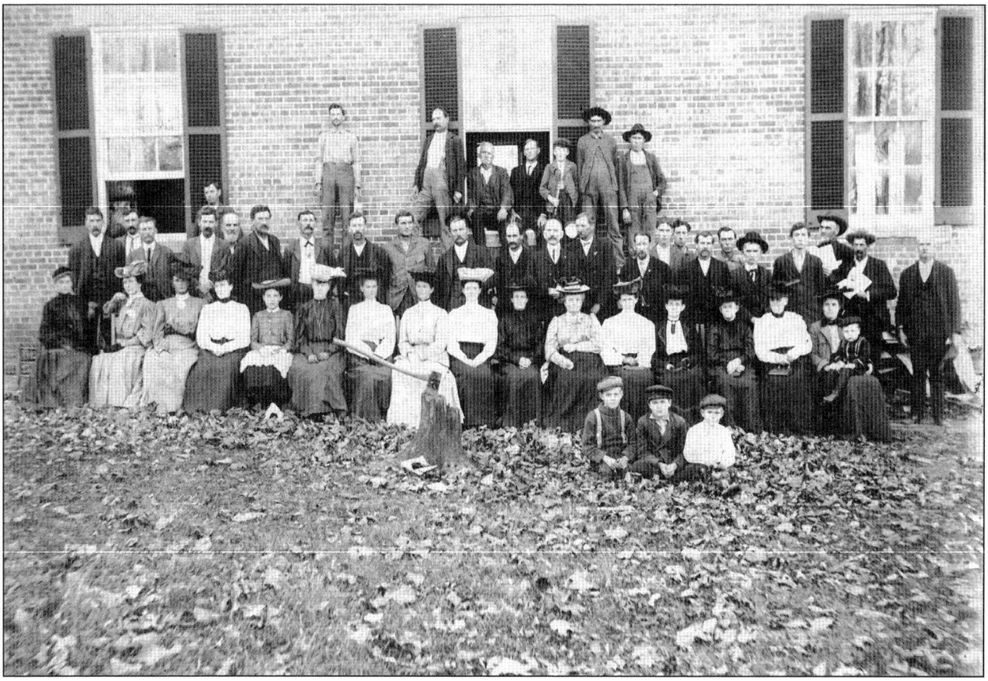

This photograph was taken in the yard next to the Metcalfe County Courthouse sometime in the early 1900s. Each summer, teachers from across the county would gather for yearly training, and this is believed to be one of these summer sessions. (Courtesy of Laurie Butler.)

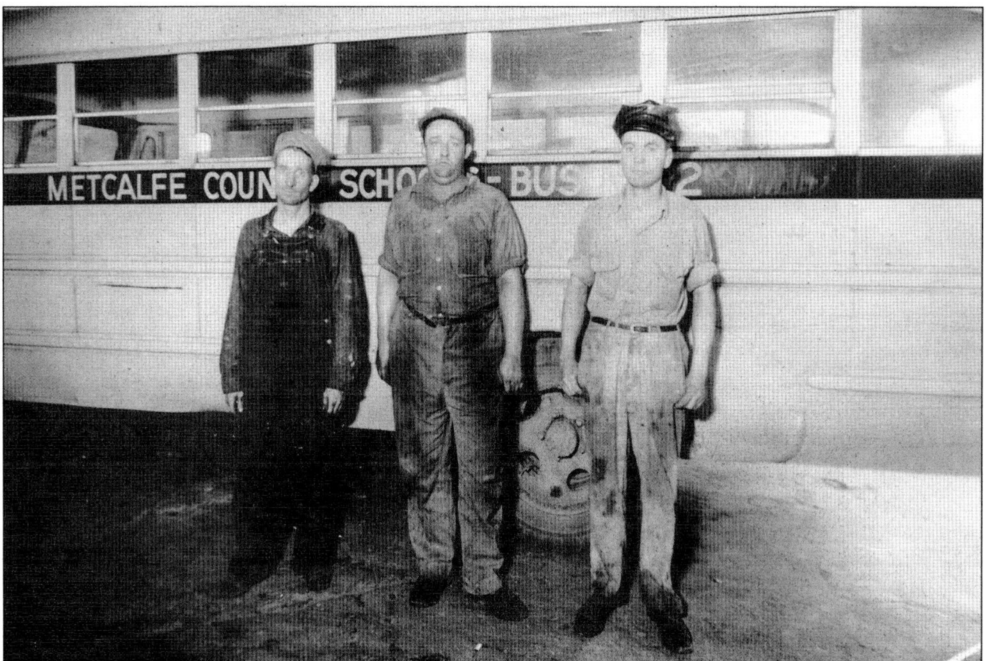

Before Metcalfe County Schools had its garage, most of the mechanical work was taken care of by local automotive garages. The three mechanics working on the bus at the Edmonton Ford Garage are, from left to right, Doc Harper, Sam Mitchell, and Robert Love. (Courtesy of Richard Young.)

Three

SULPHUR WELL

Sulphur Well developed around a well that was drilled by Ezekiel Neal in 1845 and in the years following became a prominent community supporting surrounding farms. It began attracting visitors from a wide area wishing to drink the mineral water. A large expansion of the town began to peak around 1860, just prior to the Civil War. During the war, the community was spared many of the large, destructive guerrilla raids that occurred in other parts of Metcalfe County; however, there is an account of one of the home guards from Green County being captured by Confederates near Sulphur Well.

When expansion did occur, it was due to the mineral water. During the 1800s and into the 1900s, mineral water was thought to cure a wide range of illnesses, including arthritis and even cholera. Physicians who specialized in hydropathy recommended that patients stay at health resorts for extended periods of time, drinking mineral water. This trend prompted the construction of the Beulah Villa Hotel in 1903. The concept for this type of hotel and resort was modeled after those found in Europe. The Beulah Villa was one of dozens of hotels that flourished in Kentucky, attracting visitors from across the United States.

Known for its mineral water and excellent food, the Beula Villa was purchased in 1920 by King Crenshaw, who was said to have rung the dinner bell every day for 46 years until he sold the hotel in 1968. In the early years, Metcalfe County roads were in poor condition, and travel was difficult until Kentucky Highway 70 was completed. Many guests would ride the train to Cave City, where Crenshaw would take them by car to the hotel. The hotel burned in the 1980s.

Started in the 1880s, Sulphur Well's annual Homecoming continues each August.

Although the hotels are gone, dining continues to be the main attraction for Sulphur Well, with hundreds of customers dining at the Lighthouse Restaurant each weekend or lodging in original log cabins at Cabin Creek, while weekend kayakers on the river have replaced those seeking mineral water.

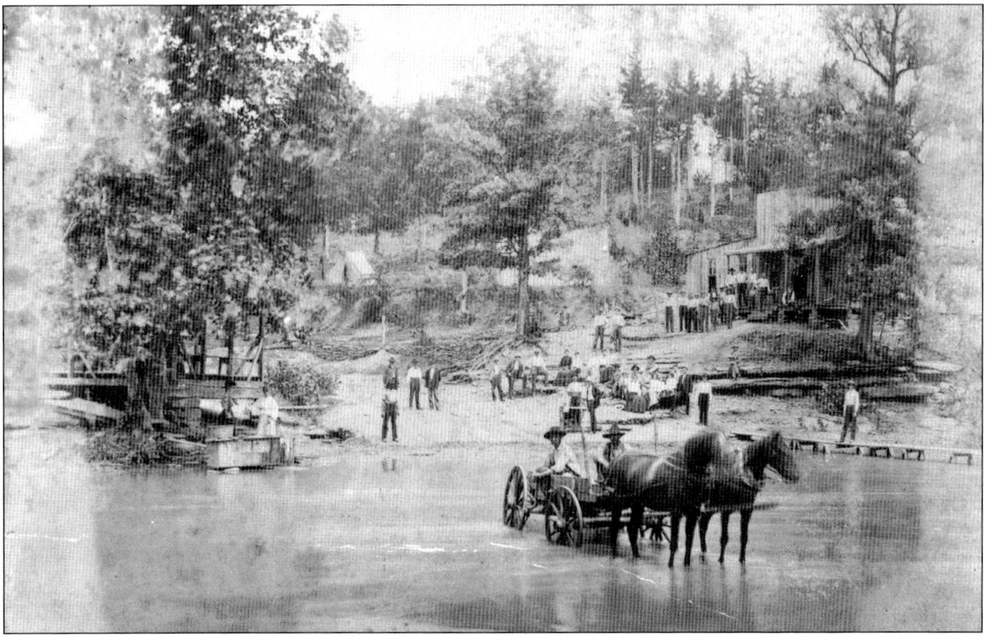

By 1878, Sulphur Well had a school. A post office was established on July 30, 1879, and in 1883, the community was reported to have a population of 100, with several stores, a hotel, and a flour mill. Note the tent and the small foot bridge where people crossed the river. (Courtesy of Cora Emma Jessie.)

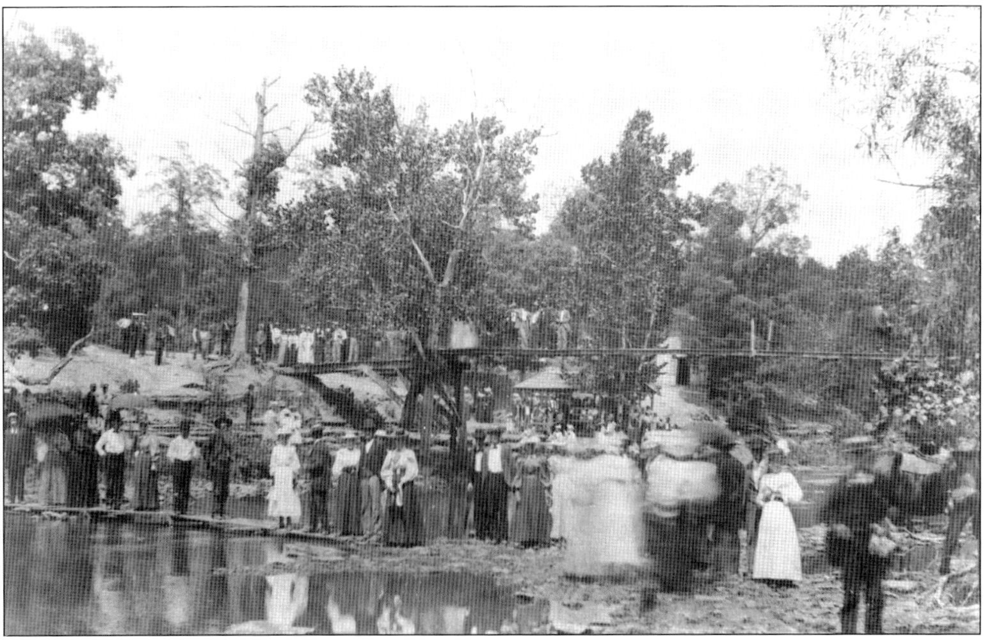

Folks gather around the river crossing at Sulphur Well during a period of low water on the South Fork of the Little Barren River. The swinging bridge, which was built during the early 1900s, was attractive to people wanting to enjoy the outdoors on Sundays and during special events. (Courtesy of Cora Emma Jessie.)

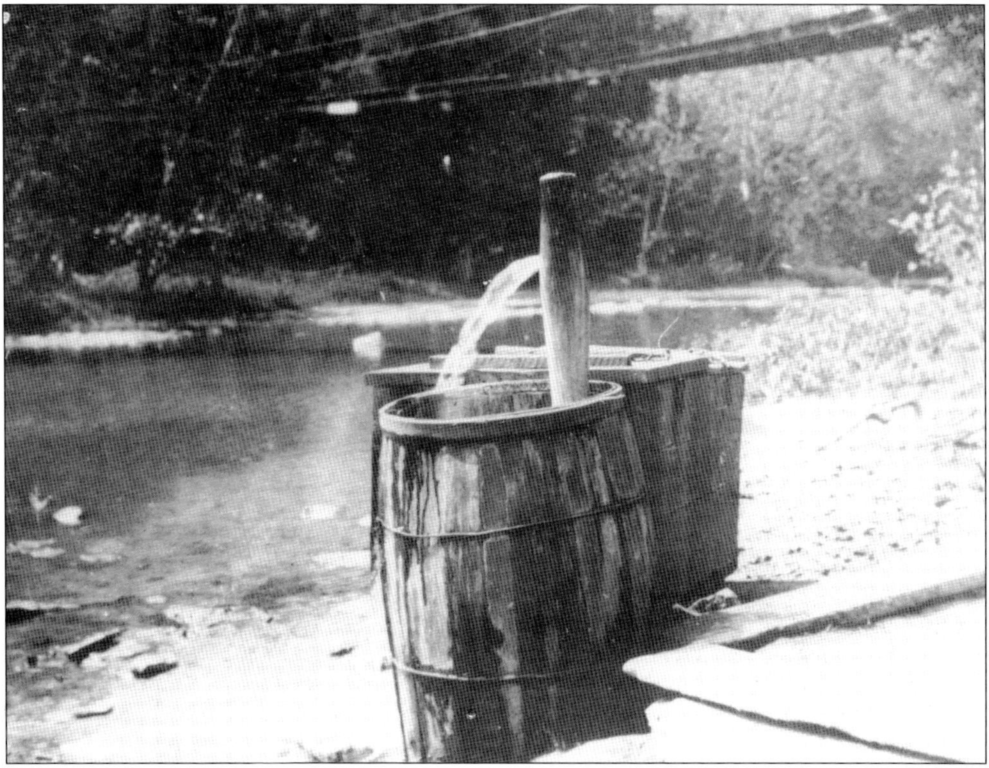

When expansion did occur in the town, it was in part due to the mineral water. During the 1800s and into the 1900s, mineral water was thought to cure a wide range of illnesses. (Courtesy of Cora Emma Jessie.)

A guest is drinking mineral water at the well. In 1907, a lawsuit between C.W. Thompson, who built the Beula Villa Hotel, and Dr. U.W. McPherson, owner of the McPherson Hotel, arose over access to the well. Thompson alleged that McPherson's Hotel did not have access to the water; however, the suit was later resolved when it was believed that Ezekiel Neal had deeded the well and two acres to all the people of Metcalfe County. (Courtesy of Cora Emma Jessie.)

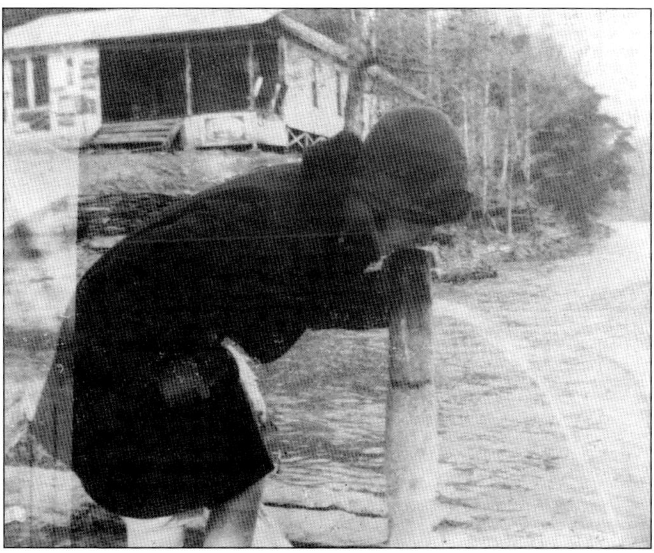

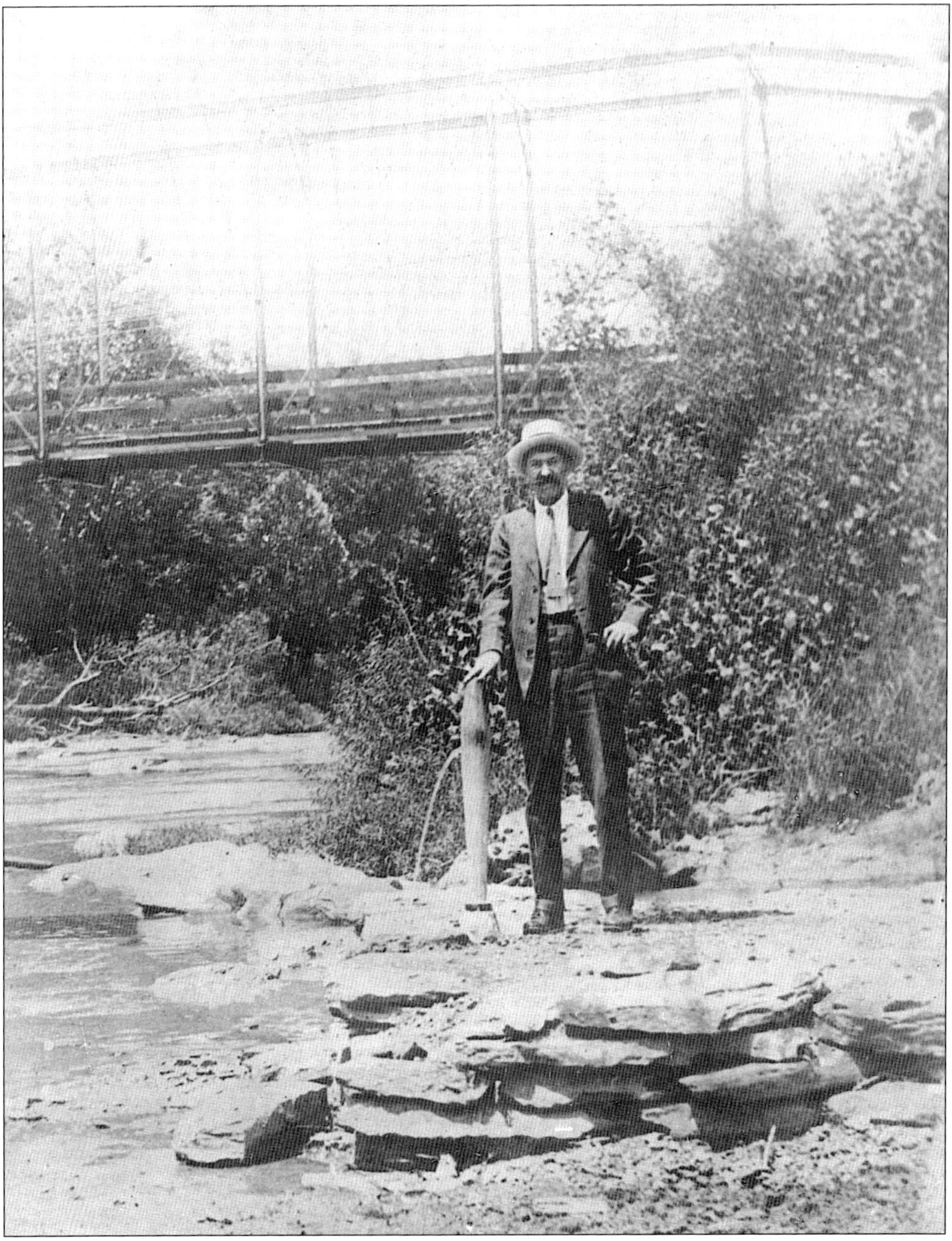

Even today, the concrete structure of the well continues being referred to as "the gum." The name comes from the practice of pushing a hollow limb or sapling from a sweet gum tree into the well, which allows water to flow above the rock, making it easier to drink. (Courtesy of Cora Emma Jessie.)

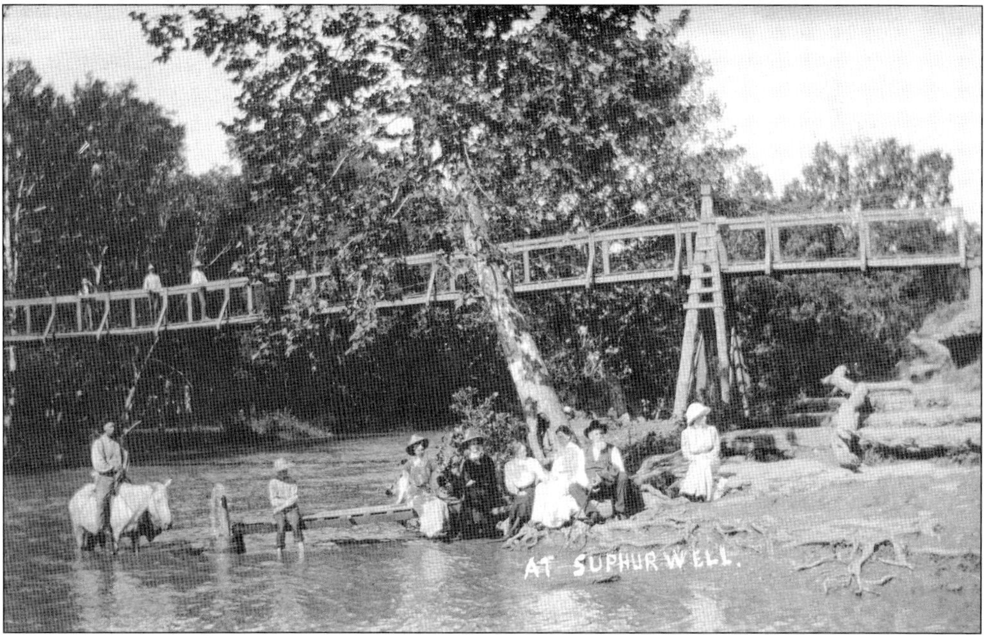

An artesian well can push water above the aquifer and in the well stem above ground level. Before the 1950s, the well ran continuously into barrels but when the well went dry in the early 1970s, the Kentucky Bureau of Highways realigned the well casing and redrilled it, allowing water to begin reflowing from the artesian well. At that time, the state improved the park and built the concrete structure that is present today. (Courtesy of Cora Emma Jessie.)

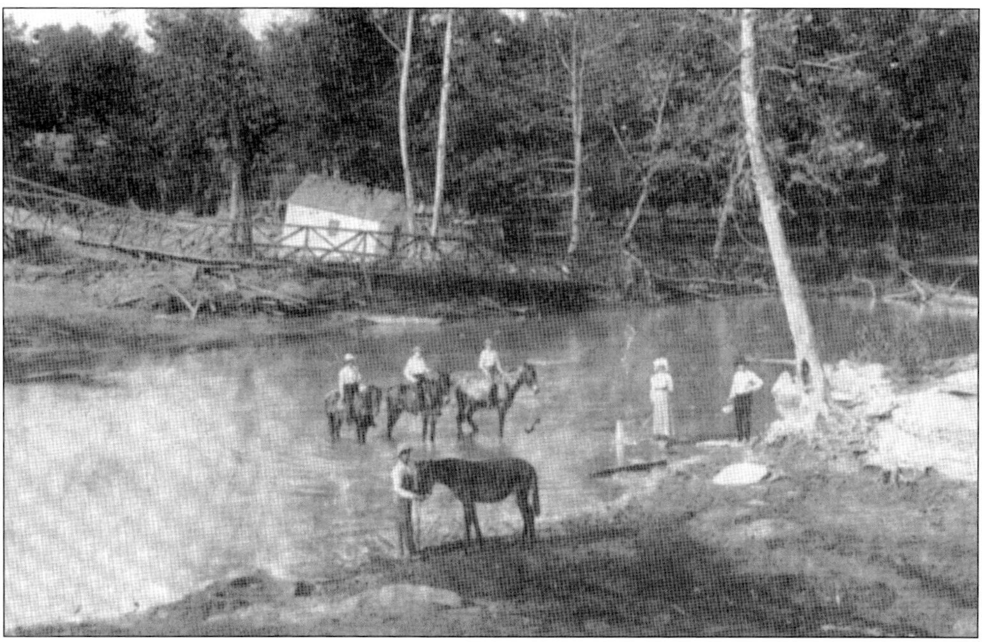

Pictured here is a view following the 1911 flood. The watershed in the South Fork of the Little Barren River is expansive and subject to large floods. Another major flood occurred in 2010; however, no residences were built along the riverbank at that time. (Courtesy of Cora Emma Jessie.)

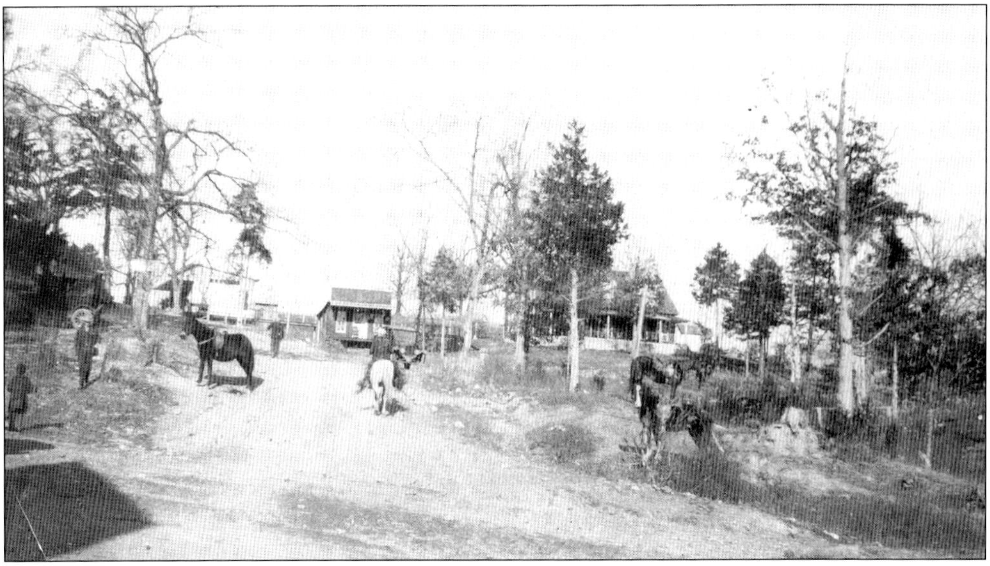

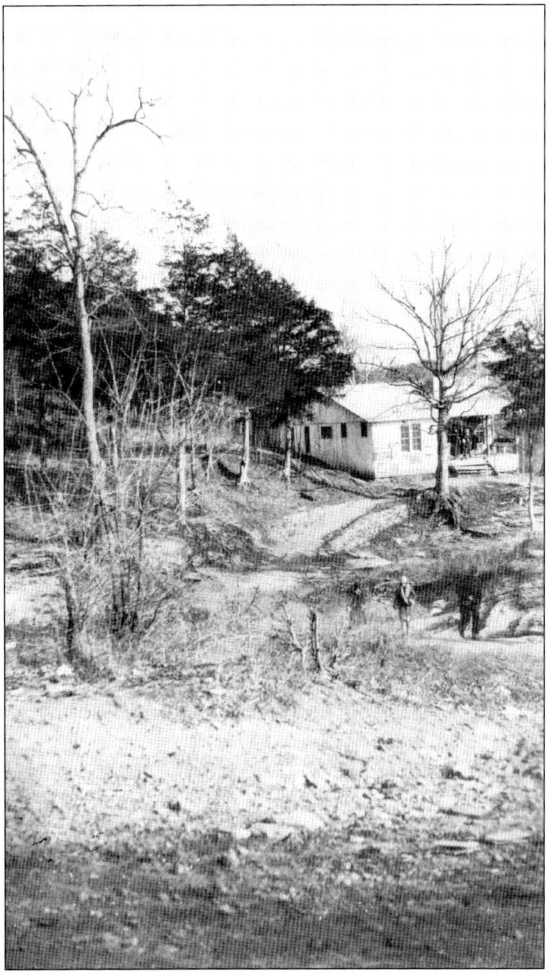

Looking east from the store and the McPherson Hotel sometime in December 1928, the road in Sulphur Well is dirt, and horses are the only transportation seen that day. It would be at least 10 years before gravel was used to surface roads, which helped improve transportation. (Courtesy of Reba Gravens Norman.)

This was the dirt road leading to the bowling alley. Sulphur Well also had a saloon and it was not uncommon for fights to break out between patrons in both establishments. One such fight in 1883 resulted in the shooting death of a man in the saloon. (Courtesy of Reba Gravens Norman.)

The owner and proprietor of the Beula Villa Hotel was King Crenshaw (left). Pictured here with a guest, Crenshaw operated the hotel until he was in his 80s. The hotel was known for numerous events, from political rallies to fox hunting championships. In 1928, Crenshaw hosted a fox horn blowing contest, a fiddler's contest, and a square dance during a fox hunt. (Courtesy of Cora Emma Jessie.)

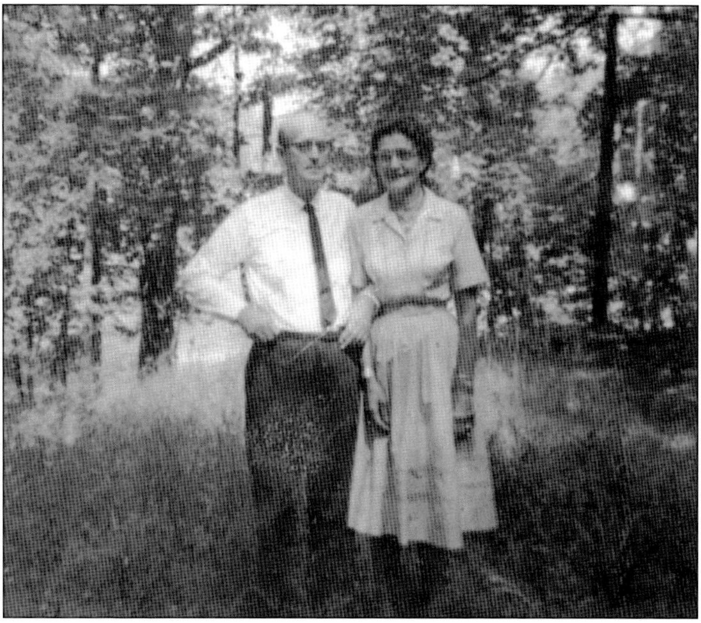

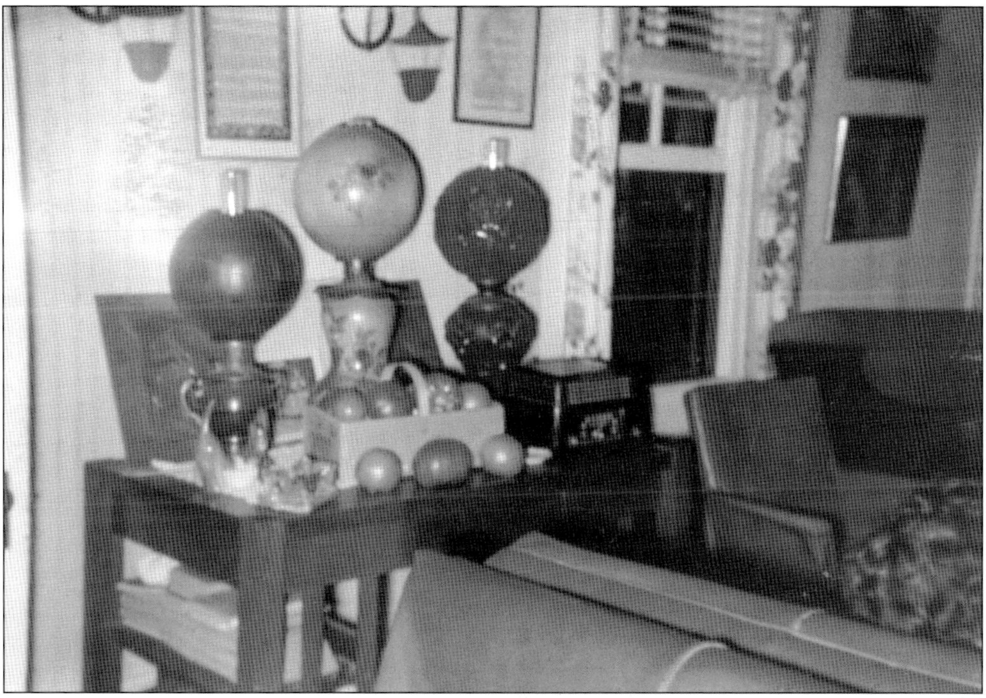

King Crenshaw loved his large antique lamp collection, which he displayed over the entire hotel. This is a photograph of the lobby in the 1960s showing lamps and boxes of fresh tomatoes for the guests. Many vegetables such as these tomatoes were grown in large gardens that the hotel staff cared for each day. (Courtesy of Dean Rowe.)

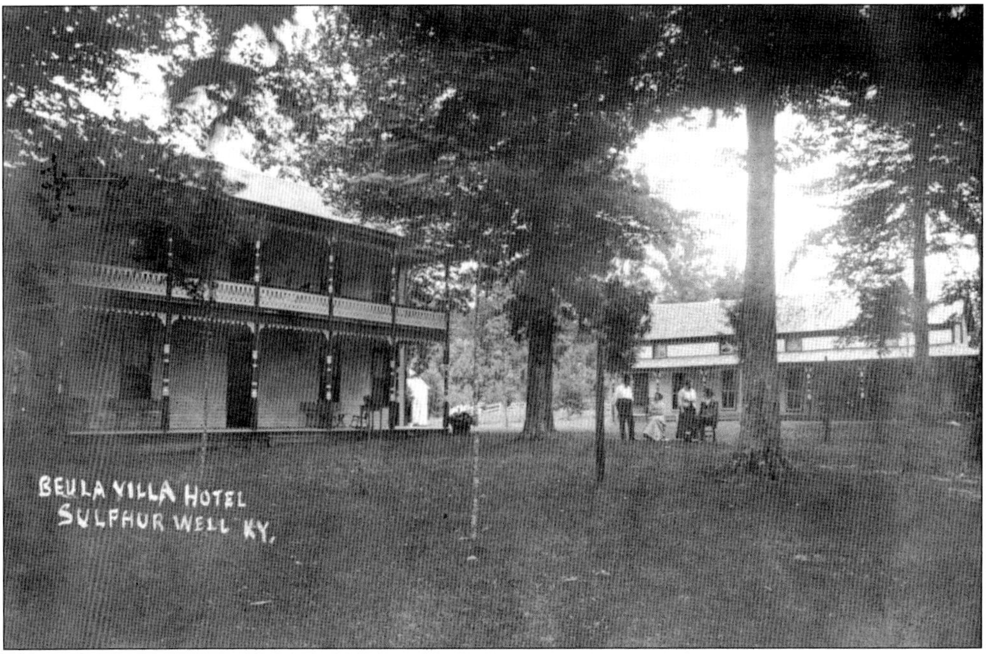

This postcard shows the yard at the Beula Villa Hotel in the early 1900s. Guests would play croquet in the yard or walk in the woods. The hotel advertised "airy rooms, spacious porches for card parties, recreation and your choice of plain water and medicinal water from the artesian well." It was a well-known destination for honeymooners and vacationers alike. (Courtesy Western Kentucky University Special Collections.)

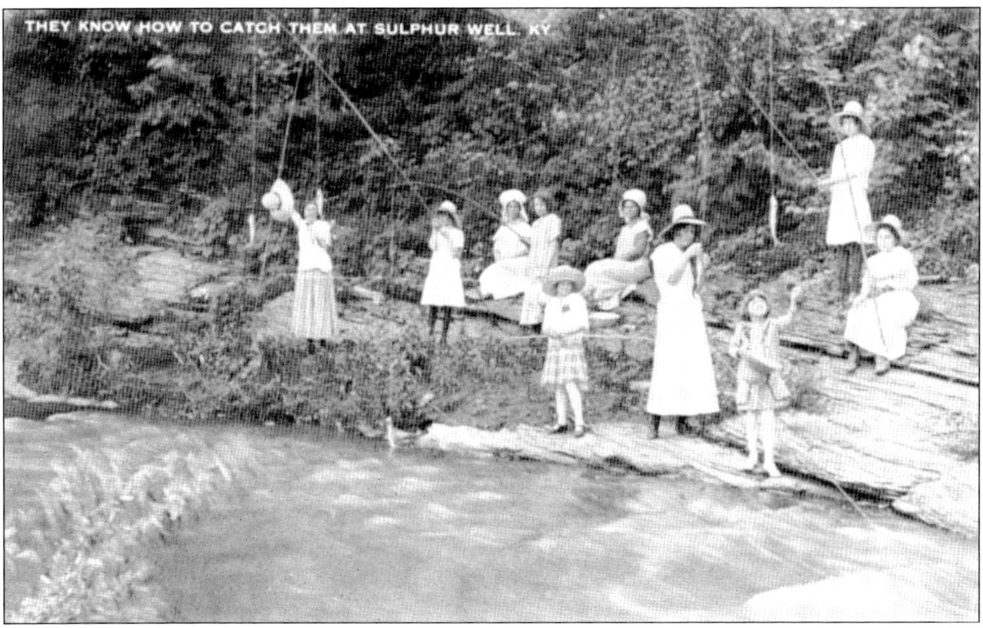

"They know how to catch them at Sulphur Well, Ky." was a postcard sold in town to promote fishing. One advertisement for the hotel boasted of good fishing and small game hunting in the nearby forests. (Courtesy of Western Kentucky University Special Collections.)

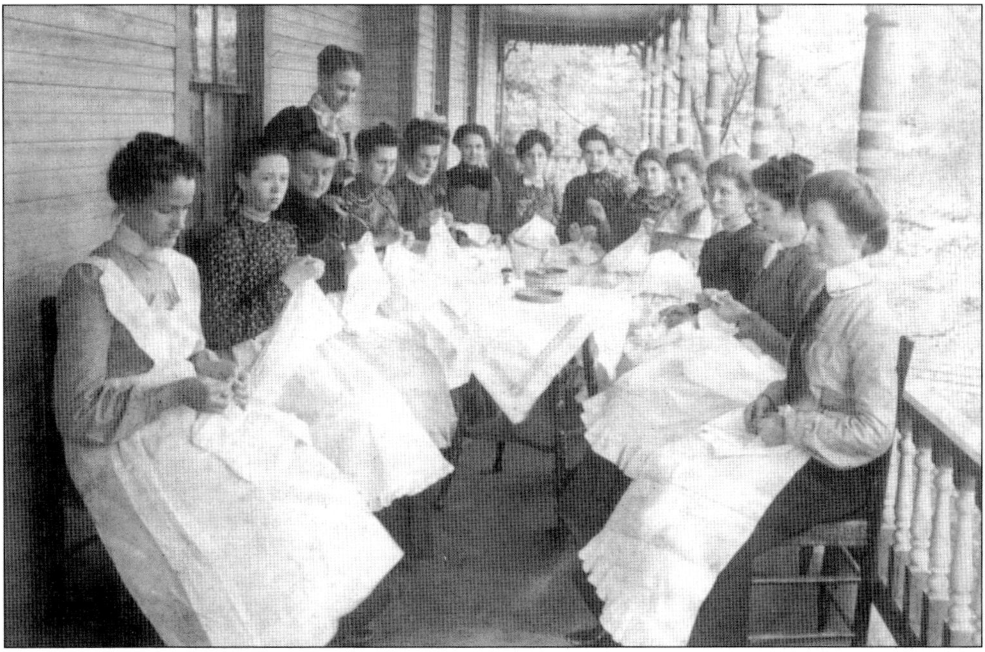

Sometime around 1910, young ladies are sitting on the massive front porch at the Beula Villa Hotel sewing and doing needlework under the watchful eye of Catlett Thompson, the wife of C.T. Thompson, who built the hotel in 1902. (Courtesy of Sherron Westerfield.)

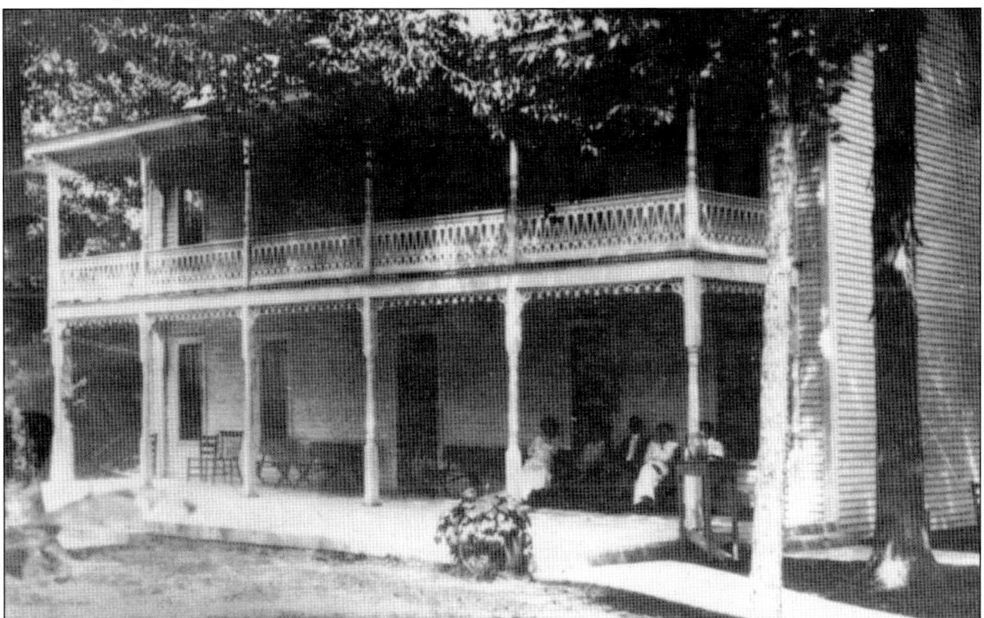

This 1930s postcard features one of Beula Villa's massive porches. Gov. Louie B. Nunn worked here after high school and said he got blisters sweeping the massive porches each morning. Upstairs and downstairs, the porches were 12 feet wide by 164 feet long, and Nunn worked seven days a week washing dishes, carrying water, and picking green beans in the hotel's gardens. (Courtesy of Western Kentucky University Special Collections.)

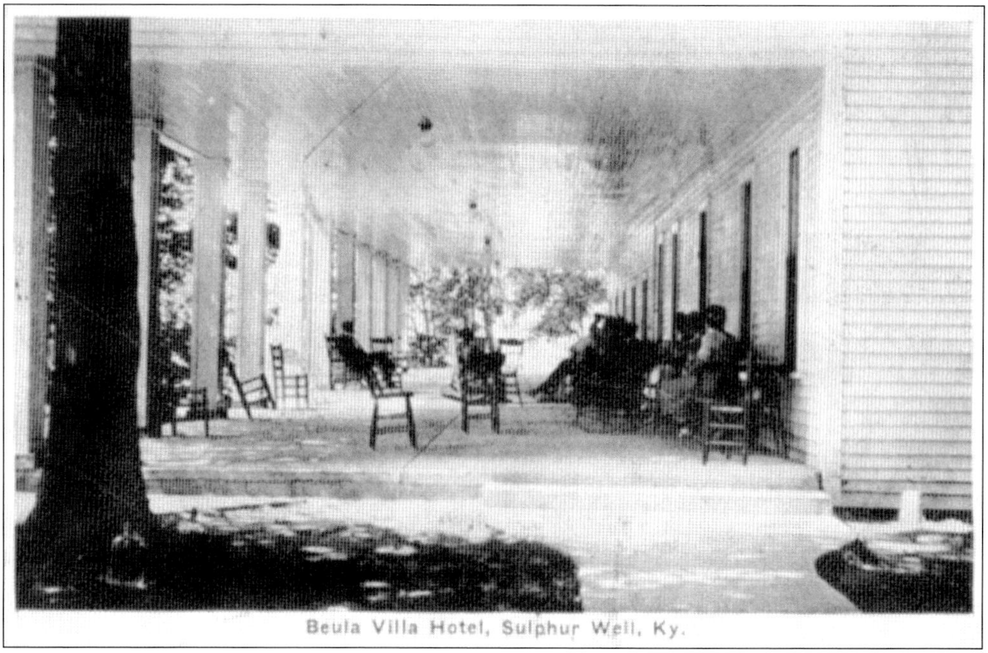

This postcard shows the semicircular main veranda at the hotel where people would wait for King Crenshaw to come out at the strike of noon and ring the big brass bell. As patrons moved into the dining room for Sunday dinner, they were greeted by tables set for 12 with starched linen and heavy flatware. Guests were served the famous fried chicken, country ham, red-eye gravy, and homegrown vegetables the hotel was famous for. (Courtesy of Western Kentucky University Special Collections.)

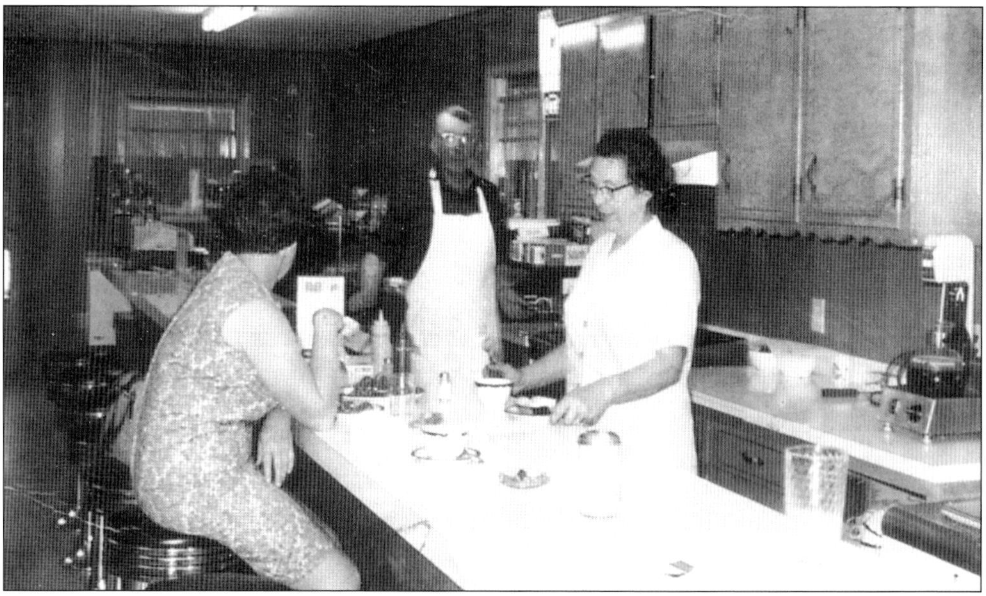

Babe and Kathleen Porter started Porters Restaurant in the late 1960s shortly after the Beula Villa closed. After running it for several years, it was sold and renamed the Lighthouse Restaurant. Just as the Beula Villa had been famous for good food, the Lighthouse has a wide following, recently being named the best non-franchised restaurant in Kentucky. (Courtesy of Cora Emma Jessie.)

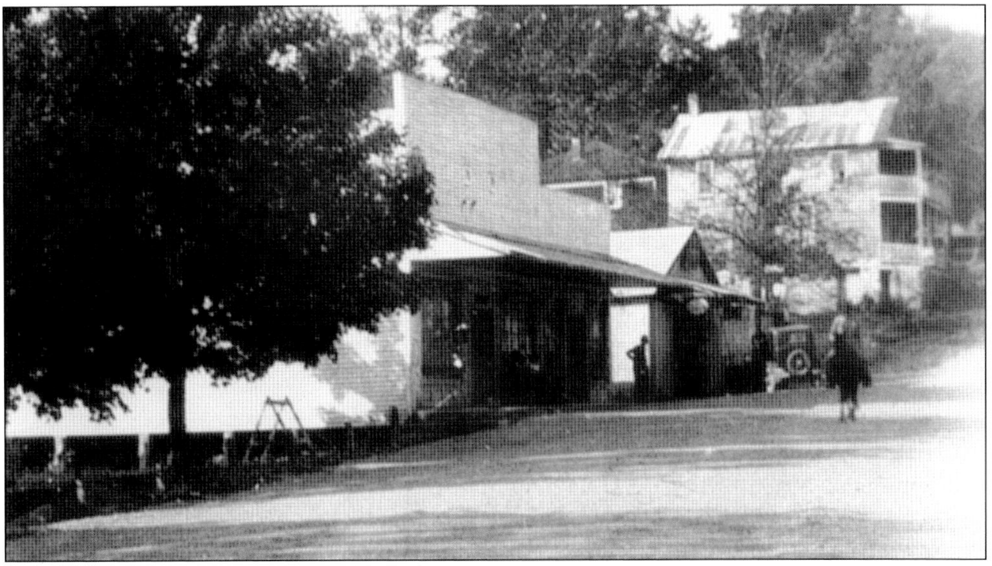

This street scene in Sulphur Well around 1935 shows both vehicles and a horseback rider. Residents used both modes of transportation well into the 1940s. The first building on the left is the Sulphur Well Country Store, and next to it is Porters Feed Supply. The large two-story building at the top of hill was the McPherson Hotel. (Courtesy of Cora Emma Jessie.)

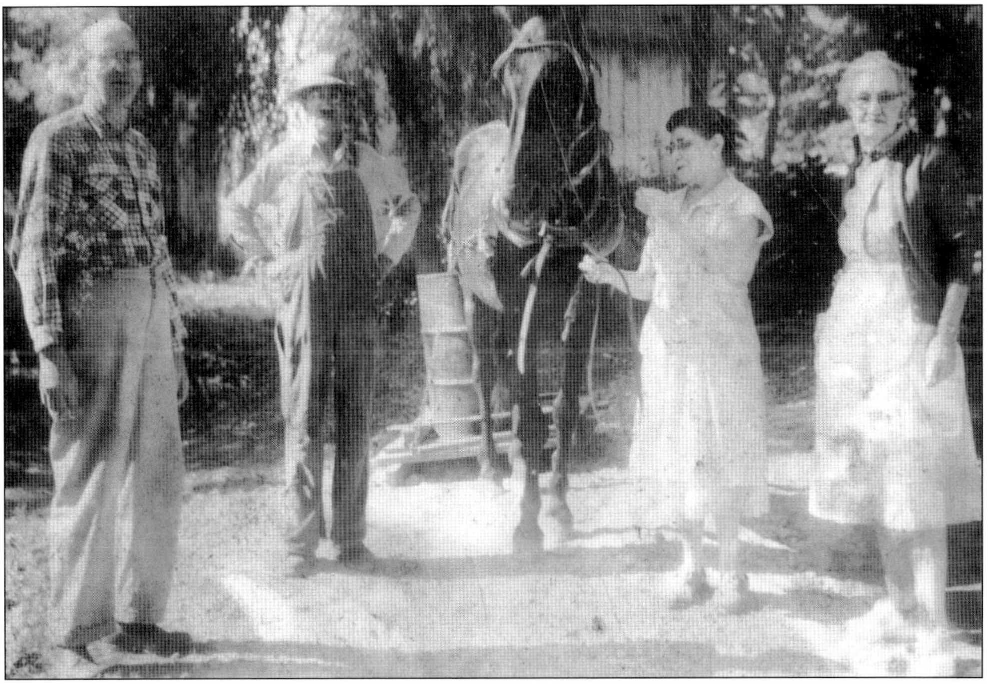

The Beula Villa Hotel was famous for its fresh country cooking. Albert Beauchamp was the main worker at the hotel. Each day he would collect food scraps from the kitchen and feed the hogs. Beauchamp also used this mule to cultivate the large garden that supplied year-round vegetables for the hotel's restaurant. The hotel also had cattle and chickens on 100 acres of land. Pictured are, from left to right, King Crenshaw, Albert Beauchamp, Ida Beauchamp, and Pearl Kidd. (Courtesy of Cora Emma Jessie.)

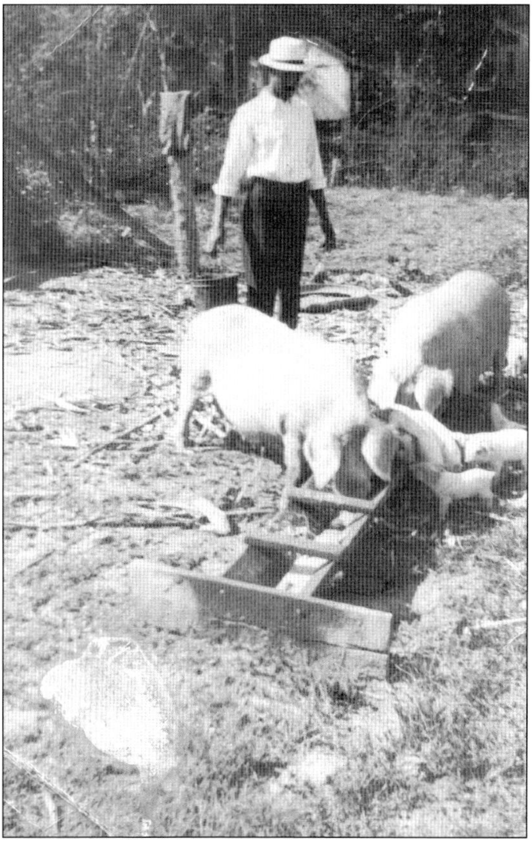

Albert Beauchamp is feeding food scraps to the Beula Villa hogs in the 1950s. Country ham dinners were a popular entrée. Into the 1960s, the hotel charged guests $6 each per night. Guests would receive three hot home-cooked meals prepared by head cook "Aunt" Ida Beauchamp and James Mitchell, head pastry cook. King Crenshaw would travel the country buying additional hams to sell at the hotel. (Courtesy of Cora Emma Jessie.)

Murrell Rowe is stirring his popular squirrel stew over the fire while John Beauchamp watches. Sulphur Well was famous for hosting political rallies in Sulphur Well Park. This rally was for Gov. Happy Chandler, who was running for a second term in 1955. Chandler, who had been governor from 1935 to 1939, was overwhelmingly elected to a second term, from 1955 to 1959. (Courtesy of Dean Rowe.)

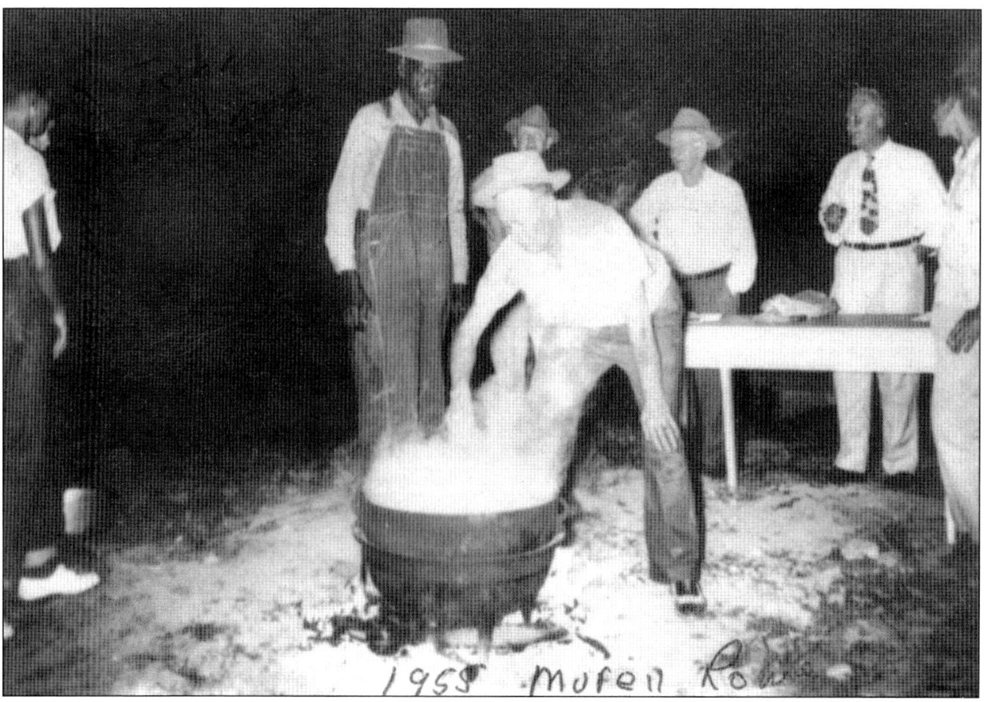

The cooks and several workers lived in servant quarters near the rear of the Beulah Villa Hotel. The wonderful food was prepared every day by Ida Beauchamp and her husband, Albert Beauchamp. James Mitchel took care of the hotel livestock and farm that supported the hotel's restaurant. (Courtesy of Cora Emma Jessie.)

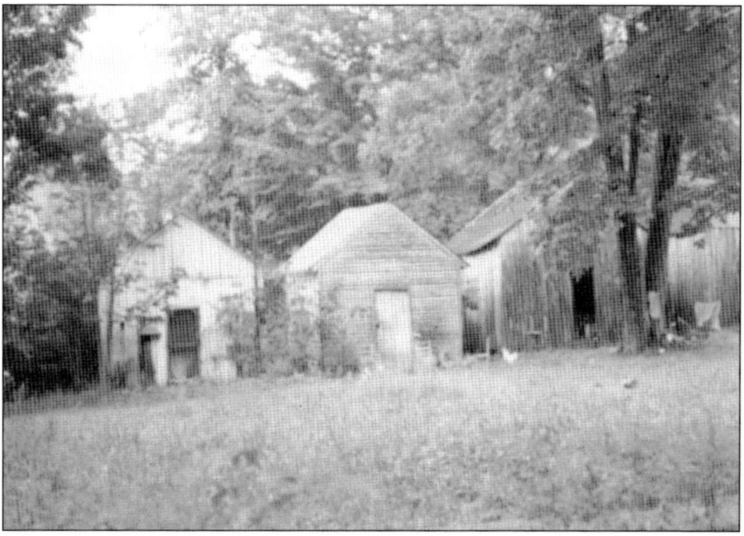

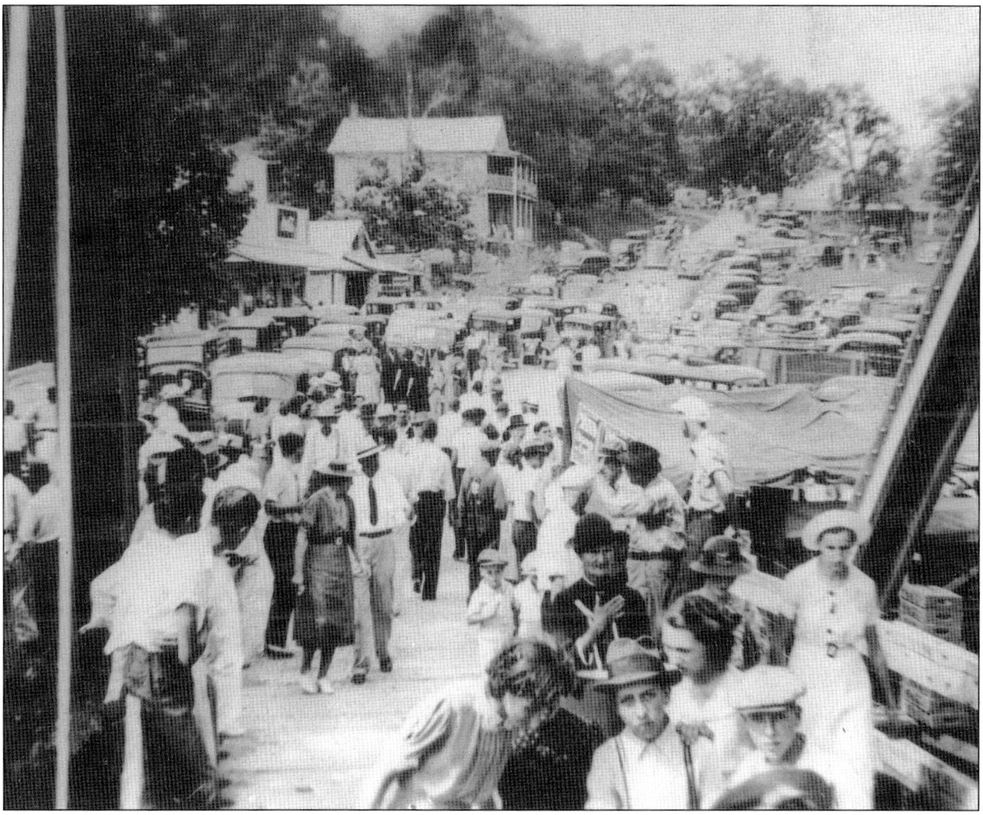

The Third Sunday in August festival was started as a homecoming by some people from Hart County sometime in the 1880s. Since then, the event has gained in popularity and by the 1940s, as shown in this photograph, was attended by hundreds of people. The event continues today, with activities all weekend. (Courtesy of Cora Emma Jessie.)

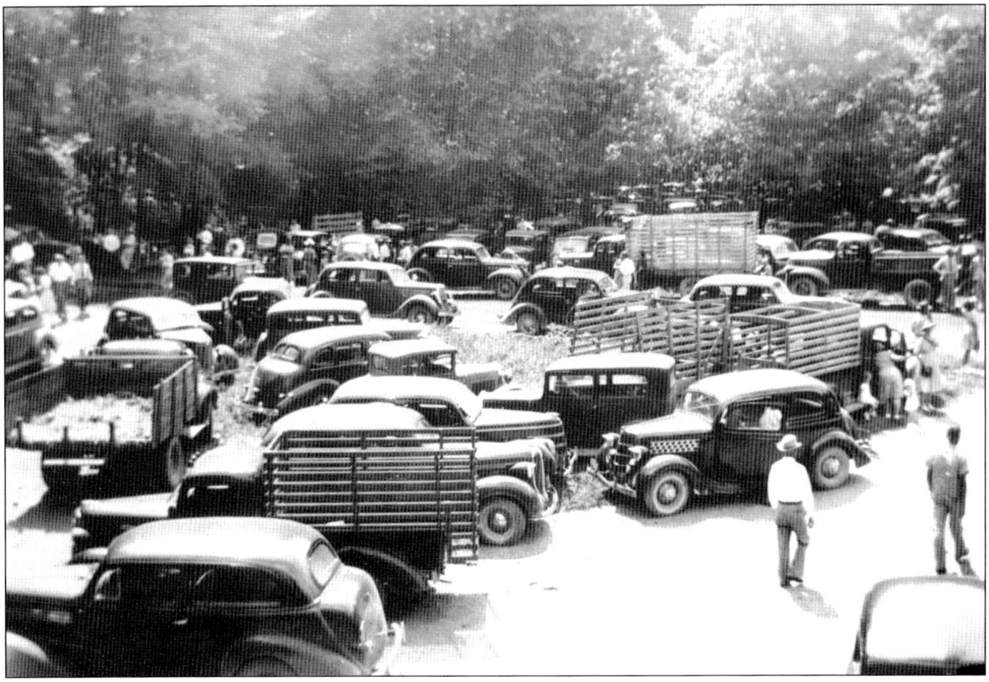

King Crenshaw said that when he started the hotel, he had to drive a Model T 18 miles on a dirt road to Cave City, where he met guests at the railroad station. By the 1940s, roads had improved and visitors came from miles around to attend events such as the Third Sunday in August in the grove. By 1968, all the guests were driving themselves to the hotel. (Courtesy of Western Kentucky University Special Collections.)

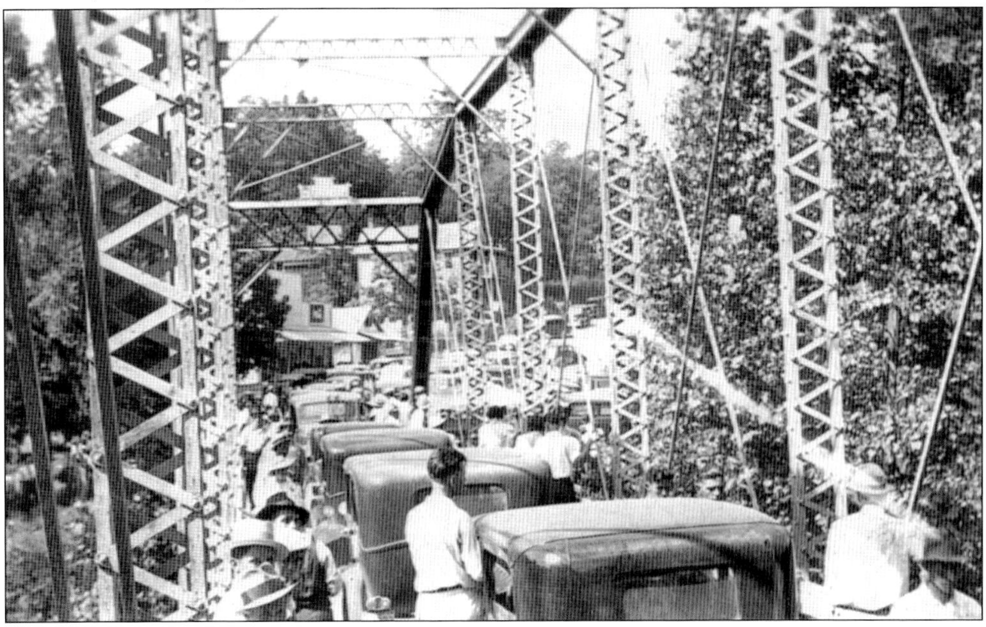

Crossing the Little Barren River was difficult prior to 1911. Metcalfe County constructed a metal truss bridge in 1911, and it served the county until the Kentucky Bureau of Highways replaced the steel bridge with a concrete one in 1949. (Courtesy of Cora Emma Jessie.)

Sulphur Well was not just a resort to spend the night at but a destination for Sunday afternoon visits. Here, Vervin and Effie Barrett enjoy an afternoon walk on the swinging bridge in 1924. (Courtesy of Vicki Harris.)

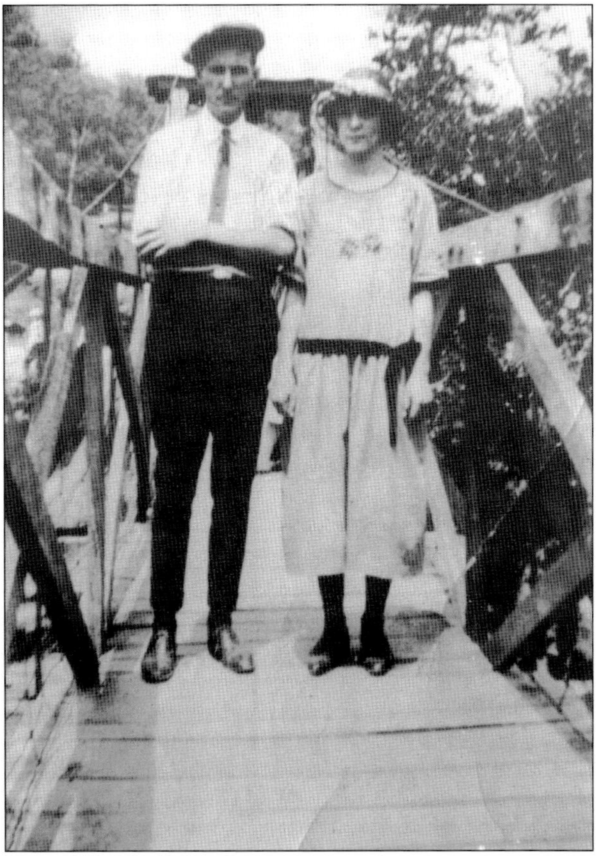

The inside of Murrell Rowe's Store is pictured here. Rowe's Store provided all the groceries local residents needed for the week, and like a lot of small country stores, customers were not charged for their purchases until their crops were sold. Murrell Rowe (right) is seen with family and locals who frequented the store in 1960. Country stores were operated by families, and many children grew up in them. Rowe had the first television in town, and many times the store would be full of people watching it, sometimes even through the windows. (Courtesy of Dean Rowe.)

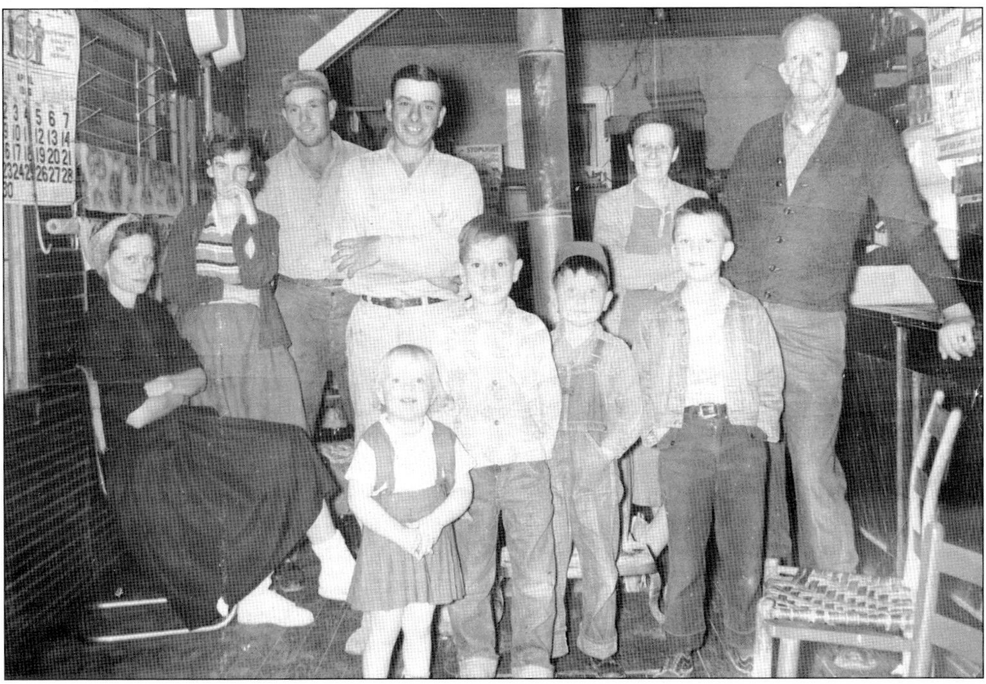

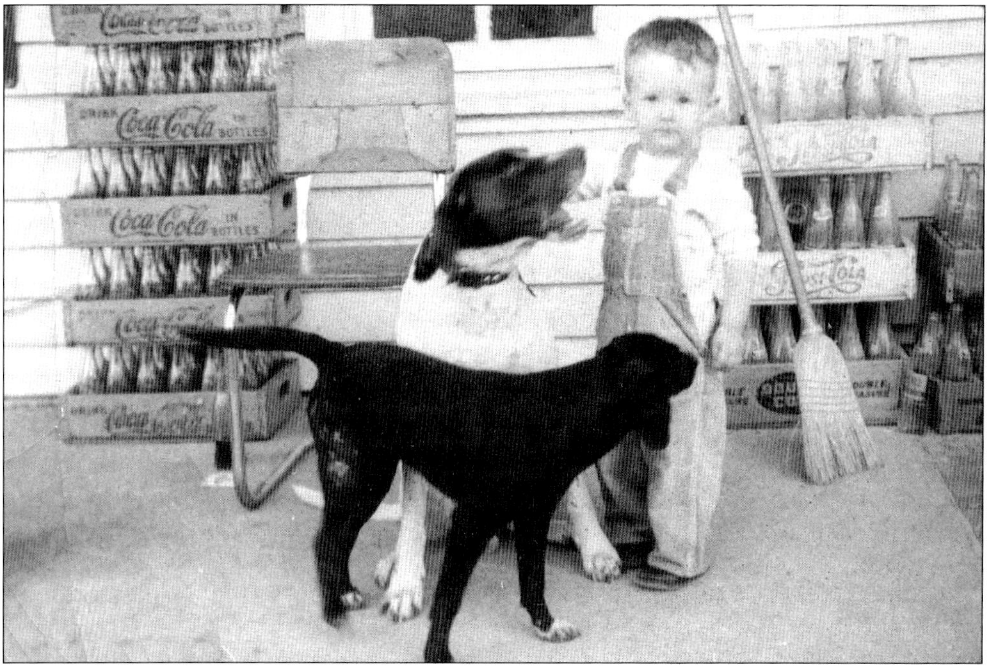

It was not unusual for kids to be at the store, and it seemed every store had at least one or two dogs. This young man on the porch is Dean Rowe, with the family dogs who would travel to the store each day with the owners. Note the soft drink bottles on the front porch. Empties were always returned for credit, which was around 3¢ per bottle. (Courtesy of Dean Rowe.)

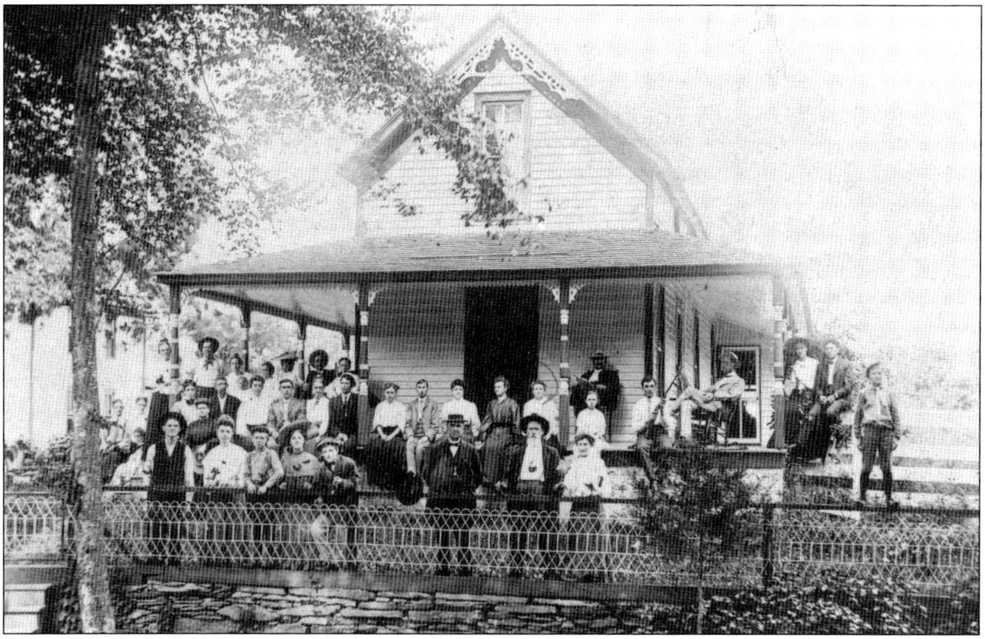

A large crowd is at the home of "Aunt Byrd" Thompson, wife of C.W. Thompson. The Thompsons, who had built the Beulah Villa Hotel in 1903, lived in this house, which was close to the hotel. The hotel had been named after C.W.'s niece Beula. Aunt Byrd lived in this house until 1954. (Courtesy of Cora Emma Jessie.)

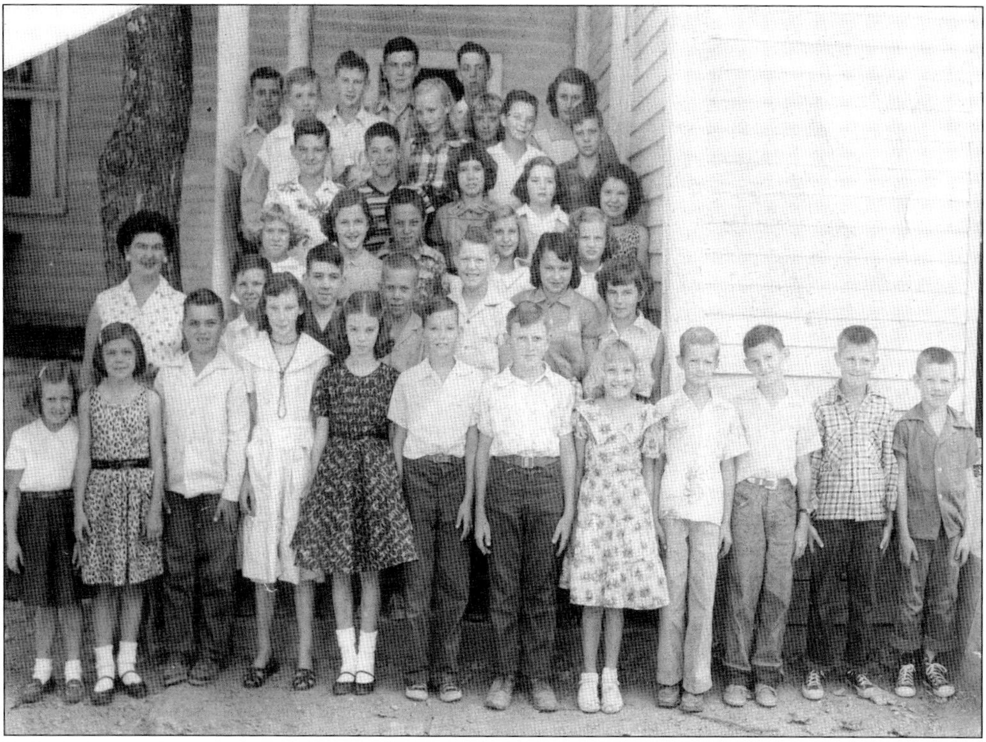

Ruby Polson, who was one of five teachers who taught grades 1–8 at Sulphur Well School, stands with her students in the 1950s. The school closed in 1959 when all students started attending the North Metcalfe School between Center and Sulphur Well. (Courtesy of Reba Gravens Norman.)

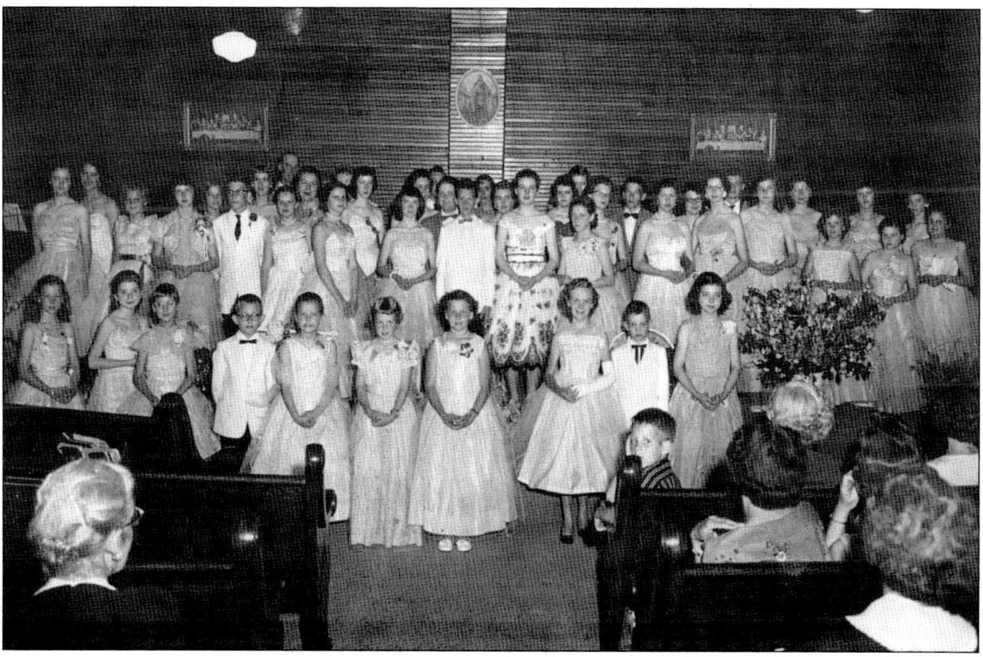

This piano recital at the Sulphur Well Methodist Church was directed by teacher Mary Ball in the late 1950s. (Courtesy of Reba Gravens Norman.)

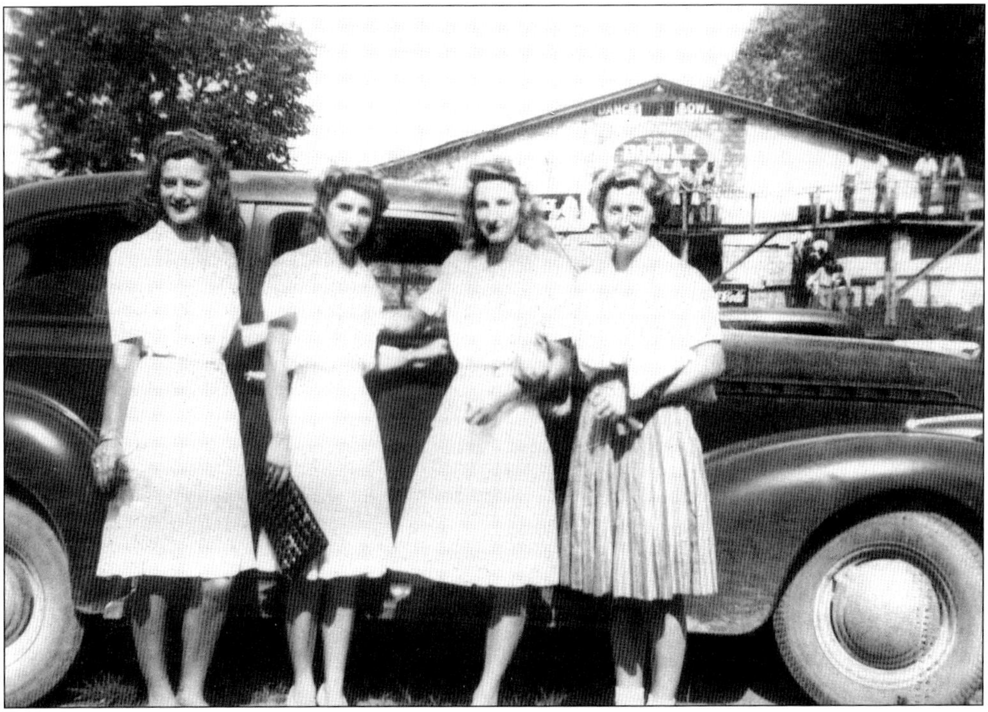

In 1943, four seniors had their photograph taken in front of the dance hall after high school graduation. They are, from left to right, Virginia Burton, Machelle Whatley, Lean Hedges, and Alyne Boston. (Courtesy of Reba Gravens Norman.)

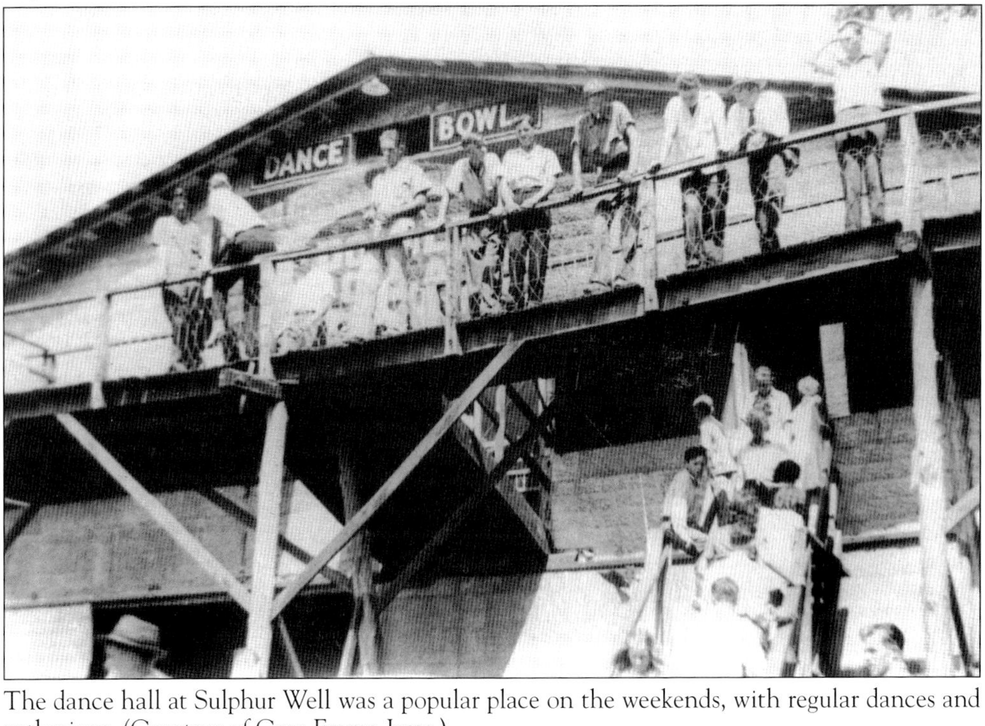

The dance hall at Sulphur Well was a popular place on the weekends, with regular dances and gatherings. (Courtesy of Cora Emma Jesse.)

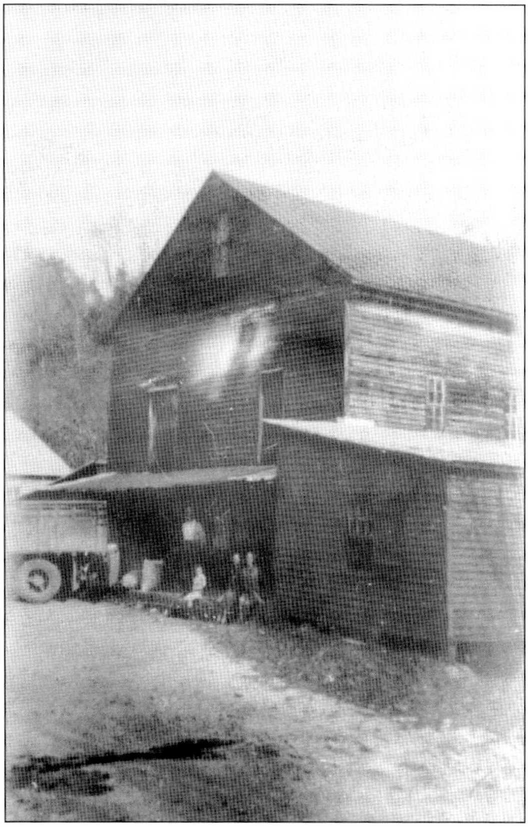

People unload grain off a truck at Marcum's Mill. Local farmers would bring corn and wheat to the mill to either sell it or have it ground. As payment, farmers would give a percentage to the mill, which was then sold. A truck would leave the mill each week making deliveries to Louisville and other locations. The flour sack below was from Sam M. Marcum and Brother near Sulphur Well. (Right, courtesy of Cora Emma Jessie; below, courtesy of Richard Hines.)

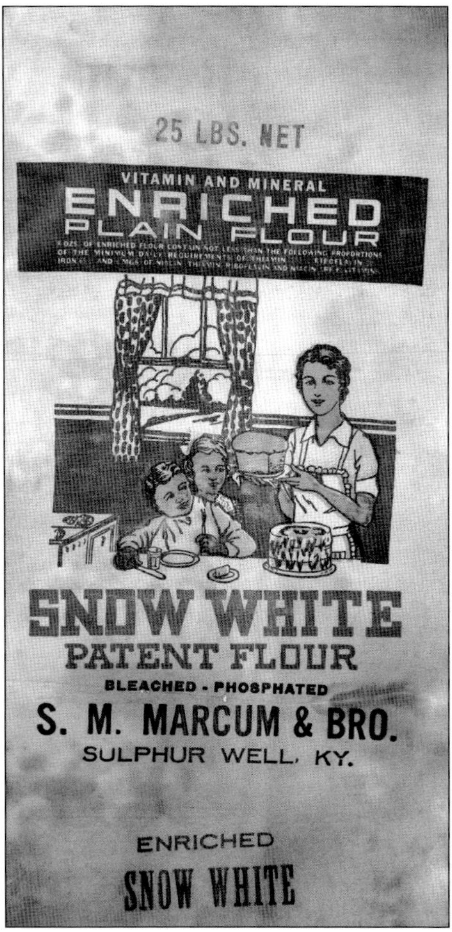

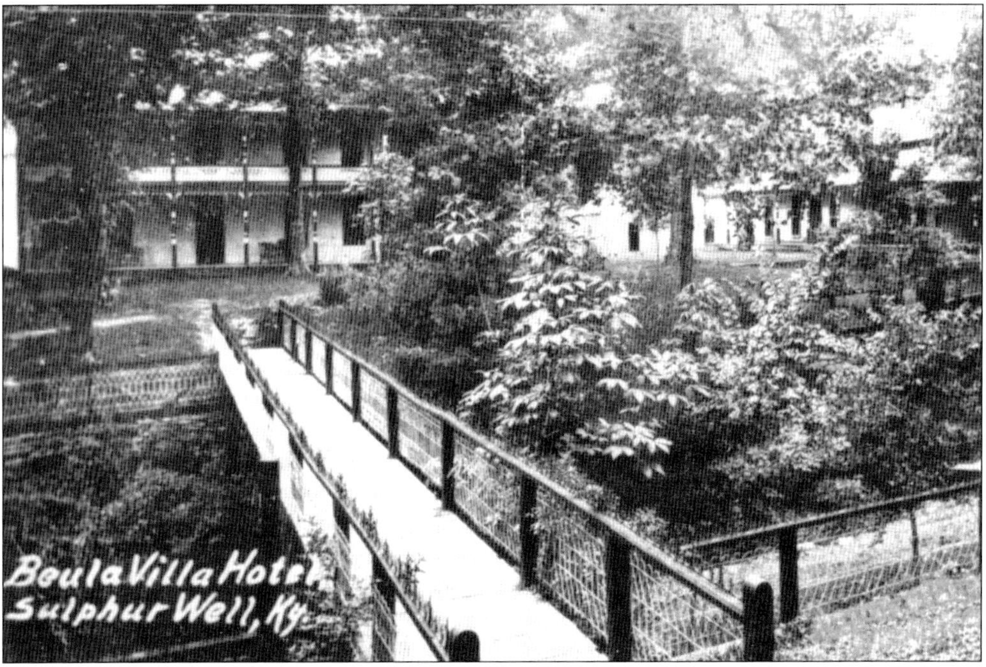

This postcard of the Beula Villa Hotel shows the bridges connecting Sulphur Well with the hotel. Employees would have to carry guests' luggage and other supplies across the bridges. Guests used these bridges each day to visit the well and for other activities. (Courtesy of Cora Emma Jessie.)

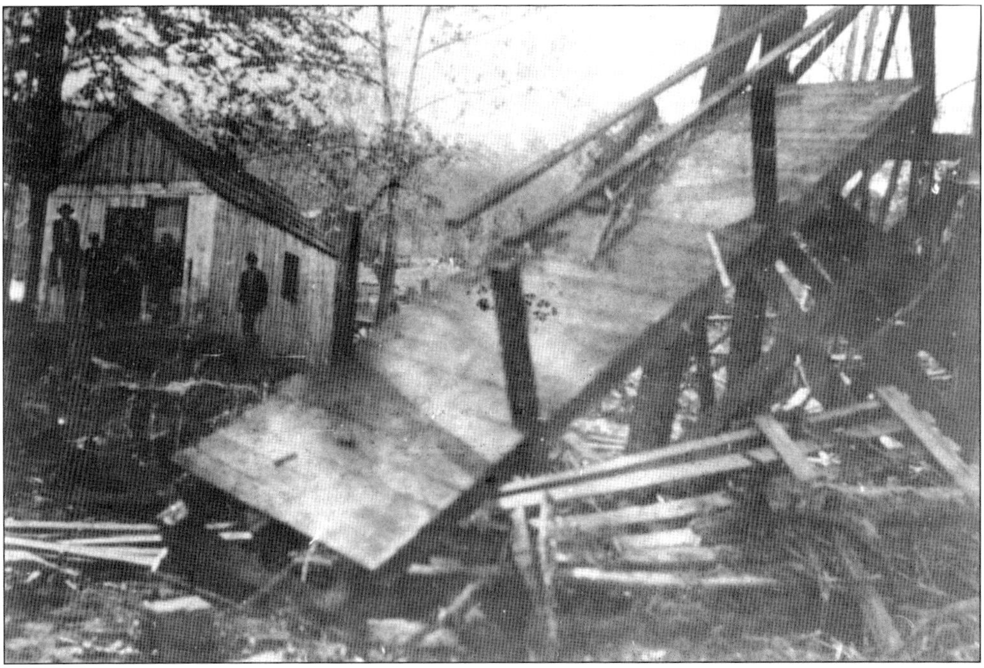

Two major floods have devastated Sulphur Well. The largest occurred in May 1911. Newspapers reported that a flood had taken both bridges across the Little Barren River along with many cottages and the pin alley. During the same flood, the estimated damage to Marcum's Mill was $2,000, and Robinson's Mill was completely washed away. (Courtesy of Cora Emma Jessie.)

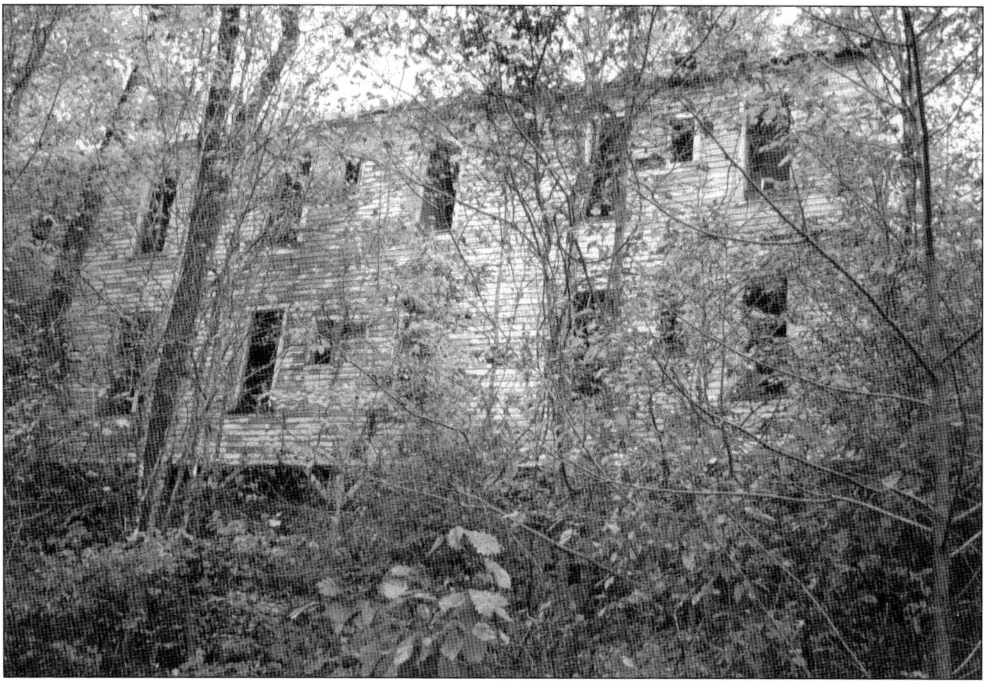

The Beula Villa Hotel came under different ownerships after it was sold by King Crenshaw. It was later abandoned, and quickly fell into disrepair. This is a photograph of the once famous hotel as it appeared in the early 1980s shortly before it was burned by an arsonist. (Courtesy of Cora Emma Jessie.)

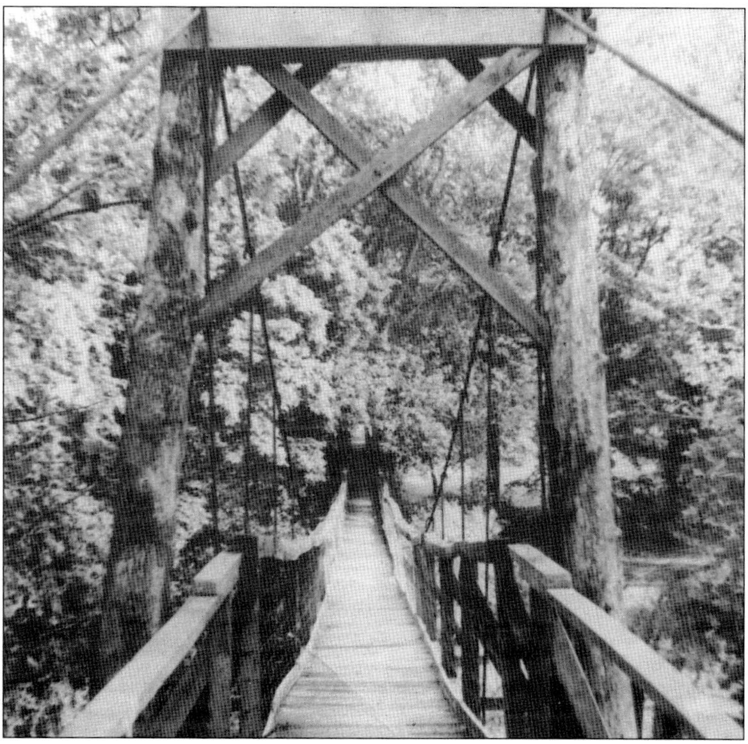

It was not unusual to use local material in building structures, such as with the bridge from the hotel across the river. On one occasion in the 1960s, the bridge partially collapsed after some boys began rocking and swinging it, dropping over 21 people onto the rock bed of the creek. (Courtesy of Cora Emma Jessie.)

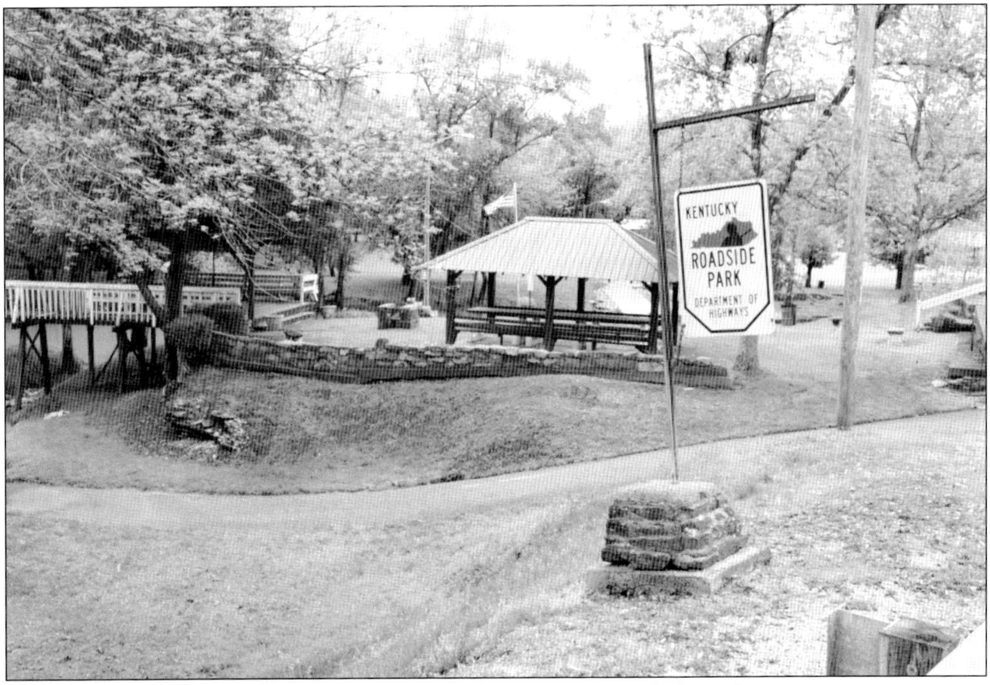

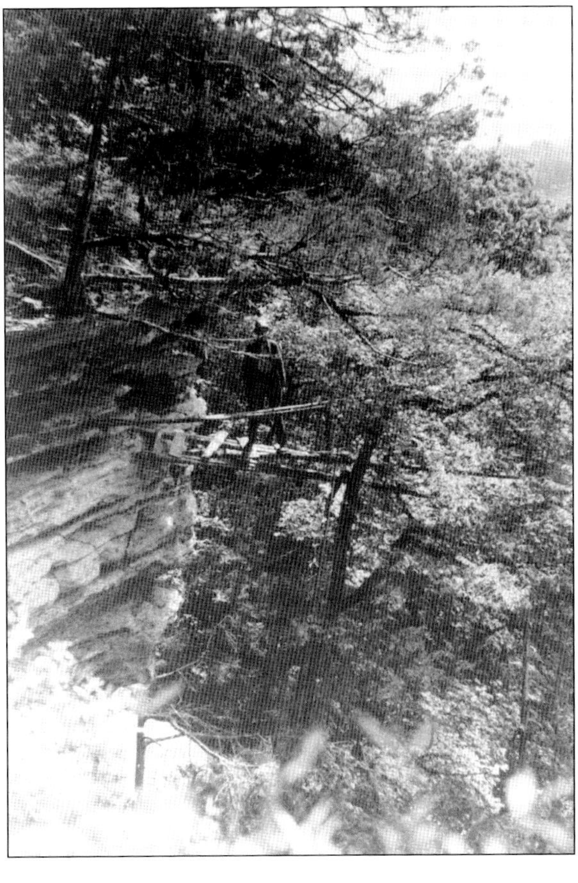

Roadside parks were once common along most of Kentucky's state highways. One of the last remaining parks is the Sulphur Well Roadside Park. Originally donated to the county by King Crenshaw in the early 1950s, it was later designated a Kentucky roadside park. The last attendant to care for the park was Dean Rowe, who worked there until the park was transferred to the Metcalfe County Road Department in the 1980s. (Photograph by Richard Hines.)

One of the most memorable characters in Sulphur Well was "Uncle" Matt Scroggy. Known for his writing and poetry, he preferred to live most of the year in a cave in a bluff overlooking the river on the outskirts of town. Access was rather precarious, and he used a series of cables and homemade red cedar ladders to reach the entrance. Scroggy is shown here standing at the entrance to his cave. (Courtesy of Cora Emma Jessie.)

Four

Summer Shade

Located in the southern portion of Metcalfe County, Summer Shade was originally in the Sartain Precinct and was later named Glovers Creek. In 1872, the postmaster changed the name to Summer Shade.

Throughout the 1800s and into the early 1900s, Summer Shade was a stagecoach stop where passengers would eat and take a break, allowing horses to be exchanged. A typical trip between Glasgow and Burkesville was an all-day affair for the Burkesville-Glasgow Stage Line, which at one time was owned and operated by Keen and Baker. Some references indicate that horses were changed at Beaumont, a few miles east of Summer Shade.

In April 1923, efforts by local citizens were underway to obtain federal funding to improve the road between Glasgow and Burkesville. By 1929, work began on what was referred to as the Cumberland Park Highway, connecting Corbin and Glasgow on the original stage route that became today's Kentucky Route 90 (KY 90).

Some of the most prominent people to come from Summer Shade include Dr. C.C. Howard, a respiratory specialist best known for establishing a system of tuberculosis hospitals across Kentucky, and baseball player Charles "Pat" Dougherty. Dougherty, who played in the Negro National League, was named a member of the 1909 All American team.

Capt. J.P. Grinstead, who was born in Summer Shade, enlisted in the Union army at the age of 15 as a private. Within a year, he received a battlefield promotion to second lieutenant, and by the end of the Civil War, Grinstead was a captain. He remained at Fort Leavenworth after the war, later serving in the Spanish-American War.

When a tree fell on 24-year-old Percy W. Bushong, he decided to finally start grammar school. Bushong not only completed grammar school, but attended both dental and medical schools in Louisville. He traveled to local patients in Metcalfe County on horseback. When World War I started, Bushong was promoted to captain in the Army Medical Corps, serving in France.

Today, Summer Shade has several manufacturing companies that utilize the extensive forest products harvested in the area.

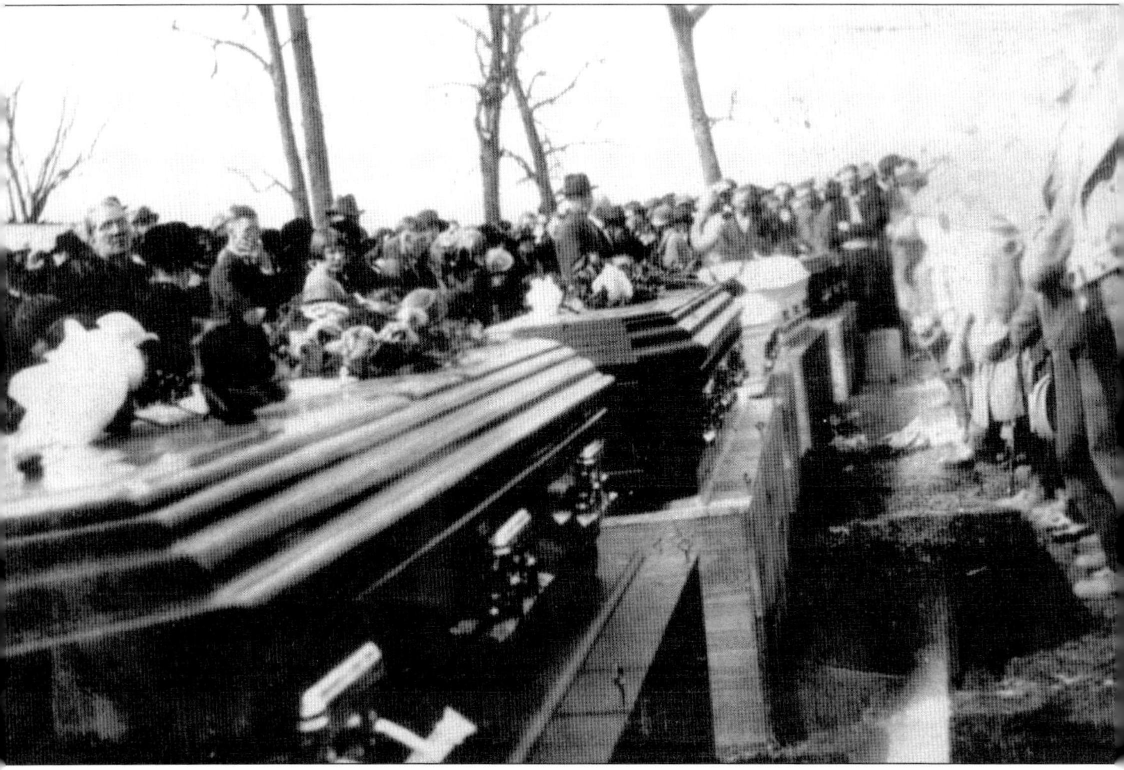

Pictured is a funeral for a Beaumont family who were killed on March 18, 1925, following a tornado outbreak that killed 848 people across five states. Newspapers reported eight killed and 50 injured in Beaumont and one killed in Bridgeport. The path of one F-4 tornado was 400 yards wide and 60 miles long. (Courtesy of Laurie Butler.)

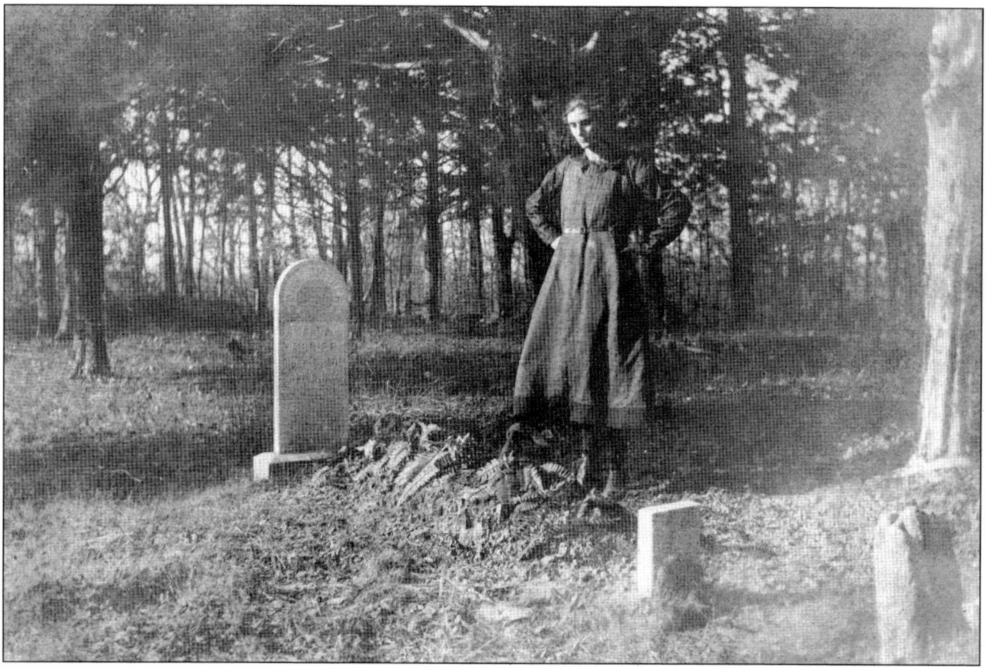

Mary Hurt is at a cemetery overseeing the gravesite of Amanda Hurt in the early 1900s. The care and oversight of gravesites was an important activity to rural Metcalfe communities. (Courtesy of Carol Hurt.)

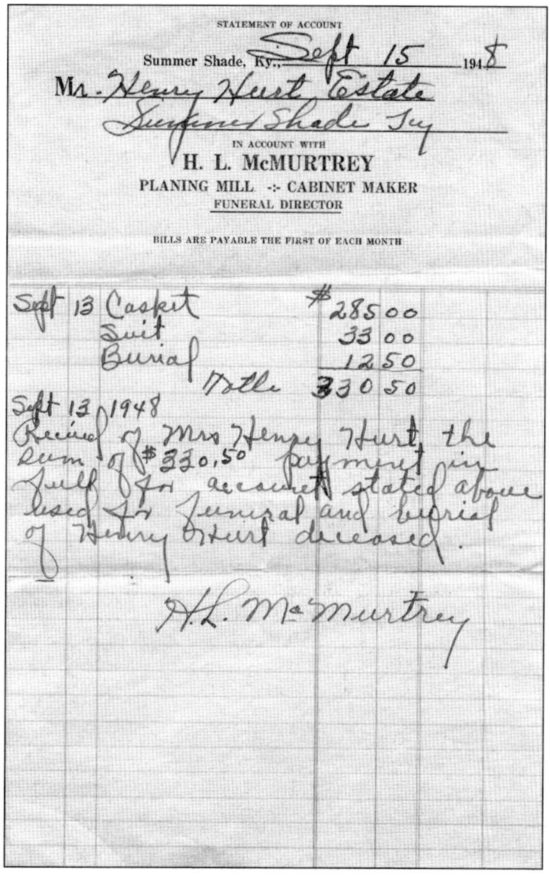

STATEMENT OF ACCOUNT

Summer Shade, Ky., Sept 15 1948

Mr. Henry Hurt Estate
Summer Shade Ky

IN ACCOUNT WITH

H. L. McMURTREY

PLANING MILL -:- CABINET MAKER

FUNERAL DIRECTOR

BILLS ARE PAYABLE THE FIRST OF EACH MONTH

Sept	13	Casket	$285 00
		Suit	33 00
		Burial	12 50
		Totle	330 50

Sept 13, 1948
Recived of Mrs Henry Hurt, the sum of $330.50 payment in full for account stated above used for funeral and burial of Henry Hurt deceased.

H.L. McMurtrey

The total funeral bill from McMurtrey's Funeral Home for Henry Hurt in 1948 was $330.50 and included a new suit, casket, and $12.50 for digging the grave. The McMurtreys also ran a cabinet shop in Summer Shade. (Courtesy of Carol Hurt.)

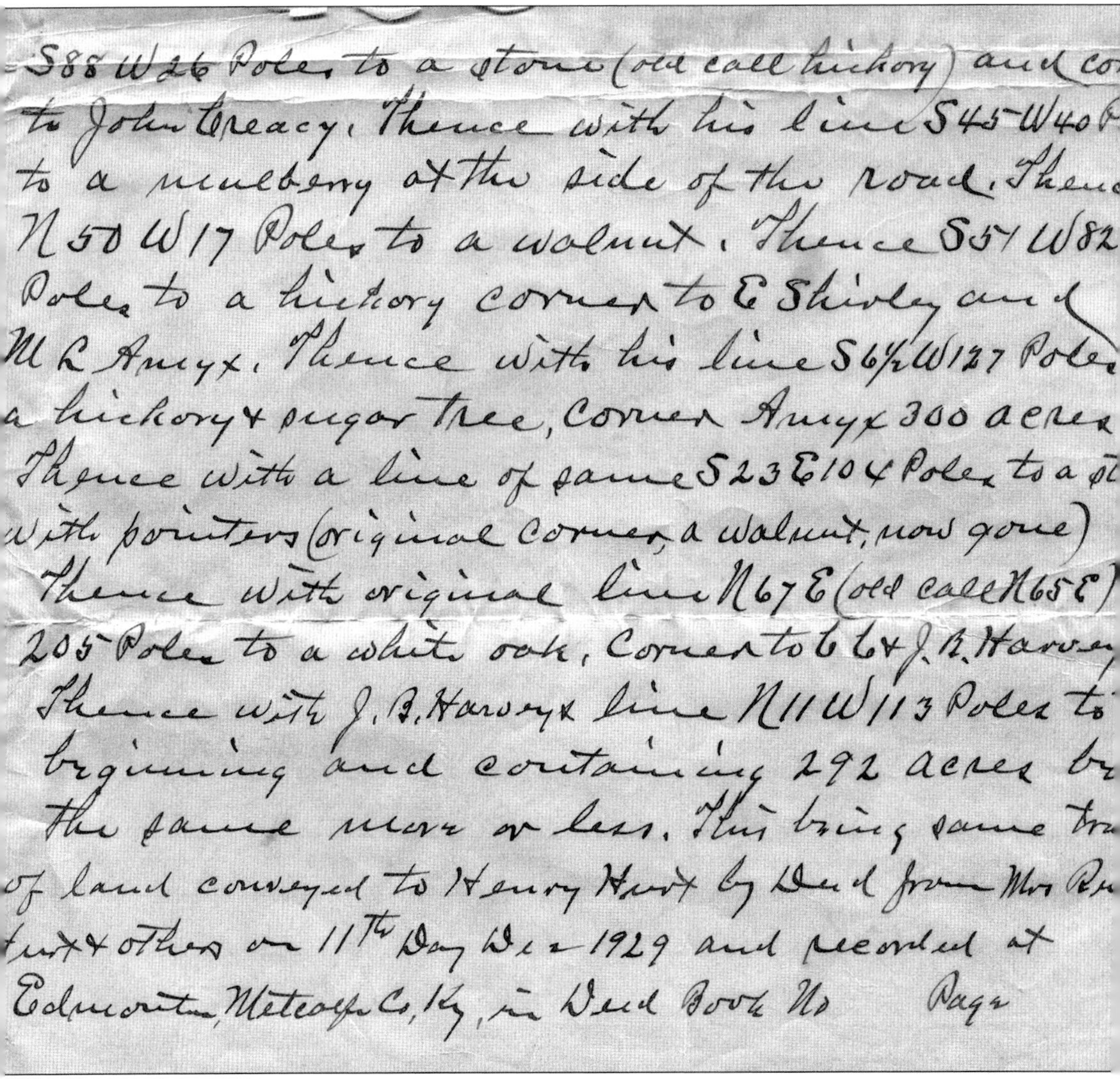

S88 W26 Poles to a stone (old call hickory) and co
to John Creacy. Thence with his line S45 W40 P
to a mulberry at the side of the road. Thence
N50 W17 Poles to a walnut. Thence S57 W82
Poles to a hickory corner to E Shirley and
M L Amyx. Thence with his line S6½ W127 Poles
a hickory & sugar tree, Corner Amyx 300 acres
Thence with a line of same S23 E104 Poles to a st
with pointers (original corner, a walnut, now gone)
Thence with original line N67 E (old call N65 E)
205 Poles to a white oak, Corner to C C & J. B. Harvey
Thence with J. B. Harveys line N11 W113 Poles to
beginning and containing 292 acres by
the same more or less. This being same tra
of land conveyed to Henry Hurt by Deed from Mrs Re
Hurt & others on 11th Day Dec 1929 and recorded at
Edmonton, Metcalfe Co, Ky, in Deed Book No Page

A deed for Henry Hurt is pictured here. Up until the early 1950s, many deeds for land were still handwritten documents. Surveyors could locate any tract of land according to the "calls." Some of the terms measuring distance include a pole, which is 16.5 feet. This form of land measurement is from an old English term, "mete and bounds," meaning measure and boundary. Calls were made between markers, which might include a rock, creek, or specified trees. (Courtesy of Carol Hurt.)

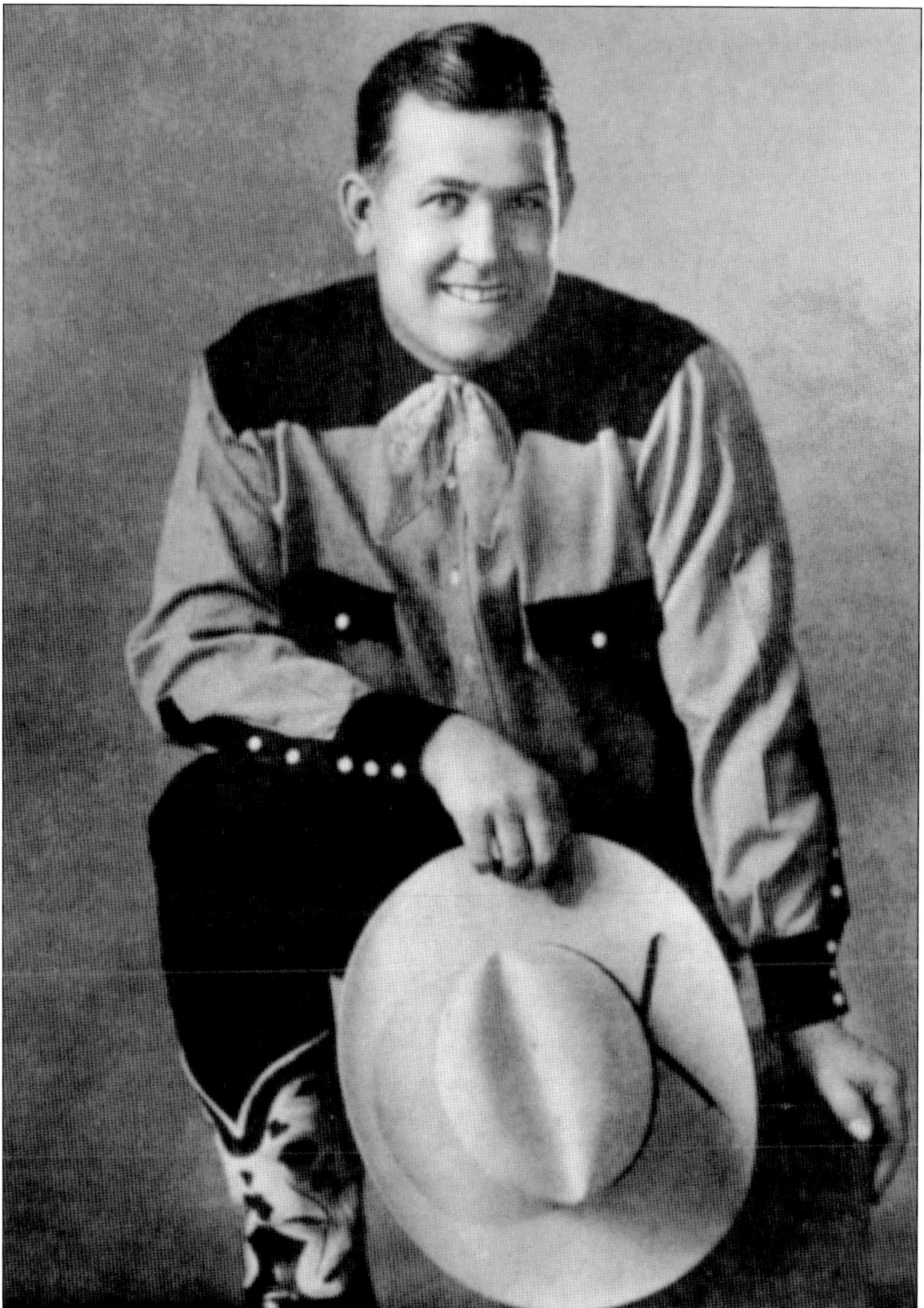

Chick Hurt, who was from Willow Shade, became a famous country singer during the 1930s. (Courtesy of Carol Hurt.)

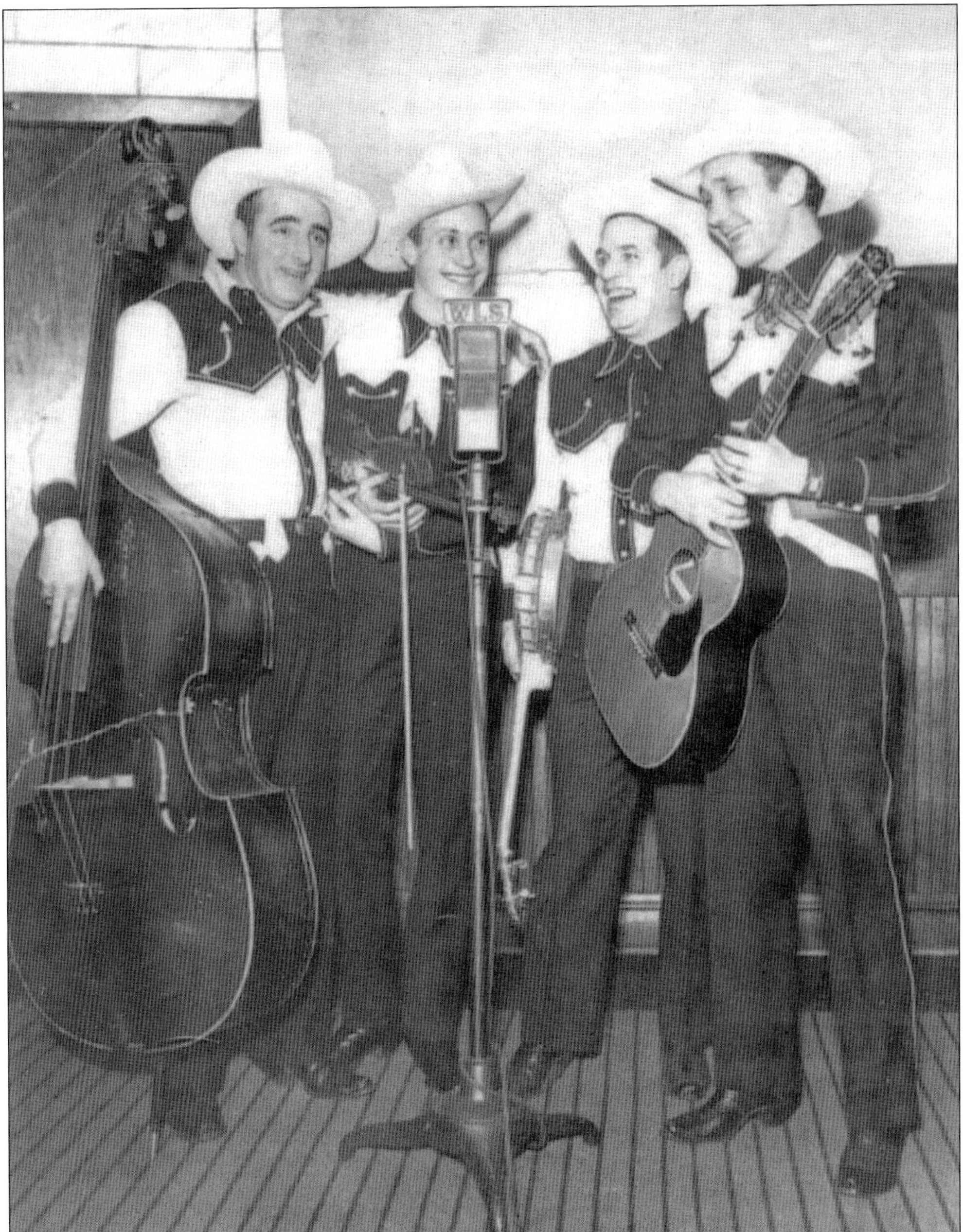

Pictured here are, from left to right, Jack Taylor, Allen Crockett, Chick Hurt, and Salty Holmes. The group was initially called the Kentucky Ramblers and began in 1931 with their radio debut on WOC in Davenport, Iowa. By 1932, the group moved to Chicago, appearing on WLS. The group's name was changed to the Prairie Ramblers by an early morning farm show called the *Prairie Farmer*. The group was influential to other artists, including Bill Monroe. (Courtesy of Carol Hurt.)

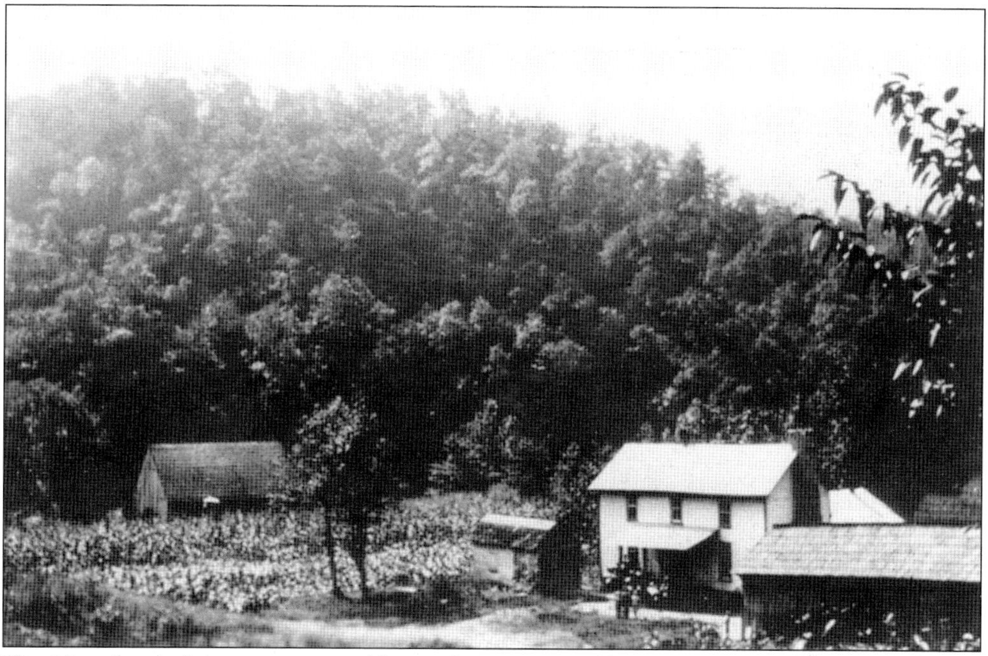

The Hurt family farm was a typical homeplace in Metcalfe County. In addition to the home, each farm had a smokehouse, corncrib, chicken coop, and a barn that was large enough to shelter cattle, mules, and that year's crop of tobacco. The family garden was essential for supplying fresh food and food that was preserved for the year. (Courtesy of Carol Hurt.)

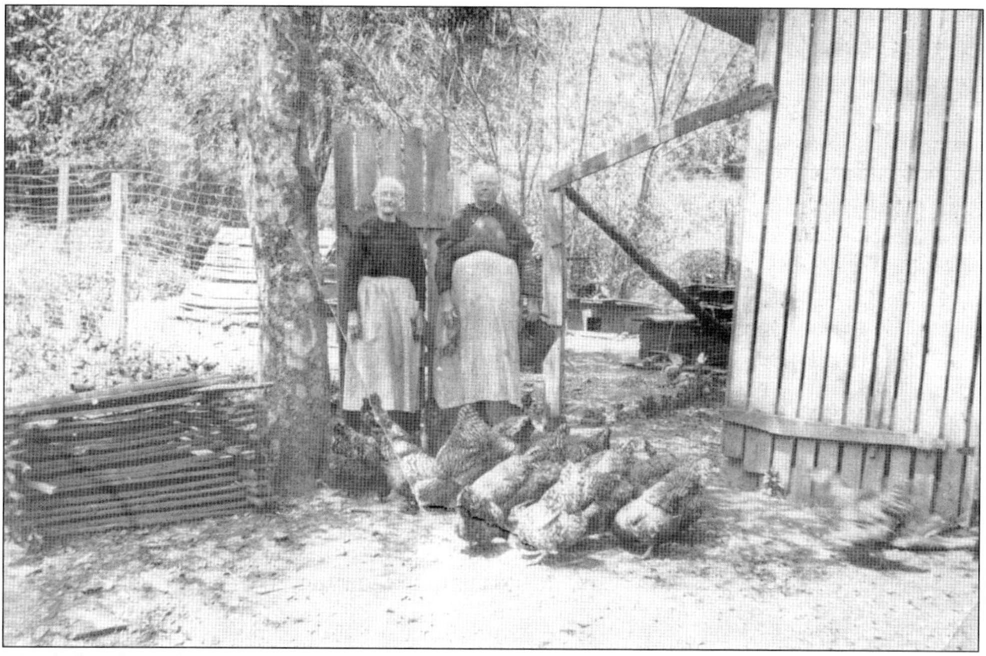

Two ladies from the Hurt family are feeding the farm's chickens, which supplied both fresh meat and eggs. Chickens and eggs were also sold or exchanged for supplies at local stores. Hucksters or peddlers would sometimes travel the area, and chickens were used as barter for needed merchandise. (Courtesy of Carol Hurt.)

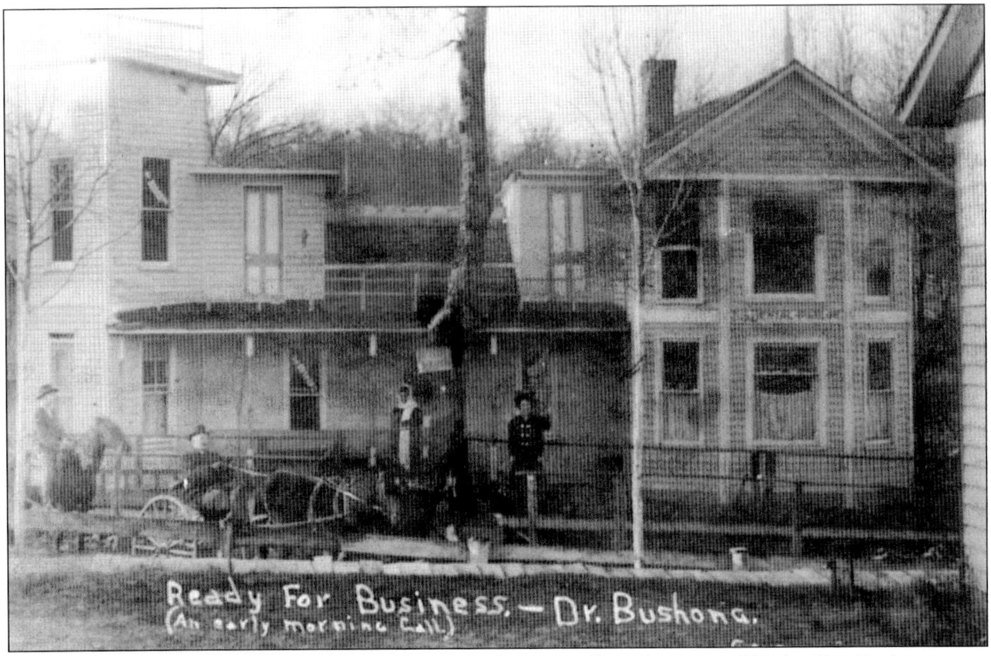

Dr. Percy Bushong leaves his office to go on a house call in Summer Shade. Dr. Bushong was famous for starting grammar school at the age of 24 after being struck by a tree. He was both a dentist and a medical doctor but later became interested in soil conservation and was a proponent of good conservation practices. He donated a portion of his 800-acre farm to the Boy Scouts for a camp. (Courtesy of Laurie Butler.)

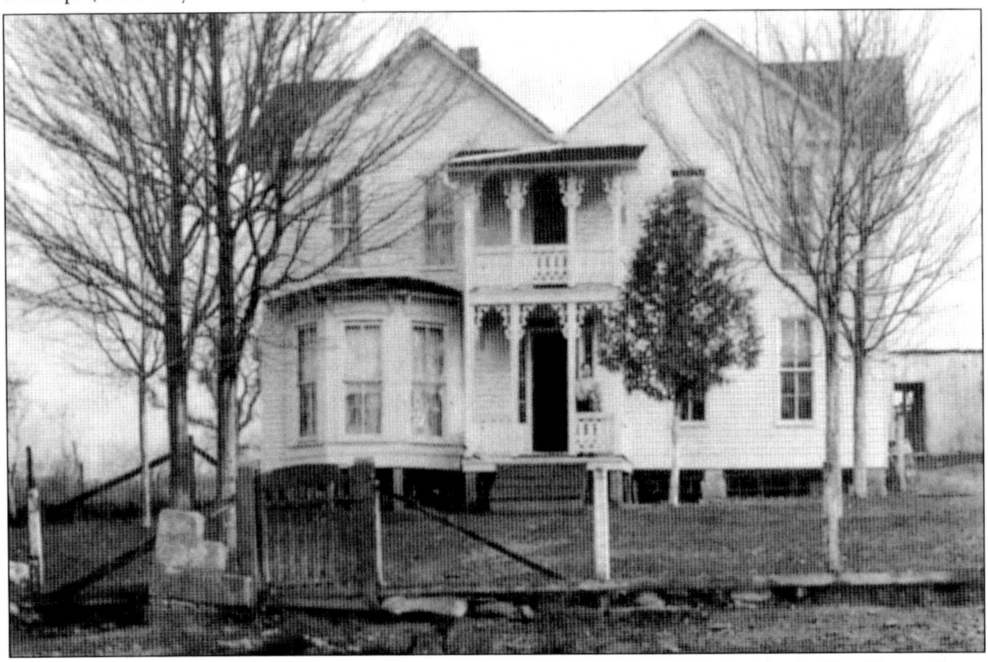

Pictured is the home of Dr. Carl Clifford Howard, who was from Summer Shade. Dr. Howard was a respiratory specialist known for establishing a system of tuberculosis hospitals across Kentucky. (Courtesy of Laurie Butler.)

Five

Farming and Natural Resources

At settlement, the area now encompassing Metcalfe County was rich in natural resources. The barrens, which started along the South Fork of the Little Barren River, were extensive grasslands with scattered groves of trees that provided opportunities for livestock grazing.

Few notes or details are available on the original numbers of elk and bison in the area, but the presence of long hunters indicates game numbers were significant. As settlement advanced, farming and grazing began immediately, and while the western portion of the county had scattered woodlands, the eastern portion was heavily wooded. Edmund Rogers spoke of the timber resources available near Edmonton. Today, those timber resources are sustaining numerous sawmills and a charcoal factory, which supply manufacturers across the state and country.

As early as 1865, oil leases were being negotiated and sold in Metcalfe County. By the late 1950s, Metcalfe was a significant producer of oil.

While wildlife was plentiful in the 1700s, by 1820, bison and later elk (1850) were extirpated from Kentucky. While white-tailed deer and turkey are a common sight today, both of these species had disappeared from Metcalfe County by the 1920s, and it was not until the 1930s that Kentucky had effective wildlife laws in place.

Kentucky began deer restoration in 1948, and by 1952, the Three Forks area in Metcalfe County was one of 10 big game management areas in the state. It was not until 1989 that turkeys were successfully established in the county. Today, both deer and turkey provide a great deal of revenue and recreation for Metcalfe County residents and visitors.

Farming has always been important, and today, Metcalfe continues as a successful tobacco producer. Metcalfe tobacco was heralded as top of the line in the 1930s, and in 1938, Metcalfe farmers were among the first in Kentucky to start cultivating and selling hybrid corn seed.

Although there are no major lakes or rivers in Metcalfe County, its position in the upper Green River watershed (Little Barren Rivers) has made it critical in the protection of the Green River over the past several decades, with many acres being set aside in the Conservation Reserve Enhancement Program.

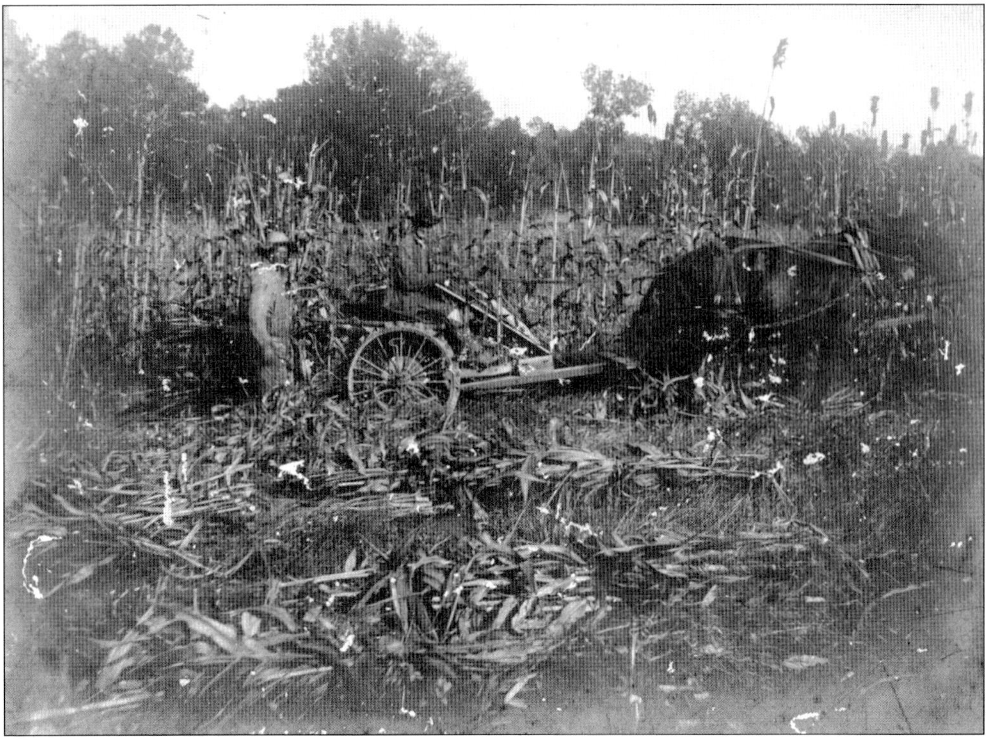

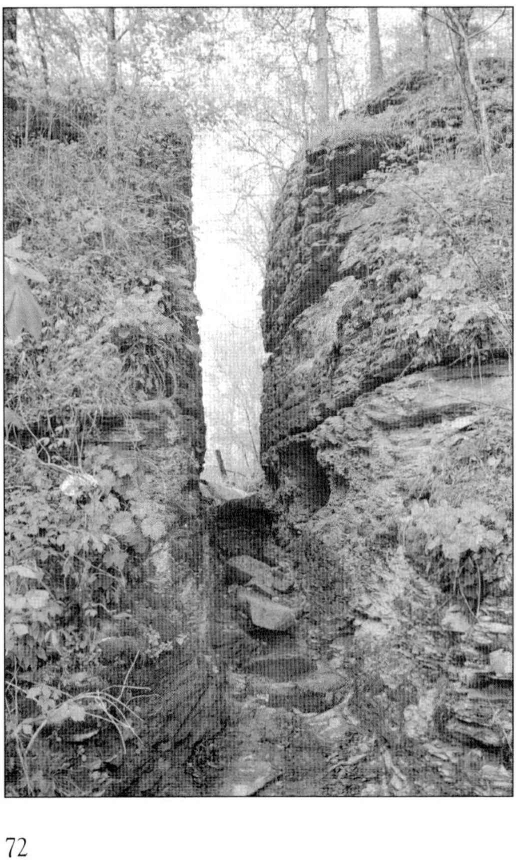

Pictured are men cutting cane and corn. Two men would be on the sled and catch stalks as they were cut. When sufficient stalks were cut, the horse was stopped, and the workers would fashion the stalks into corn shocks. The machine was used to harvest feed corn, a tougher grade of corn used for animal feed. The ears of corn were left on the stalk for the livestock. In 1910, Metcalfe County farmers grew 23,594 acres of corn with an average yield of 16.7 bushels per acre. (Courtesy of Freddie Ray.)

The Cut was at Rockland Mills, a thriving community with several businesses and mail delivery twice a week. A gristmill, which had been constructed on the South Fork of the Little Barren River, was located where the river made a large bend and only separated by a narrow rock formation. Prior to the Civil War, slaves were used to cut a gap in the rock allowing overflow from floodwaters to flow into the adjacent river bottom. Rockland Mills and the mill are now gone. (Photograph by Richard Hines.)

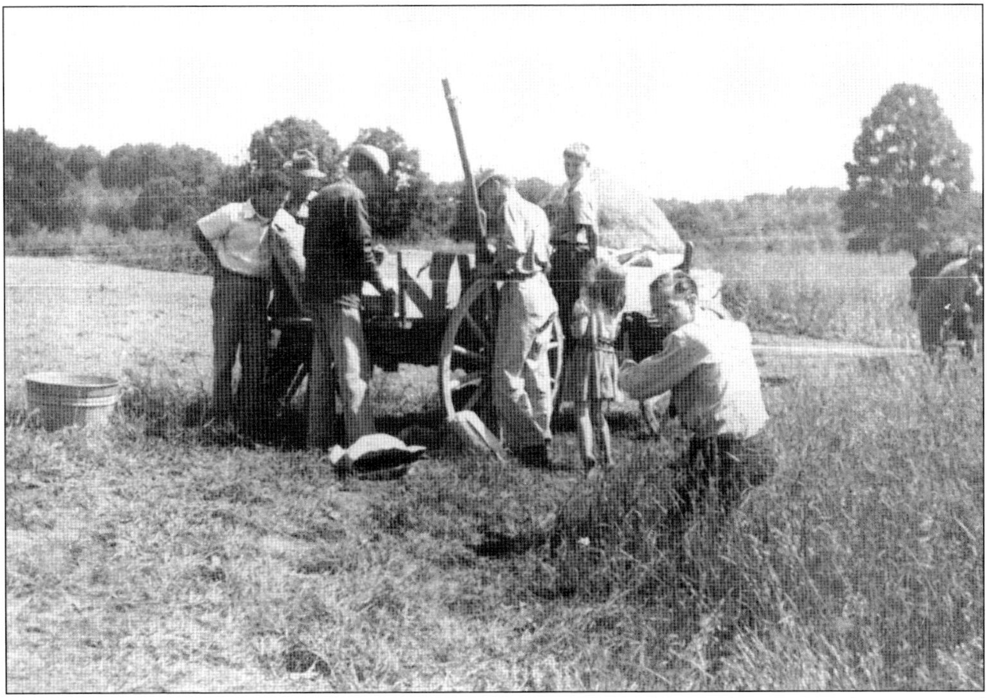

University of Kentucky Extension Service agents are teaching farmers how to use dynamite and other explosives for agriculture work. (Courtesy of University of Kentucky Extension Service.)

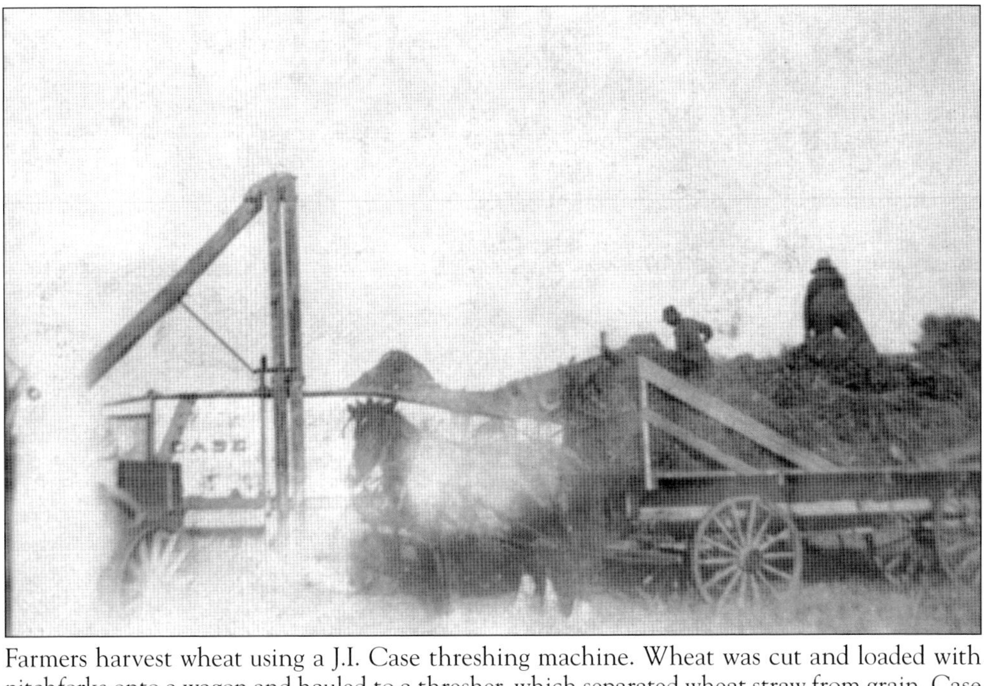

Farmers harvest wheat using a J.I. Case threshing machine. Wheat was cut and loaded with pitchforks onto a wagon and hauled to a thresher, which separated wheat straw from grain. Case began building these machines in the 1840s; however, by the mid-1920s, combines replaced them. In 1910, Metcalfe County had 3,391 acres of wheat with an average yield of 8.6 bushels per acre. (Courtesy of Carol Hurt.)

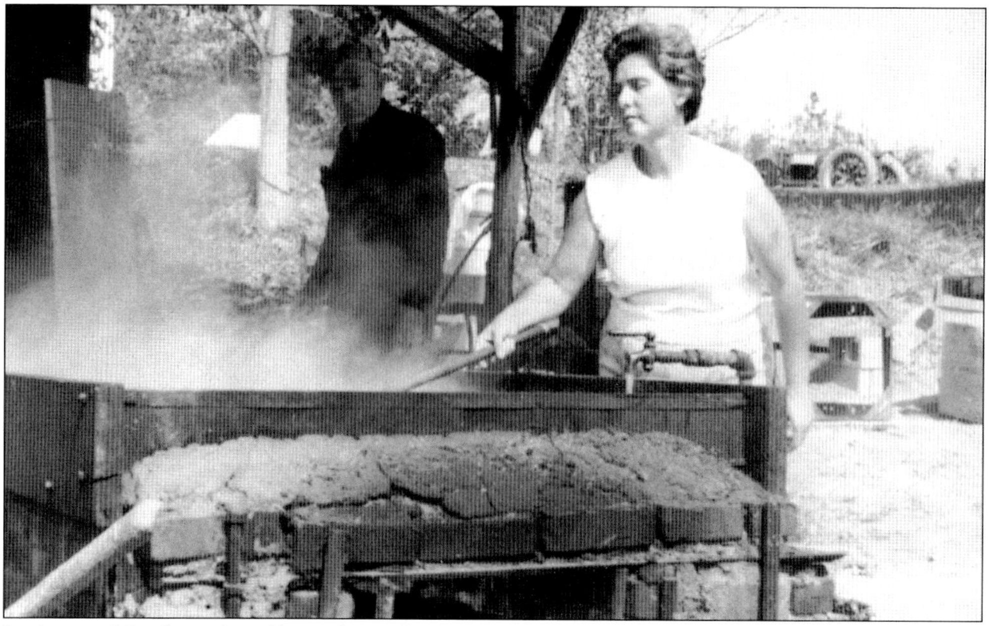

Luther and Darlene Atwell are shown boiling sorghum. Each fall, farmers would grow sorghum cane. It was used to process sorghum molasses by pressing cane stalks and extracting the sweet juice, which was boiled into concentrate to make molasses. Here, Darlene Atwell is stirring the liquid until it becomes sorghum. The remaining cane stalks were fed to livestock, and seed heads were fed to poultry. (Courtesy of Cora Emma Jessie.)

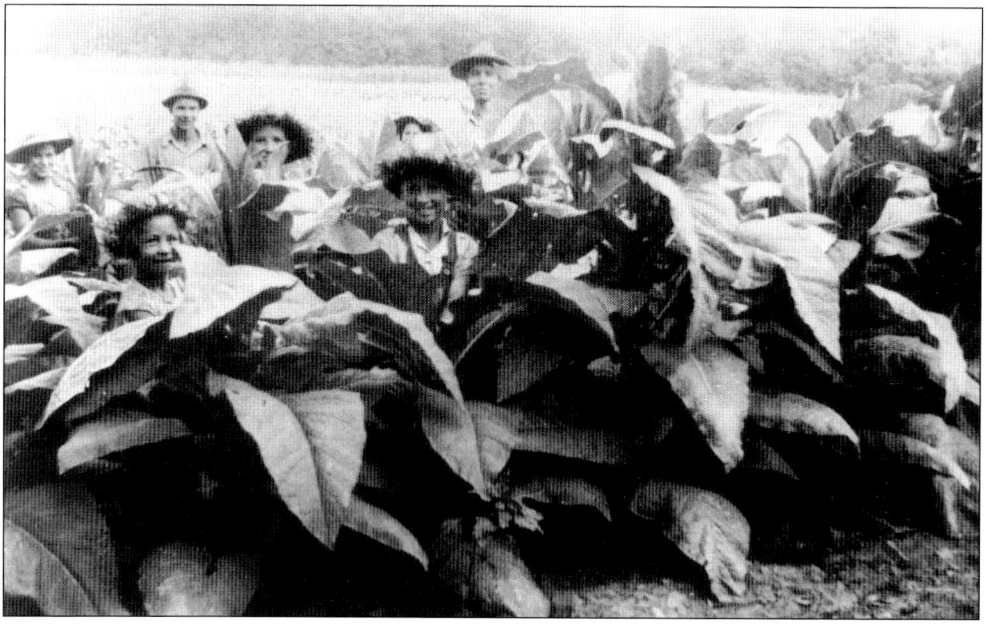

Each August through September, families growing tobacco would "top" their tobacco, which was done soon after flowers began opening. This required breaking flower stems out of the top of each plant and spraying a sucker control chemical. When not topped, tobacco poundage yields would drop by as much as 20–25 pounds per acre per day up to harvest. Here, the Parke family is topping tobacco around 1946. (Courtesy of Chris Parke.)

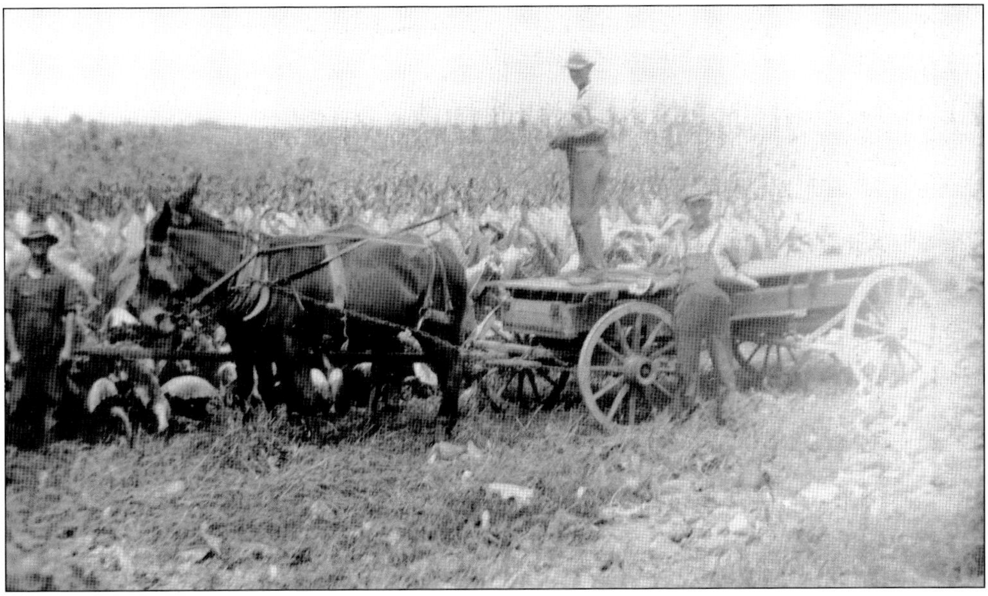

A typical fall scene in Metcalfe County around 1937 shows fields after the tobacco was topped, cut, and speared onto sticks. Each stick typically held six stalks. Workers would load the tobacco onto wagons and haul it to nearby barns, where it was hung to be air cured. (Courtesy of Vicki Harris.)

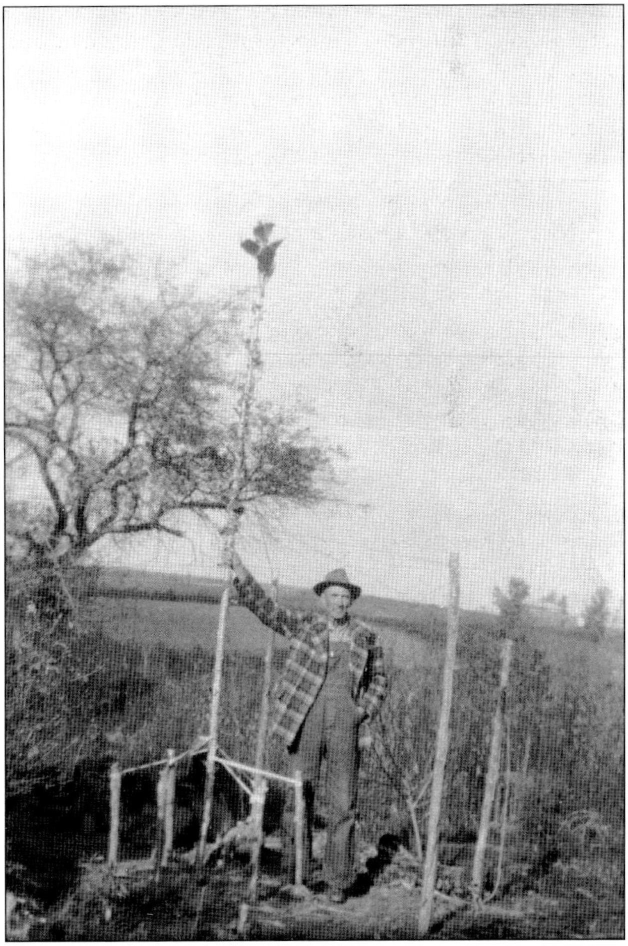

This 12-foot tobacco stalk with leaves stripped off in 1956 is believed to be Maryland Mammoth. Beginning in 1938, a tobacco support program was established that restricted tobacco production on farms. When the program ended in 2004, the price support was based on poundage; however, in earlier years, it was determined by acreage. Some farmers attempted to grow high poundage on limited acres by using this variety. (Courtesy of Vicki Harris.)

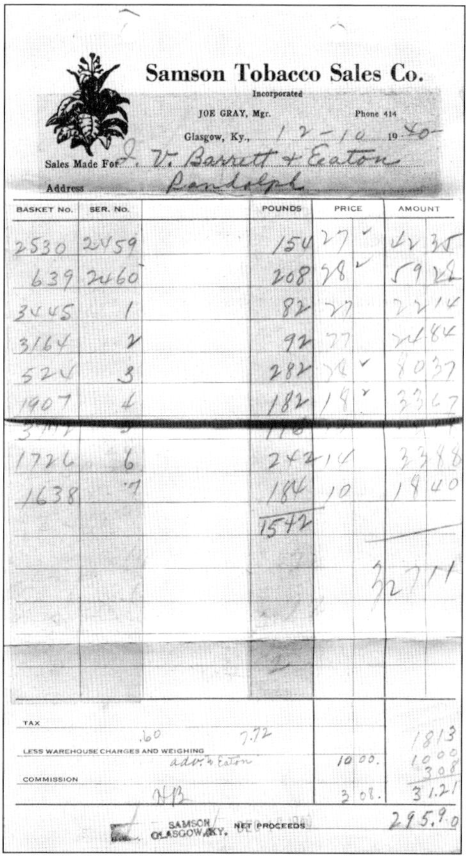

Samson Tobacco Sales Co.
Incorporated
JOE GRAY, Mgr. Phone 414
Glasgow, Ky., 12-10 1940
Sales Made For J. V. Barrett + Eaton
Address Randolph

BASKET NO.	SER. NO.		POUNDS	PRICE	AMOUNT
2530	2459		154	27	41 35
639	2460		208	28	58 24
3445	1		82	27	22 14
3164	2		92	27	24 84
524	3		282	28	80 37
1907	4		182	18	33 67
[illegible]	5		[illegible]		
1726	6		242	14	33 88
1638	7		184	10	18 40
			1542		
					327 71

TAX .60 7.72 18 13
LESS WAREHOUSE CHARGES AND WEIGHING adv. to Eaton 10 00. 10 00
COMMISSION 3 08. 3 08
31 21
SAMSON GLASGOW, KY. NET PROCEEDS 295.90

A receipt from Samson Tobacco Sales Co. in Glasgow shows one farm's entire income for 1940. This tobacco crop netted 5.9¢ a pound. Once the check was received, bills at local stores were paid off, a small amount was set aside for Christmas, and the rest was saved to buy next year's seed and supplies. (Courtesy of Gary Richardson.)

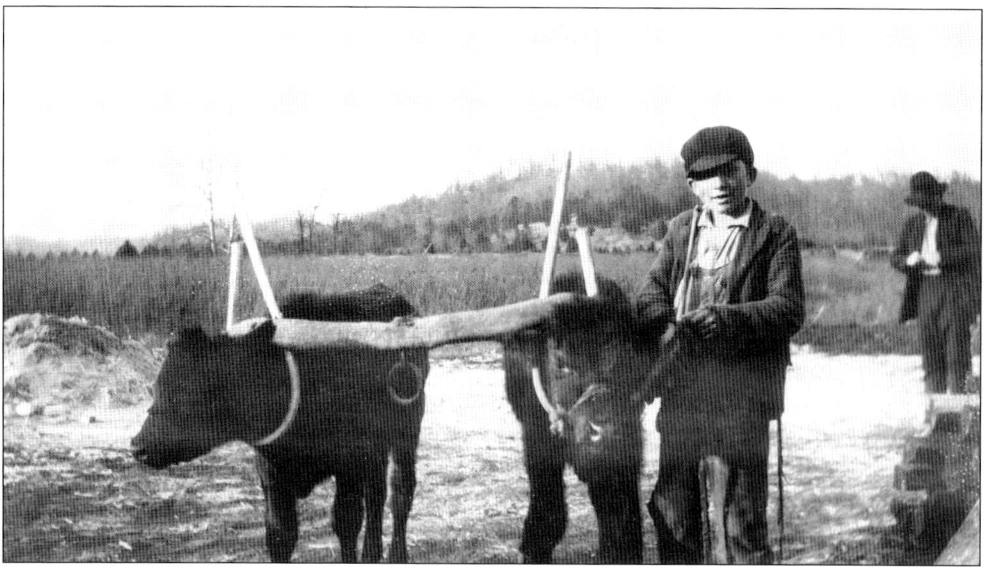

Young oxen are being trained for farm work sometime in the 1920s. An ox is a castrated bull or steer used for heavy farm work, including plowing and pulling wagons and logs. When mature, oxen weigh between 1,500 to 1,700 pounds, depending on the breed. These oxen appear to be possibly South Devon, a favorite breed for draft use. (Courtesy of Richard Young.)

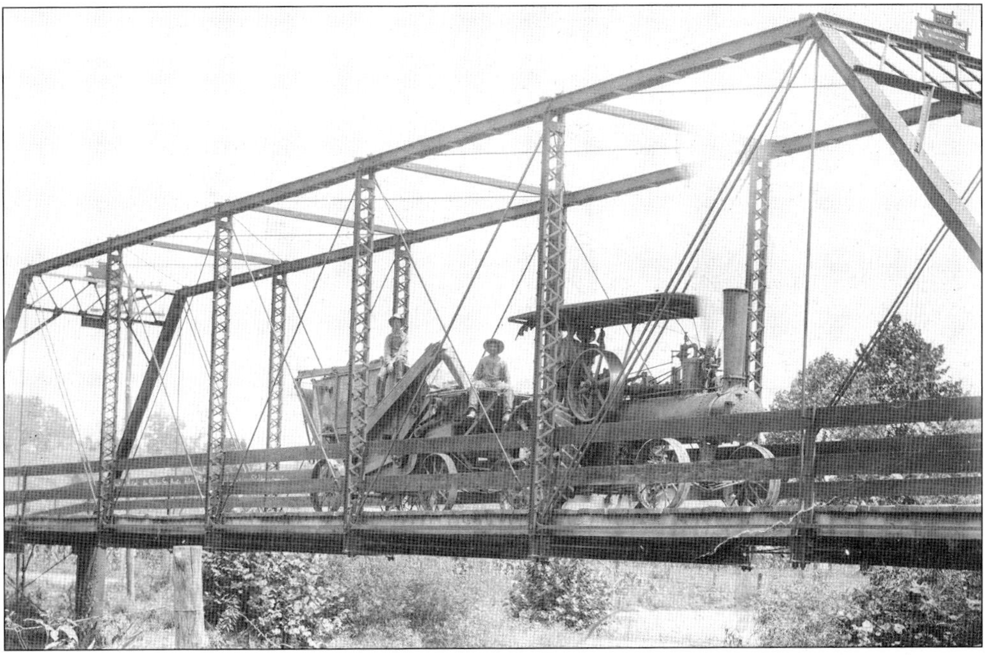

Edd Grider (driver) is crossing the East Fork of the Little Barren River on the Sparks Bridge on a steam tractor and wheat separator. Steam tractors were first built around 1880. This machine is a Geiser Eclipse steam tractor built in Waynesboro, Pennsylvania, between 1912 and 1924. This tractor and separator traveled through the area harvesting wheat each year. (Courtesy of Richard Young.)

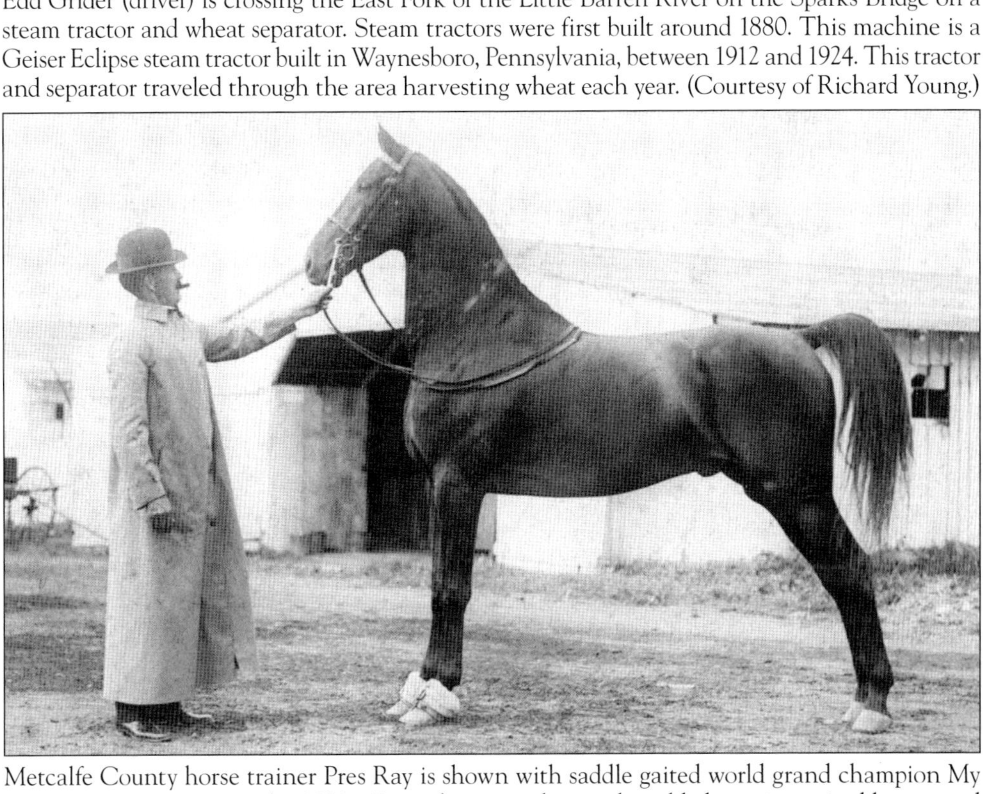

Metcalfe County horse trainer Pres Ray is shown with saddle gaited world grand champion My Major Dare sometime in the 1920s. Ray, who trained several world champion gaited horses and harness horses, including Sunflower in 1915, was sought out by horse owners across the United States hoping to develop championship blood in their stables. (Courtesy of Freddie Ray.)

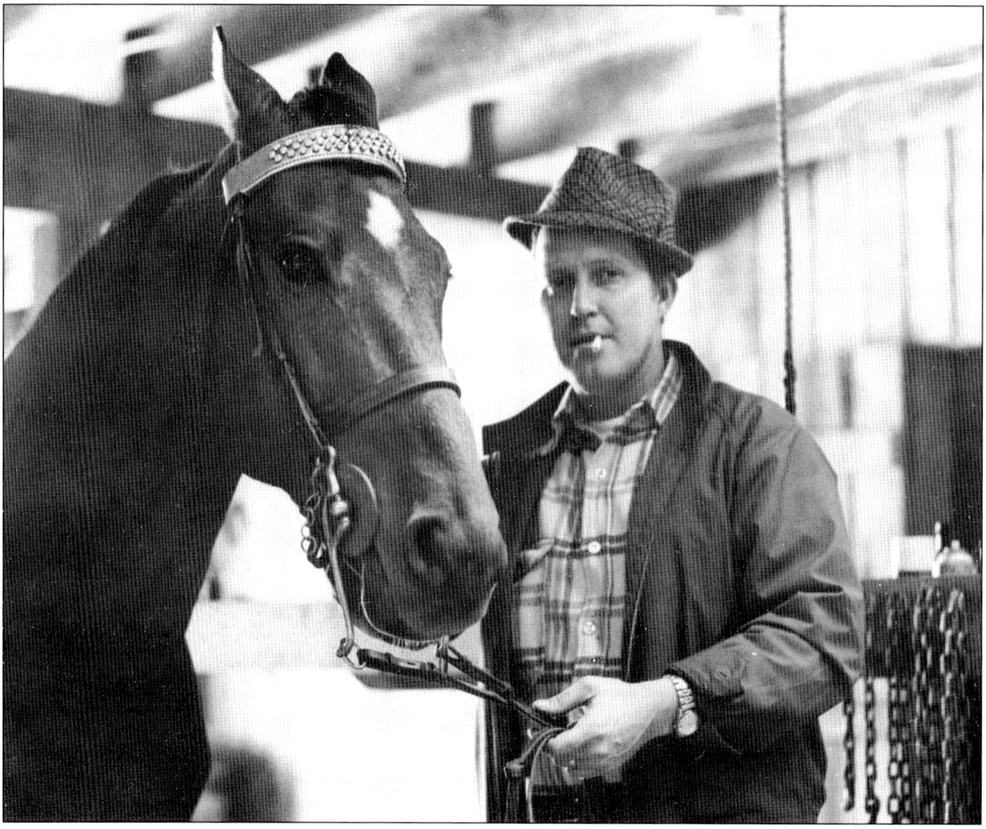

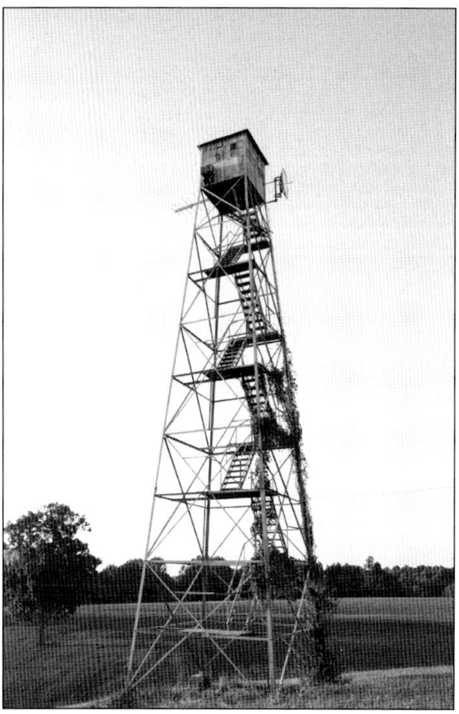

Freddie Ray is shown with Old Hickory Traveler, a champion Tennessee walking horse. Ray was a well-known horse trainer who trained horses across the southeastern United States. He operated a 20-stall training barn in Metcalfe County until 1977, when the barn burned. Horses have always played an important role in Metcalfe County for transportation, pleasure riding, and farm work. In 1910, Metcalfe County's 9,000 residents owned 2,495 horses. (Courtesy of Freddy Ray.)

Of the original 165 forest fire lookouts across Kentucky, the Mell Lookout in the Mell Ridge community is one of only a few that remain. Erected in the 1940s, these five- to six-story-high towers were located on high-elevation sites that enabled personnel in multiple towers to triangulate the location of forest fires. Most lookout towers were closed in the 1970s. (Photograph by Richard Hines.)

When Tom Emberton began his campaign for governor of Kentucky, he spent time at numerous farm supply stores, including the Edmonton Farm Center. (Courtesy of Tom Emberton.)

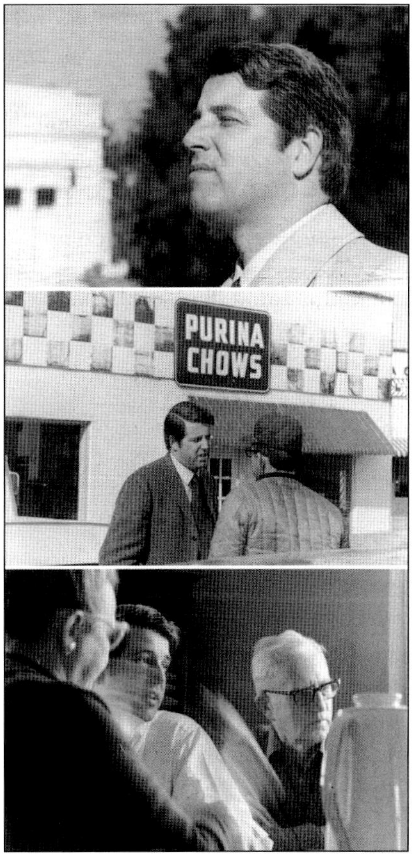

A farm truck is getting gas at a service station where today's Burkmann Feeds is located. Trailers, which are common today, were rare in the 1950s. No matter the size, most farm trucks had wooden racks for hauling livestock. Many of these racks were manufactured in Summer Shade by the McMurtry family. While oak is a stronger wood, the preferred material for racks was sassafras because it was lighter. (Courtesy of Richard Young.)

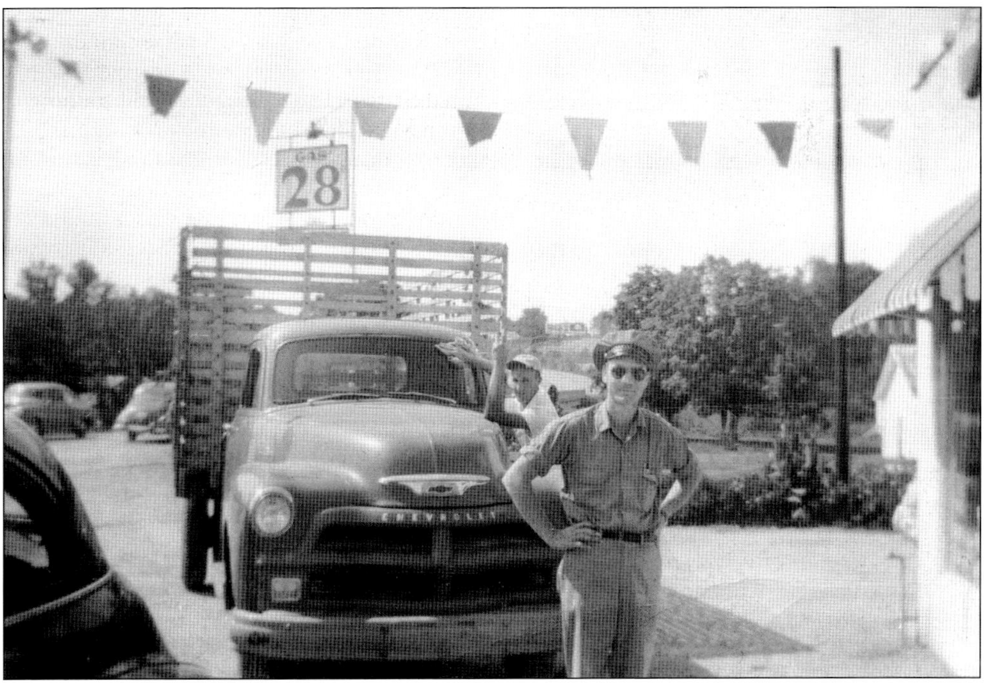

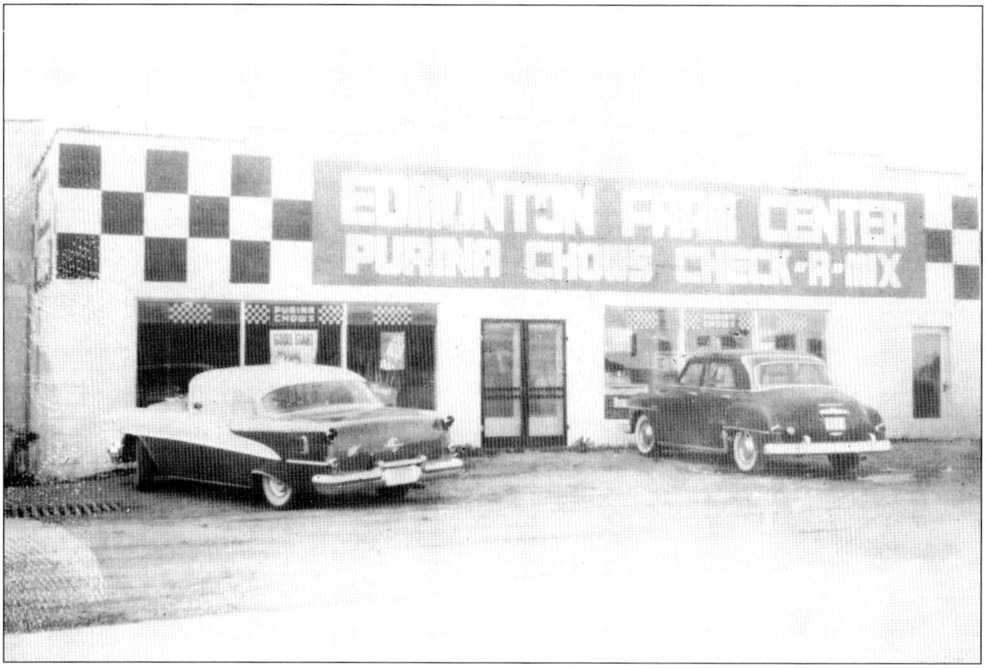

Farms needed supplies, and the Edmonton Farm Center was one of the larger stores in Edmonton. This building is currently the home of Burkmann Feeds. (Courtesy of Richard Young.)

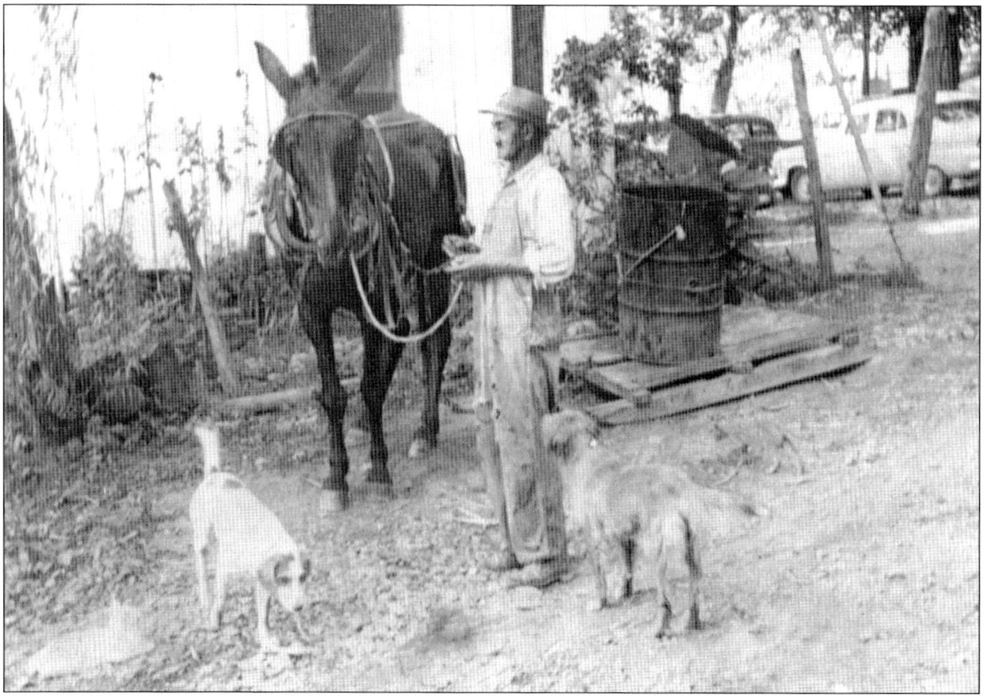

This mule is pulling a homemade wooden sled. Much cheaper than wagons, these sleds were used year-round to haul items around the farm. This sled was used every day to take food scraps and slop from the Beula Villa dining hall to the hog lot. (Courtesy of Cora Emma Jessie.)

Mules were essential on every farm. Whether pulling single bottom plows with one mule, pulling large equipment with four mules, or using a pair of mules to pull wagons, all mules were an important asset. Farmers not only raised crops to sell but had to plan on growing enough grain and forage to keep their mules healthy. (Courtesy of Carol Hurt.)

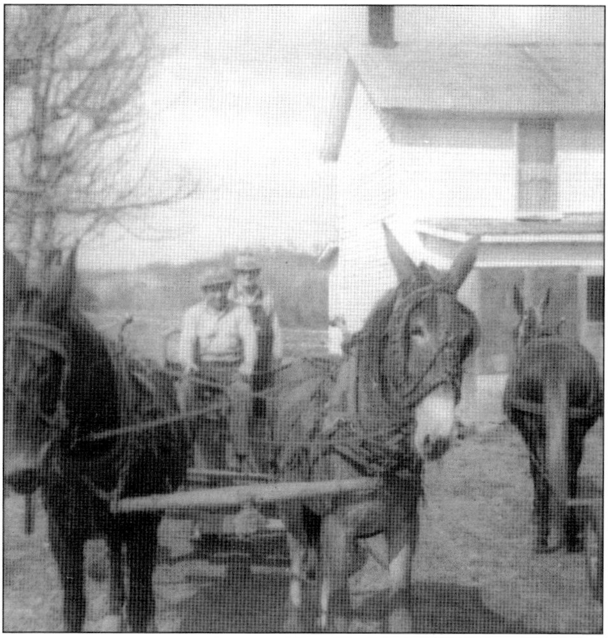

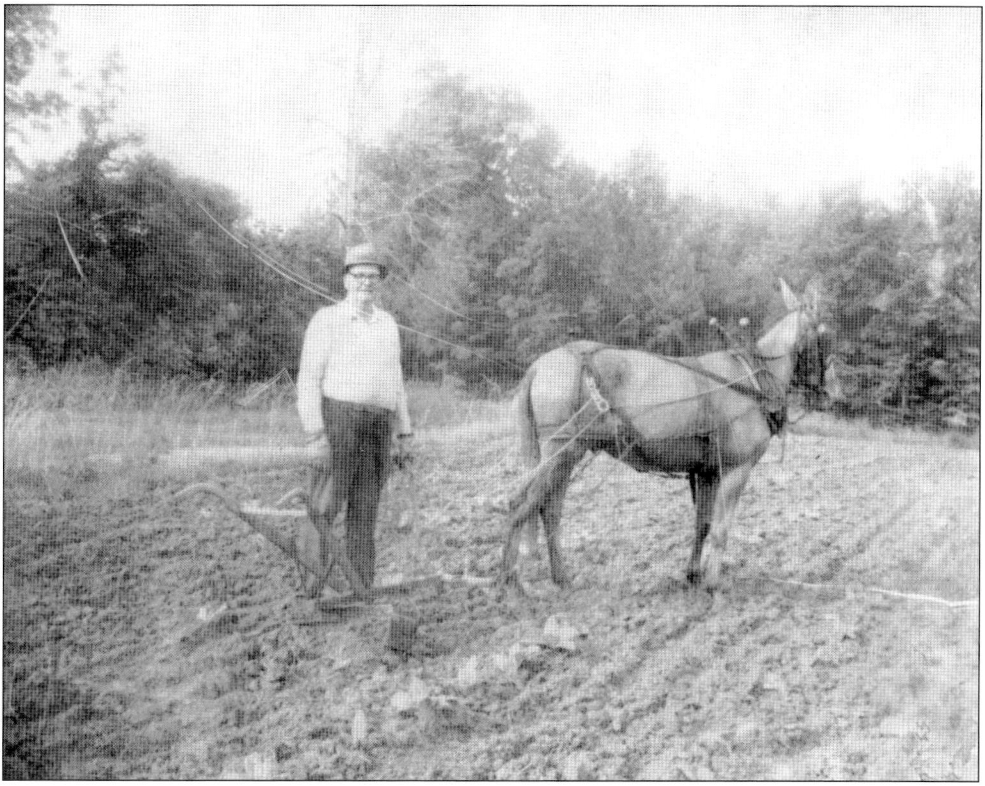

In 1946, William Froggett is preparing tobacco ground with his mule. Mules were essential for every Metcalfe County farm and were being used on many farms well into the early 1950s. Mules and horses began being replaced with tractors beginning in the late 1940s. (Courtesy of Danny Froggett.)

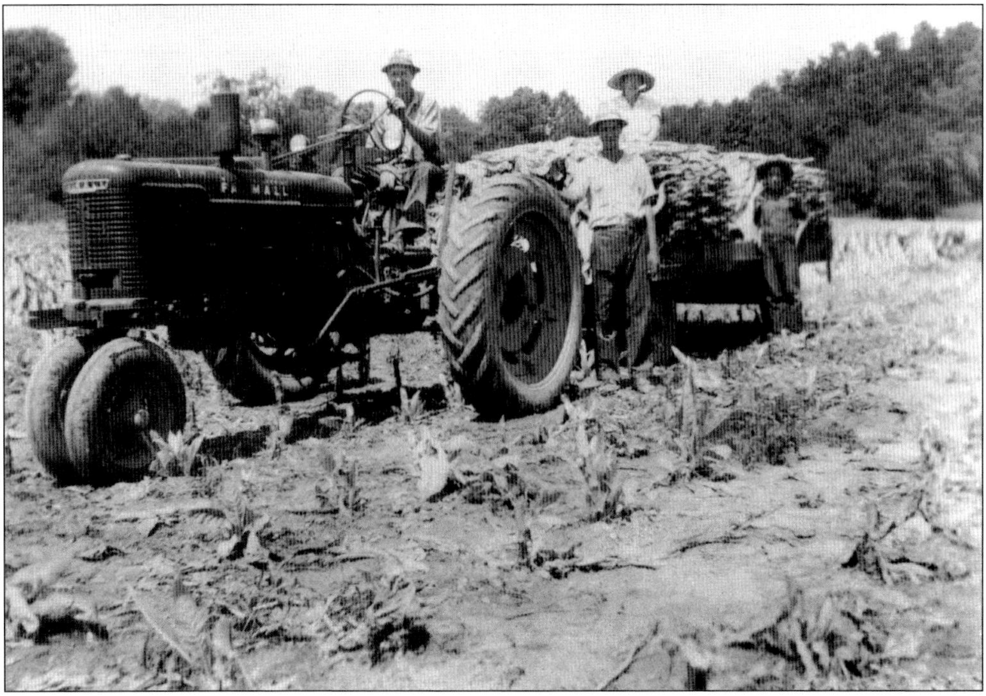

Tractors later replaced mules. Once the crop was cut and speared onto sticks, it was hauled to the barn. The Parke family is shown here hauling out tobacco in 1946. That year, the family had a great crop and received 50¢ per pound. From left to right are James Parke (driving), Wallace Parke, Rebecca Parke, and Jesse Parke. (Courtesy of Chris Parke.)

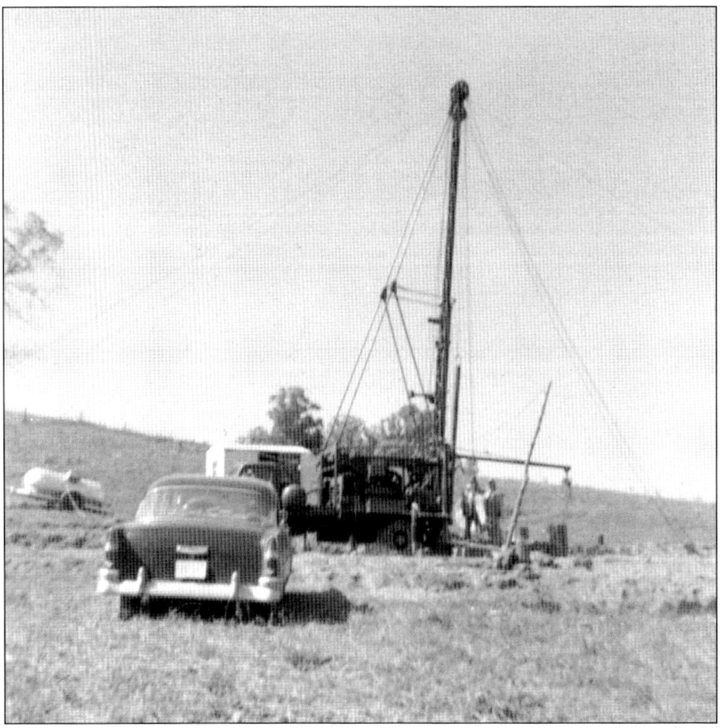

The Bucyrus Erie No. 22 cable tool drill rig is drilling an oil well in Metcalfe County. Oil production picked up in 1959, with some wells reaching several hundred barrels per day. The white building by the rig is called a "doghouse." It is where crews slept while the rig drilled 24 hours a day. Since records have been kept, there have been over 4,000 oil and gas well permits issued in Metcalfe County. (Courtesy of Western Kentucky University Special Collections.)

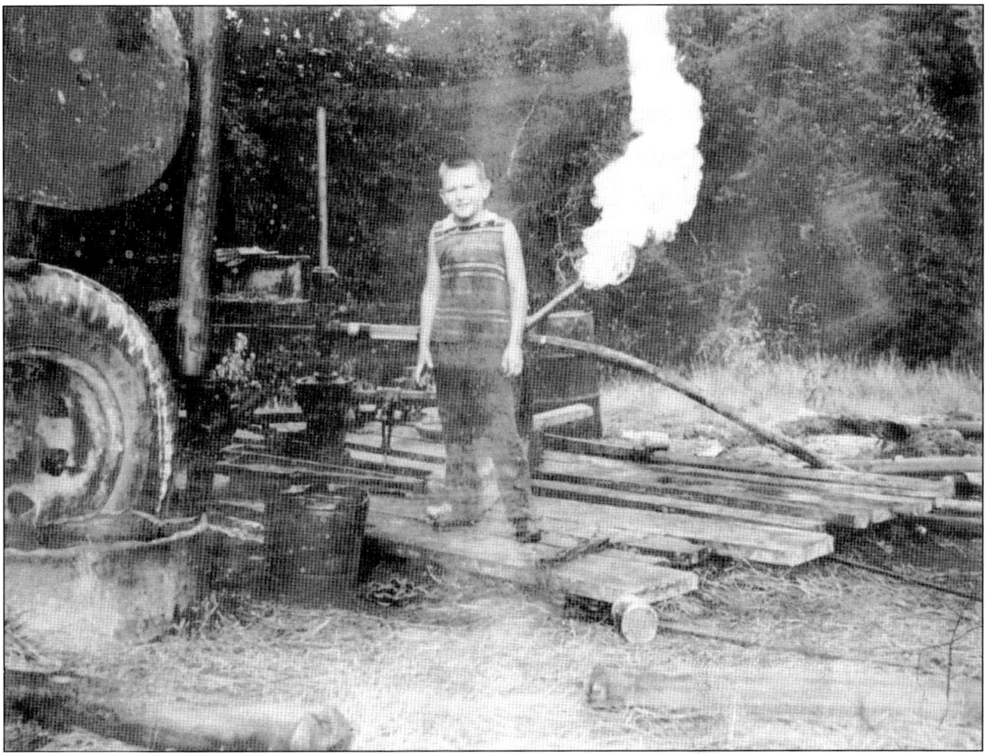

One of Metcalfe County's most successful oilmen is Doug Smith. Smith, now Edmonton mayor, got his start in the oil business at a young age. Here, he is helping on a drilling rig that was operating on his grandfather's farm. (Courtesy of Doug Smith.)

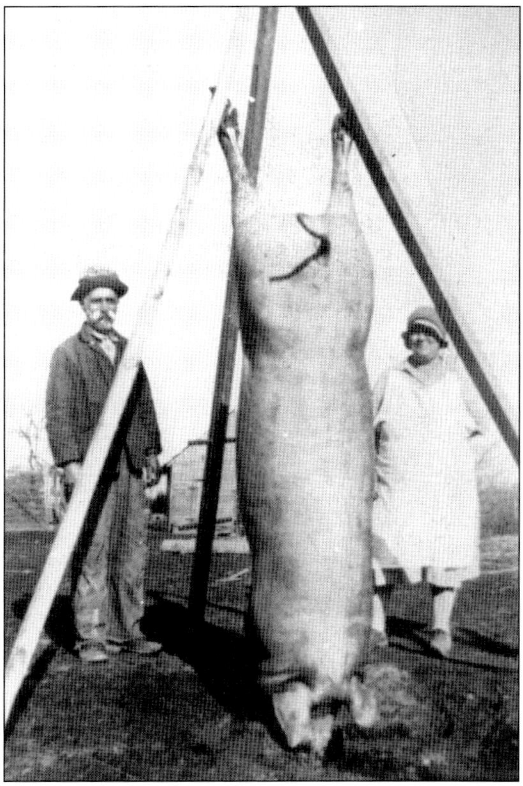

Hog killing time was a routine chore for each farm. As weather began to cool in the fall, farmers would kill one or more hogs for the next year's supply of meat. When the hog was hung up, it was usually on a gambrel, which hooked into each leg allowing the hog to be lifted and dressed. The term "gambling the hog" was used to describe using a gambrel to hang up the hog. (Courtesy of Western Kentucky University Special Collections.)

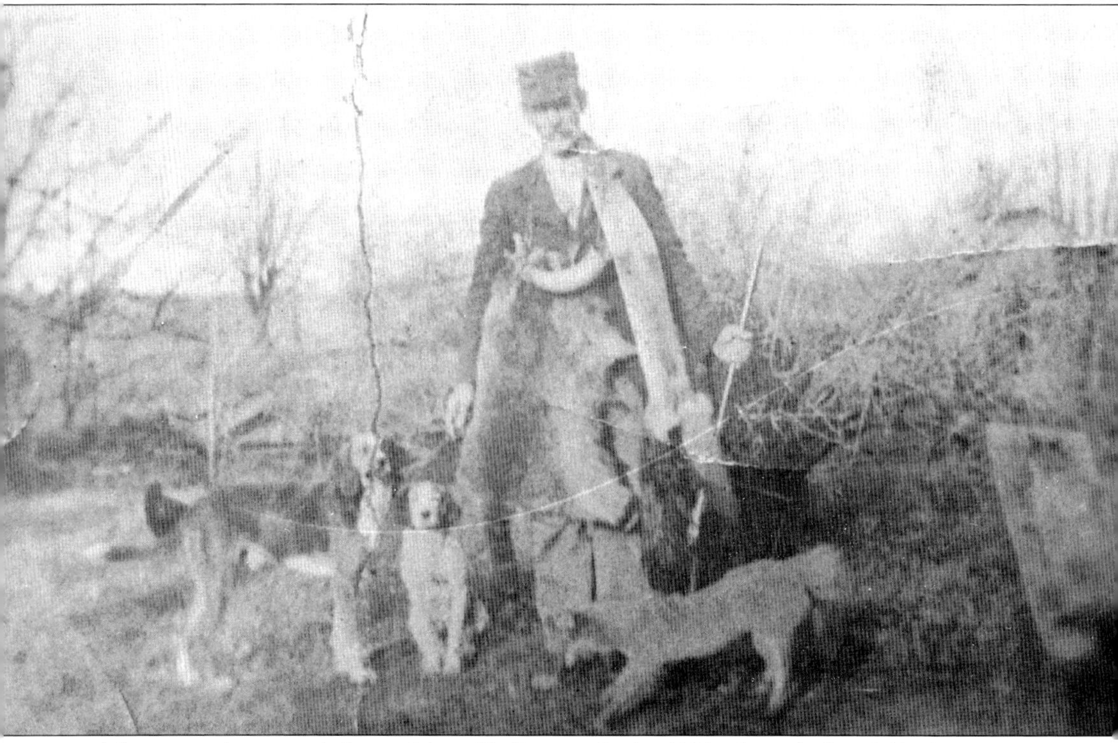

A hunter is shown with furs in Metcalfe County. In the 1920s through the 1960s, fur prices were high enough that skilled hunters and trappers could supplement family farm income from the sale of fur. During the Great Depression, corn averaged 16 bushels per acre and was selling for 80¢ a bushel. At the same time, a top-grade mink pelt could bring almost as much money ($10) as an acre of corn ($12.80), and red fox pelts could bring $4 each. (Courtesy of Western Kentucky University Special Collections.)

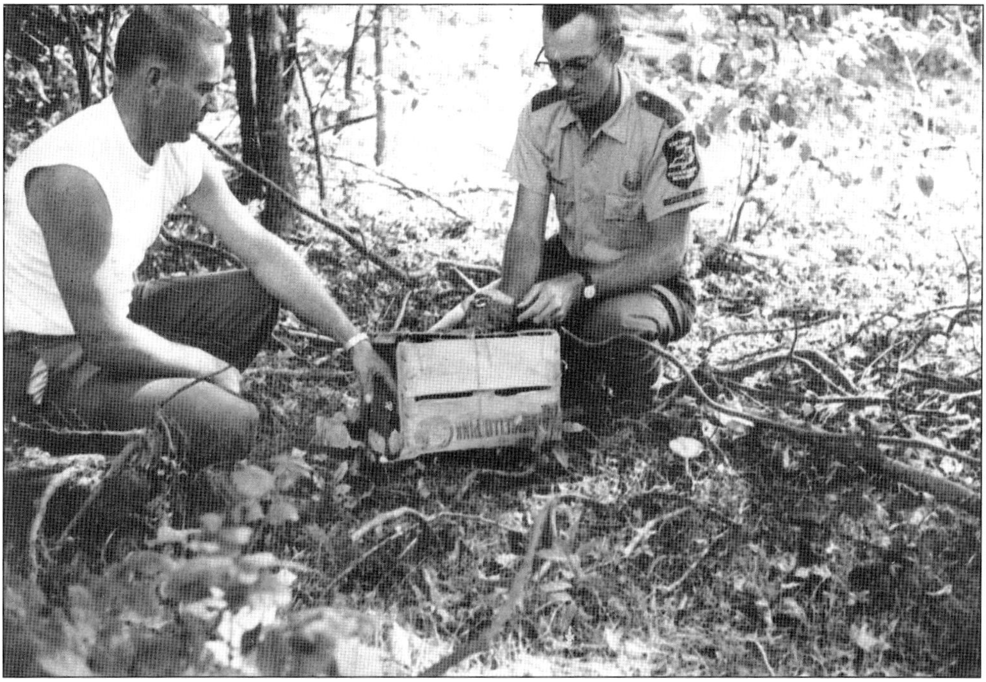

Metcalfe County conservation officer Wendell Stephens is pictured with a local landowner releasing a pen-reared quail. Of the various programs the Department of Fish and Wildlife conducted, this was one of the most popular, but a failure. Quail numbers had already began declining in the 1950s due to planting and expansion of KY-31 fescue grass. As fescue acreage increased, quail numbers plummeted across Kentucky and the southeastern United States. (Courtesy of Wendell and Misti Stephens.)

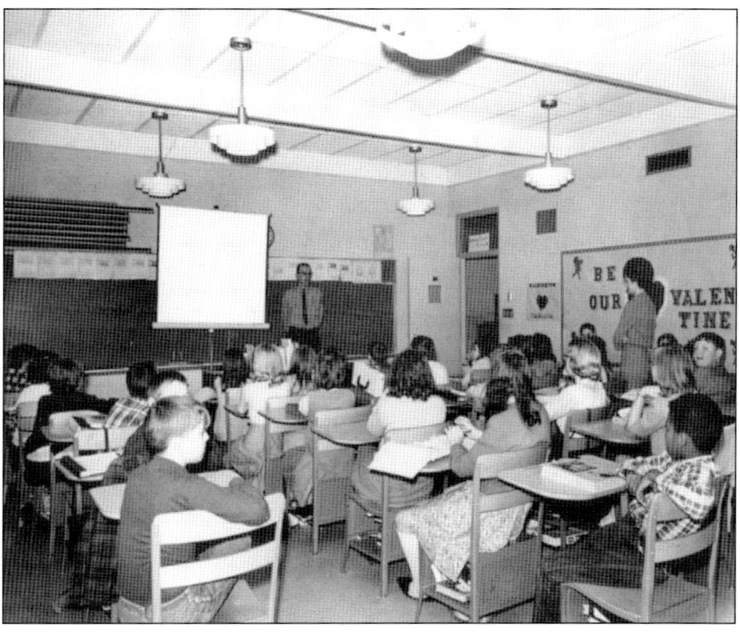

Another part of each conservation officer's job was helping teach monthly fish and wildlife programs in fifth and sixth grade classes in Kentucky schools. Here, Wendell Stephens is teaching students about local fish and wildlife resources. (Courtesy of Wendell and Misti Stephens.)

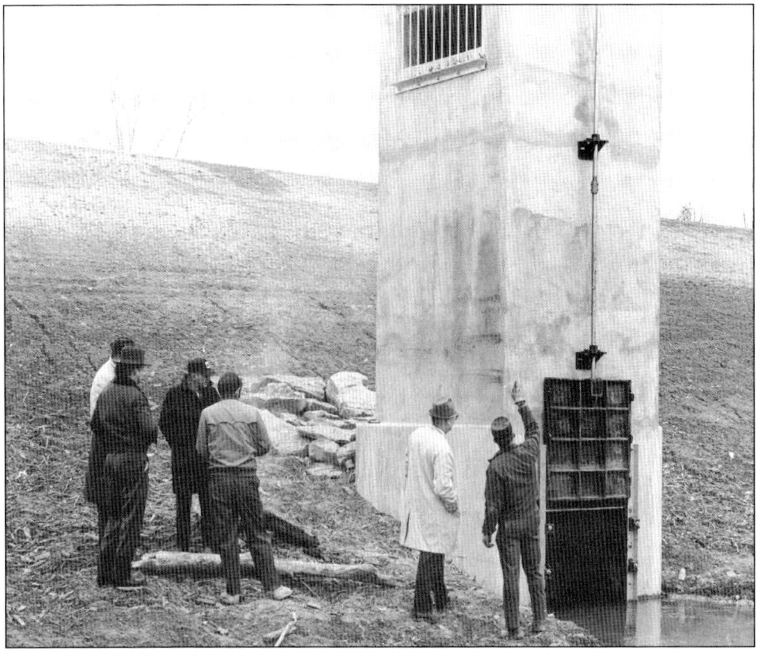

The new county lake dam and water control structure is inspected by officials prior to completion and flooding of the new lake. The Metcalfe County Rod & Gun Club was a large organization and played a significant part in managing club grounds and helping solicit funds for fish and wildlife in the county. (Courtesy of Wendell and Misti Stephens.)

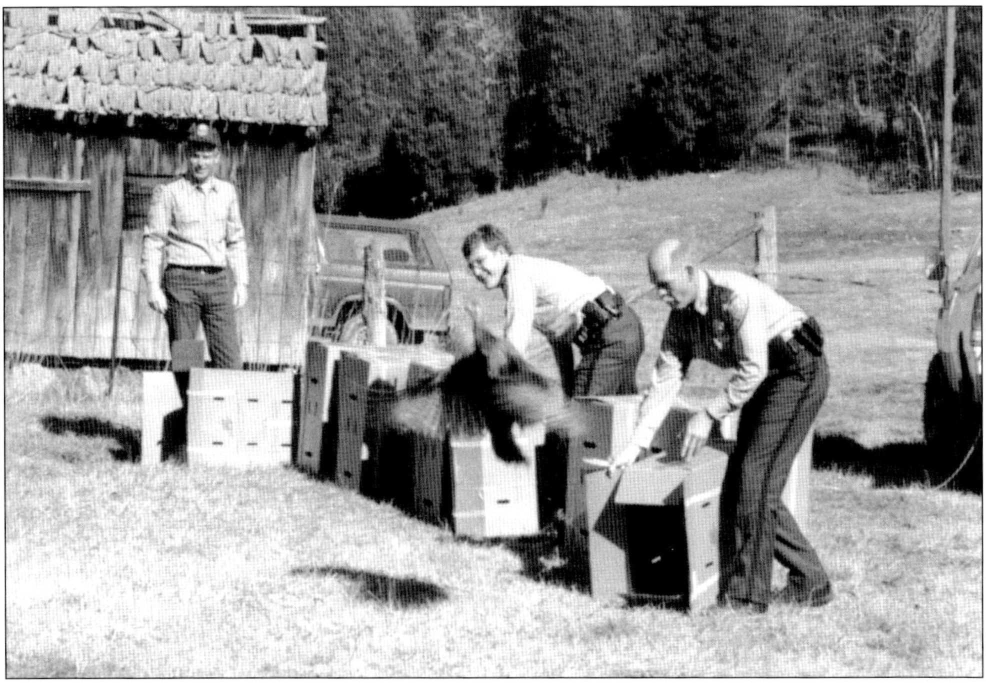

Wild turkeys were killed out of Metcalfe County and Kentucky by the late 1920s, and it was not until 1980 that the Kentucky Department of Fish and Wildlife Resources began trapping and relocating wild turkeys in the state. One of the Metcalfe County releases took place on the Metcalfe County–Cumberland County line around 1989 with birds that were trapped on the Bluegrass Army Depot in Madison County. (Photograph by Richard Hines.)

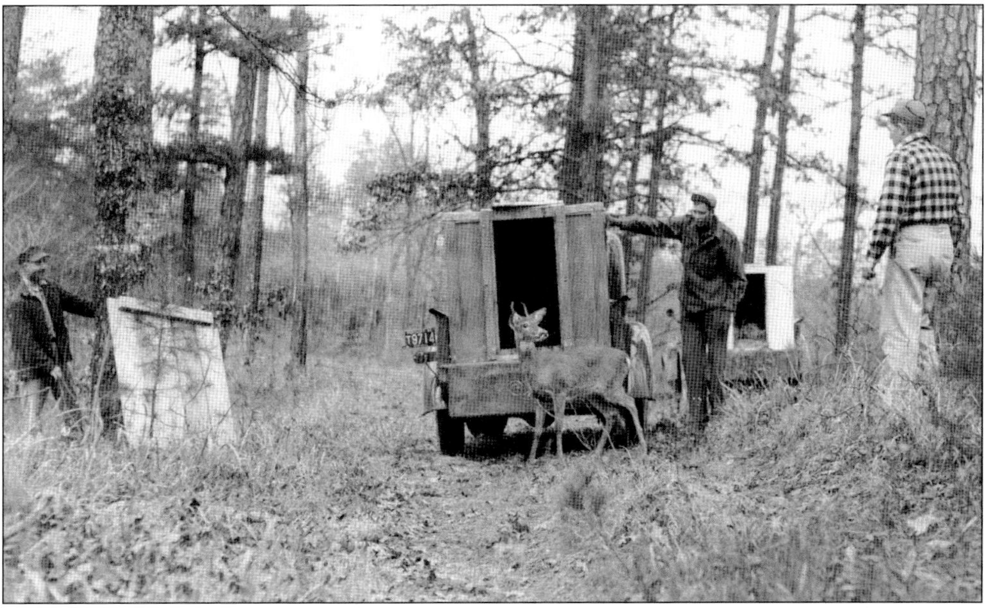

With the exception of two locations, white-tailed deer were extirpated from Kentucky by the 1920s. The long process of restoring deer began in 1945. One of the earlier deer stockings in Kentucky took place in 1948 on the Adair, Cumberland, and Metcalfe County lines in an area called Three Rivers, which was one of 10 designated big game refuges in Kentucky. Deer were trapped on the Kentucky Woodlands National Wildlife Refuge and released across Kentucky. Conservation officer Wendell Stephens helped with additional stockings in the 1960s. (Courtesy of the Kentucky Department of Fish and Wildlife Resources.)

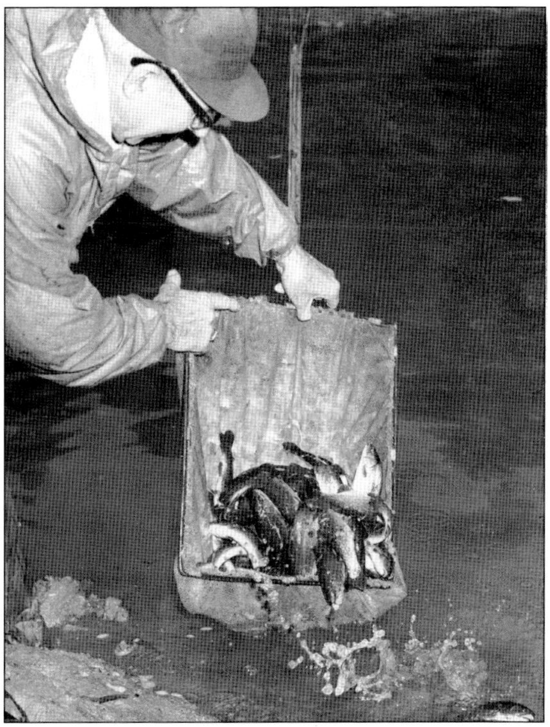

The Kentucky Department of Fish and Wildlife Resources began stocking Metcalfe County Lake in the early 1970s with rainbow trout each winter to provide fishing opportunities for local anglers. Under normal circumstances, trout cannot survive due to high water temperatures, however, by releasing them during the winter months, water temperatures remain cold enough for them to survive. (Courtesy of Wendell and Misti Stephens.)

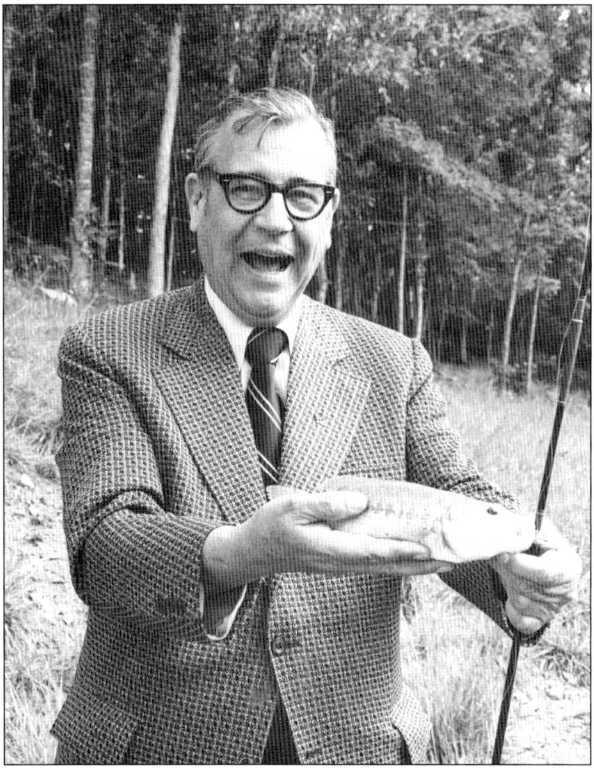

Congressman Tim Lee Carter (1910–1987), who served in the House of Representatives from 1965 to 1981 and represented Metcalfe County, was attending an event at the Metcalfe County Rod & Gun Club when it is said he caught his first largemouth bass. During World War II, he was an Army doctor and later had a practice in Tompkinsville. (Courtesy of Wendell and Misti Stephens.)

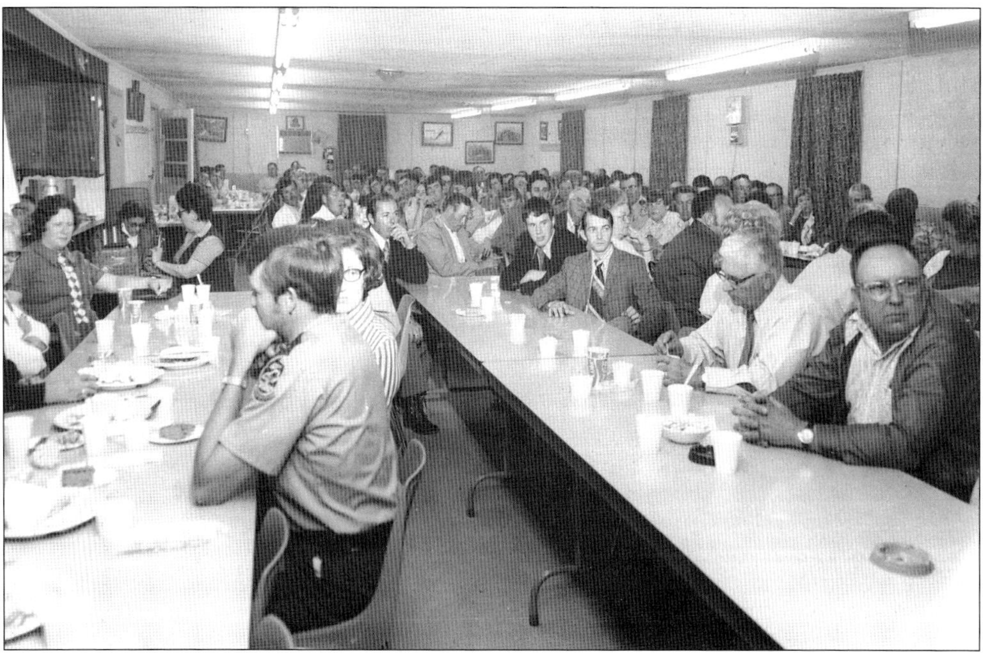

Dinners at the Metcalfe County Rod & Gun Club were big events, and many officials and local residents attended these cookouts. The club was also affiliated with the League of Kentucky Sportsmen, and on a statewide basis this gave the club a tremendous amount of leverage in providing Metcalfe County with resources. (Courtesy of Wendell and Misti Stephens.)

Six

Military Service to the Country

Most of Metcalfe County was settled following the Revolutionary War by soldiers who were granted military land patents for serving in the Continental Army.

Within a year of the establishment of Metcalfe County, the Civil War broke out, and men from the county answered the call; around 100 were listed as serving in the Union army. Several also served in the Confederate army. One of the last surviving Civil War widows was Elvira Page. Although she was born in 1877, she married William Page, a Civil War veteran, in 1903, making her one of the last Civil War widows in the United States.

One Civil War veteran was 15-year-old J.P. Grinstead from Summer Shade, who enlisted as a private. Within a year, Grinstead received a battlefield commission to second lieutenant, and by the end of the war, he was promoted to captain. After the war, he remained at Fort Leavenworth, Kansas, where he was considered for the position of Kansas adjutant general.

In World War I, World War II, Korea, and Vietnam, Metcalfe County men answered the call, serving in every branch and theater of operations. The importance of those who served was clearly demonstrated in 1946 when a memorial was established on the courthouse square and again in 1968 when Billy Smith was killed in Vietnam. Smith was Metcalfe County's first casualty in that war. On that day, Mayor Stanley Butler required that all businesses in the city be closed during the funeral.

Another former resident was Maj. Gen. Charles Henry, who retired after a 33-year career in the Army. General Henry is in the Quartermaster Hall of Fame at the Pentagon.

From privates to generals and from the Revolutionary War to the Gulf War, those who served are well represented and well respected by the residents of Metcalfe County, who owe so much to these individuals who have helped make life in the county what it is today.

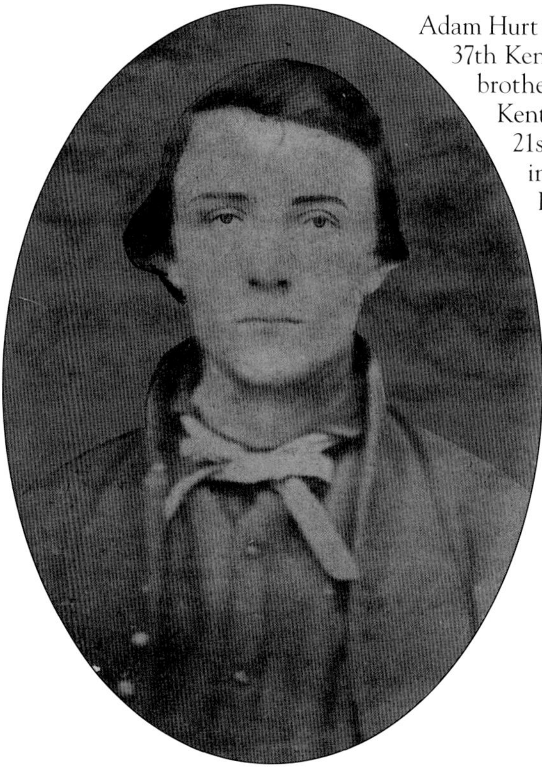

Adam Hurt served in the Union army in 1861 with the 37th Kentucky Mounted Infantry Regiment. Other brothers who served were Anguish in the 37th Kentucky Mounted Infantry Regiment, Isaac in 21st Kentucky Infantry Regiment, Lafayette in the 3rd Kentucky Infantry Regiment and Battery "A" 1st Kentucky Light Artillery, and Washington in the 13th Kentucky Calvary. The Hurt family was told that two family members were captured and nearly died in a Confederate prisoner of war camp. (Courtesy of Carol Hurt.)

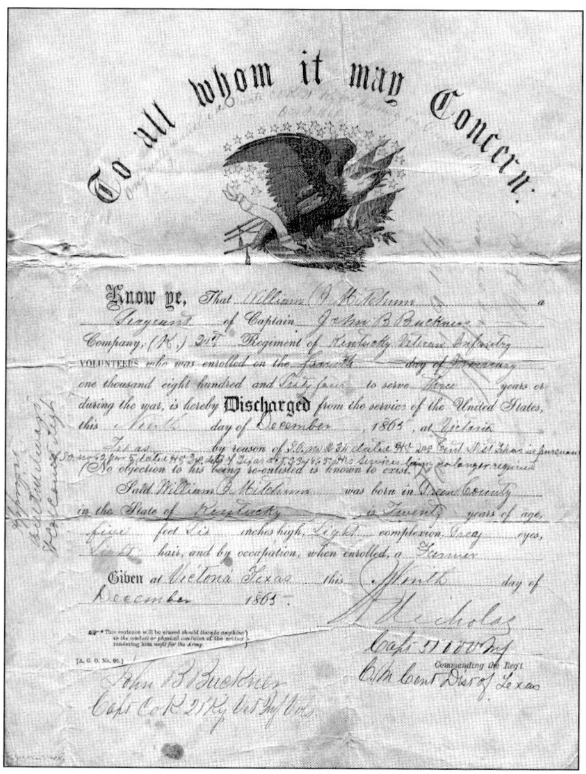

To all whom it may Concern.

Know ye, That William B. Mitchum a Sergeant of Captain John B Buckner Company, (K.) 21st Regiment of Kentucky Veteran Infantry VOLUNTEERS who was enrolled on the fourth day of [illegible] one thousand eight hundred and Sixty four to serve Three years or during the war, is hereby **Discharged** from the service of the United States, this Ninth day of December, 1865, at Victoria Texas by reason of [illegible] No objection to his being re-enlisted is known to exist.*

Said William B. Mitchum was born in [illegible] County in the State of Kentucky, is Twenty years of age, five feet Six inches high, Light complexion, Gray eyes, Light hair, and by occupation, when enrolled, a Farmer

Given at Victoria Texas this Ninth day of December 1865.

*This sentence will be erased should there be anything in the conduct or physical condition of the soldier rendering him unfit for the Army.

[A. G. O. No. 99.]

John B Buckner
Capt Co K 21 Ky Vet Inf Vols

[illegible]
Capt 5? USC Inf
Commanding the Reg't
[illegible] Cent Dist of Texas

During the Civil War, soldiers who were discharged from service were required to have discharge papers in their possession. This paper was for William Mitchum, who was with the 21st Kentucky Infantry Regiment. The 21st saw action in many locations across Kentucky and had been under General Sherman's command during the latter part of the war. Mitchum was discharged in Texas on December 9, 1865. (Courtesy of Henry and Bonnie Froggett.)

Ivy Luther Smith was born in 1894 and died in 1969. Smith served during World War I in France. He is shown here at left with a friend somewhere in France. (Courtesy of Doug Smith.)

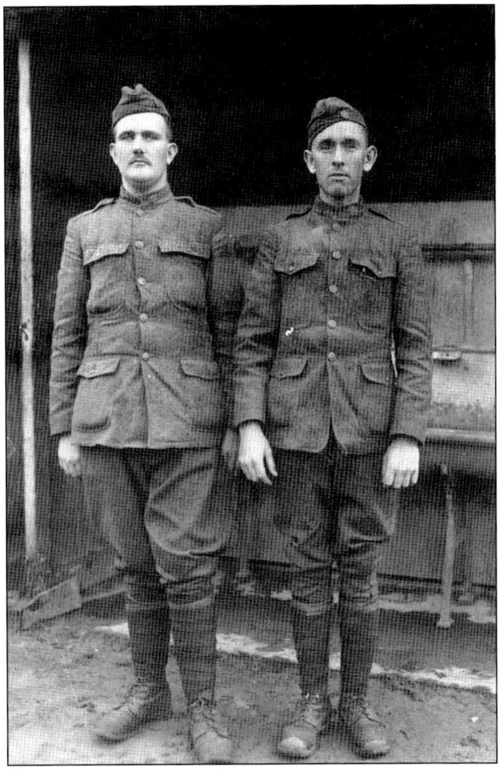

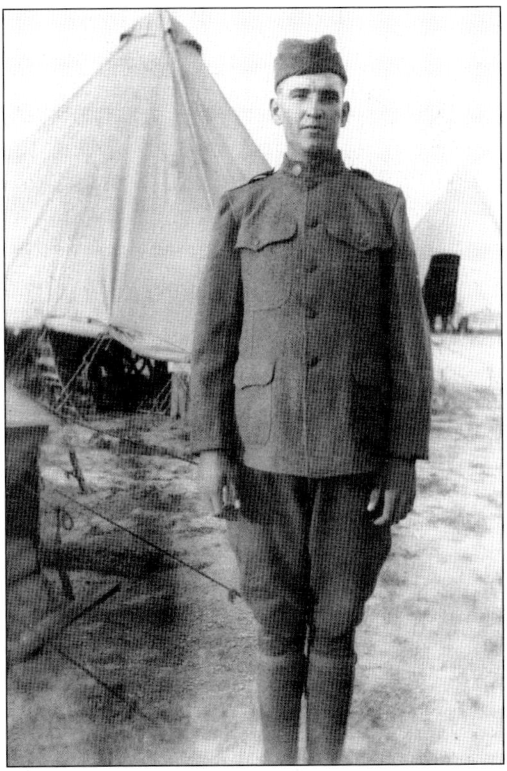

Joe Bailey served in France during World War I in 1914, and never mentioned his war experiences. He was well-known for his care and love of the horses and mules he would raise and train. After his divorce, he built a cabin inside his barn where he lived with the animals he loved. Locals also knew they could occasionally buy whiskey from Bailey. One of his horses was over 30 years old and known as the oldest horse in Metcalfe County. (Courtesy of Vicki Harris.)

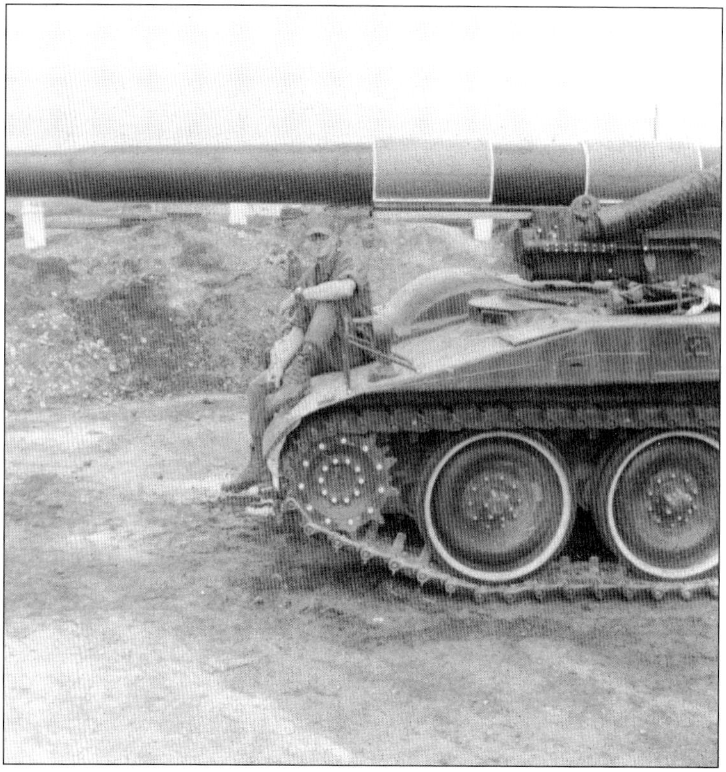

Specialist Stanley Ray Harbison, a 1966 graduate of Metcalfe County High School, served in Germany from 1968 to 1969 as a member of an Honest John missile crew. He served in Vietnam in 1970, where he was assigned to an artillery unit. This photograph shows one of his assignments on Fire Base Nancy, manning a 175-mm artillery piece in the northern section of Vietnam near the demilitarized zone. (Courtesy of Stanley Harbison.)

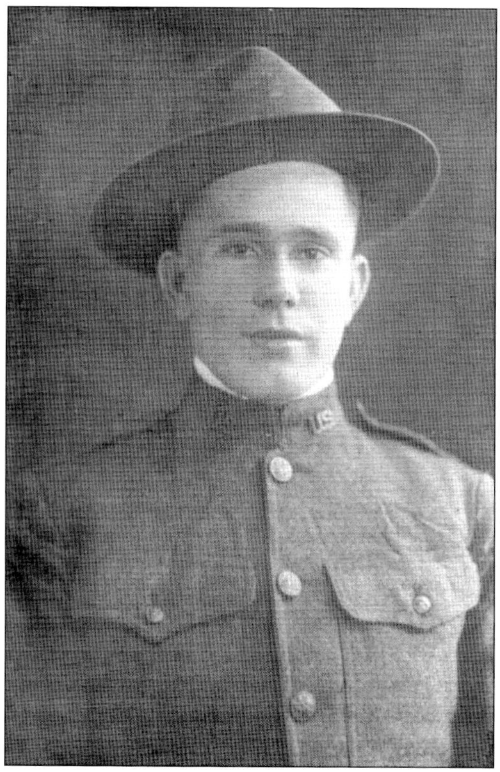

Rollin G. Simmons enlisted in the US Army in 1918. Just as he was moved to France, he contracted the flu and was held in a hospital for several months. In the process, he was separated from his unit, and could not contact family (nor could they contact him) until he returned home. (Courtesy of Roger and Gail Simmons.)

Frank Henry (1895–1963) was a private first class who served with the 326th Field Artillery. The 326th fought in the largest battle in the history of the US Army, the Meuse-Argonne Offensive in 1918. This battle was the last major offensive of World War I. Henry was later assigned to the 217th Military Police. (Courtesy of Doug Smith.)

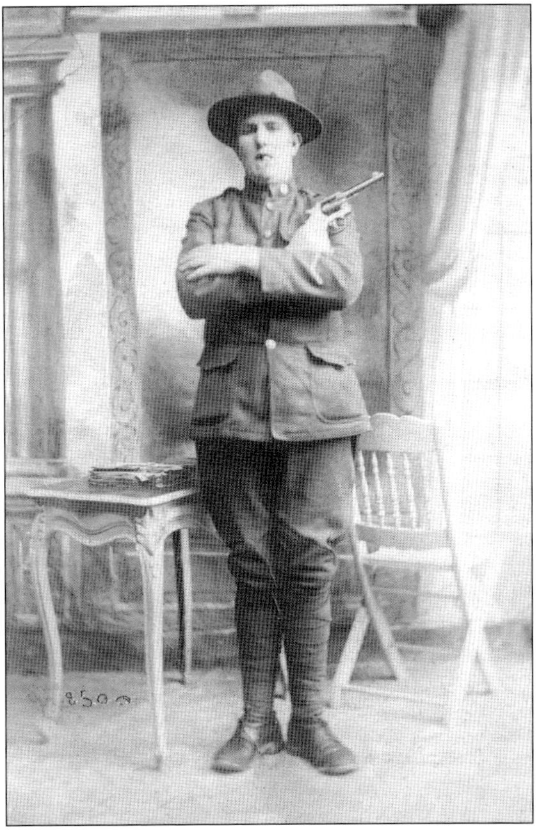

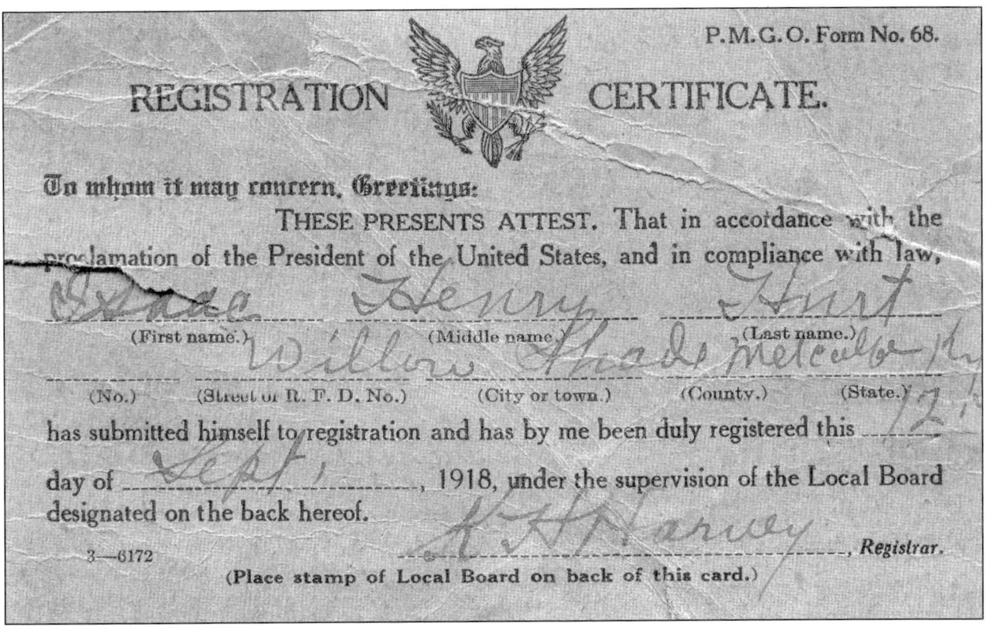

P.M.G.O. Form No. 68.

REGISTRATION CERTIFICATE.

To whom it may concern, Greetings:

THESE PRESENTS ATTEST. That in accordance with the proclamation of the President of the United States, and in compliance with law,

Isaac Henry Hurt

(First name.) (Middle name.) (Last name.)

Willow Shade Metcalfe Ky

(No.) (Street or R. F. D. No.) (City or town.) (County.) (State.)

has submitted himself to registration and has by me been duly registered this 12

day of Sept, 1918, under the supervision of the Local Board designated on the back hereof.

3—6172

H H Harvey, Registrar.

(Place stamp of Local Board on back of this card.)

This is the World War I draft registration certificate for Isaac Hurt. In May 1917, the Selective Service Act was passed, authorizing the president to increase numbers in the military. Draftees were selected from men between 18 to 45 years old. (Courtesy of Carol Hurt.)

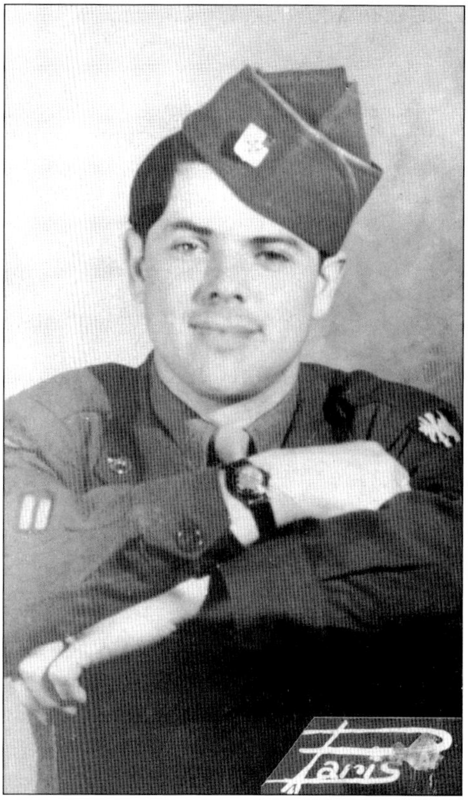

During World War II, Ceburn Ray Martin from the Goodluck community served in the Third Army under General Patton and was on the front lines until their unit reached Germany. Martin was there when several concentration camps were liberated, including Dachau, the camp in operation for the longest period of time. At the close of the war, he was assigned to the military police holding captured German SS troops during the war trials. (Courtesy of Tudor Martin.)

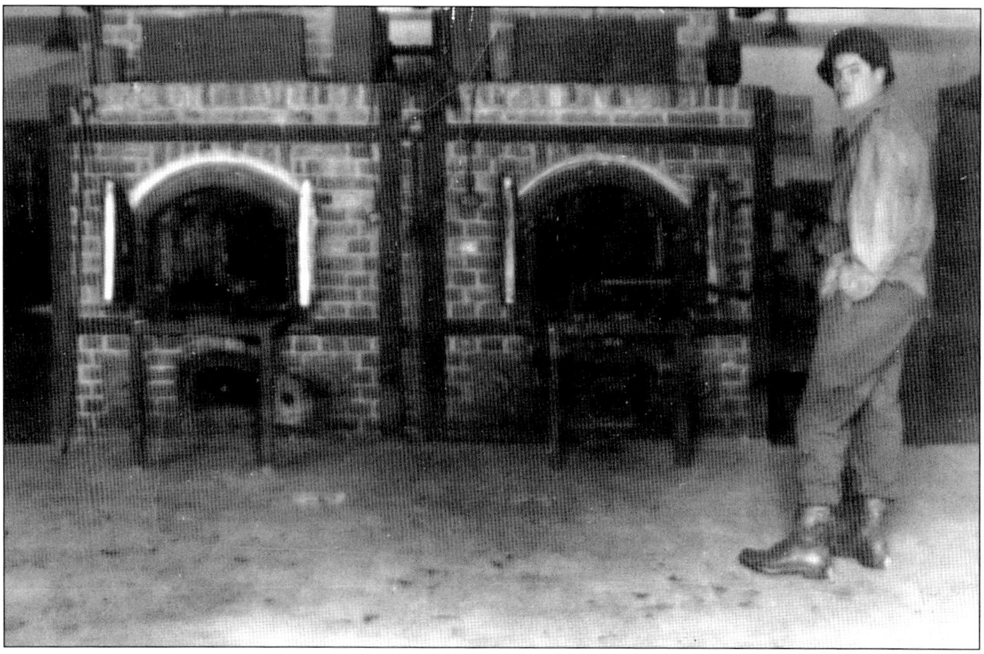

Ray Martin was there when American troops reached Dachau. The Martin family said that what he had seen haunted him the remainder of his life. This photograph was taken in front of ovens used to cremate Jewish prisoners. (Courtesy of Tudor Martin.)

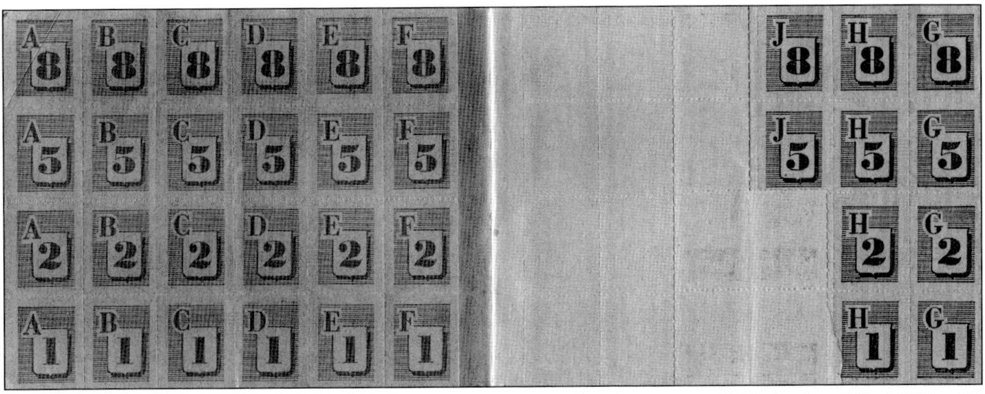

War ration stamps were a result of a rationing program that began in 1943 during World War II. Extending into 1946, stamps were used for products that were in short supply, including shoes, gasoline, sugar, and rubber from tires (and even mileage on vehicles). Rationing was needed to assure that soldiers on the front would have what they needed. (Courtesy of Gary Richardson.)

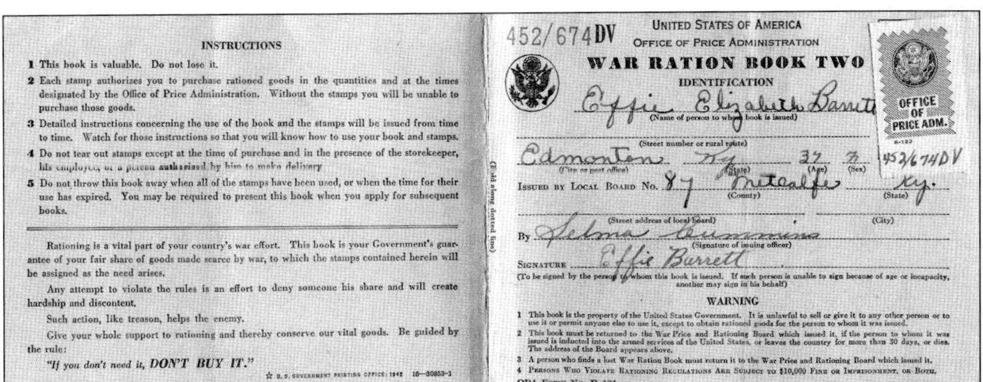

INSTRUCTIONS

1 This book is valuable. Do not lose it.

2 Each stamp authorizes you to purchase rationed goods in the quantities and at the times designated by the Office of Price Administration. Without the stamps you will be unable to purchase those goods.

3 Detailed instructions concerning the use of the book and the stamps will be issued from time to time. Watch for those instructions so that you will know how to use your book and stamps.

4 Do not tear out stamps except at the time of purchase and in the presence of the storekeeper, his employee, or a person authorized by him to make delivery.

5 Do not throw this book away when all of the stamps have been used, or when the time for their use has expired. You may be required to present this book when you apply for subsequent books.

Rationing is a vital part of your country's war effort. This book is your Government's guarantee of your fair share of goods made scarce by war, to which the stamps contained herein will be assigned as the need arises.

Any attempt to violate the rules is an effort to deny someone his share and will create hardship and discontent.

Such action, like treason, helps the enemy.

Give your whole support to rationing and thereby conserve our vital goods. Be guided by the rule:

*"If you don't need it, **DON'T BUY IT.**"*

☆ U. S. GOVERNMENT PRINTING OFFICE: 1942 16—30853-1

(Fold along dotted line)

452/674DV

UNITED STATES OF AMERICA

OFFICE OF PRICE ADMINISTRATION

WAR RATION BOOK TWO

IDENTIFICATION

Effie Elizabeth Barrett
(Name of person to whom book is issued)

(Street number or rural route)

Edmonton Ky 37 F
(City or post office) (State) (Age) (Sex)

OFFICE OF PRICE ADM.

452/674DV

ISSUED BY LOCAL BOARD NO. 87 Metcalfe Ky.
(County) (State)

(Street address of local board) (City)

By Selma Cummins
(Signature of issuing officer)

SIGNATURE Effie Barrett
(To be signed by the person to whom this book is issued. If such person is unable to sign because of age or incapacity, another may sign in his behalf)

WARNING

1 This book is the property of the United States Government. It is unlawful to sell or give it to any other person or to use it or permit anyone else to use it, except to obtain rationed goods for the person to whom it was issued.

2 This book must be returned to the War Price and Rationing Board which issued it, if the person to whom it was issued is inducted into the armed services of the United States, or leaves the country for more than 30 days, or dies. The address of the Board appears above.

3 A person who finds a lost War Ration Book must return it to the War Price and Rationing Board which issued it.

4 PERSONS WHO VIOLATE RATIONING REGULATIONS ARE SUBJECT TO $10,000 FINE OR IMPRISONMENT, OR BOTH.

OPA Form No. R-121 16—30853-1

Each person in Metcalfe County as well as across the United States was required to have a signed ration book before they could purchase a long list of items that were being rationed to assure that military forces were supplied first. (Courtesy of Gary Richardson.)

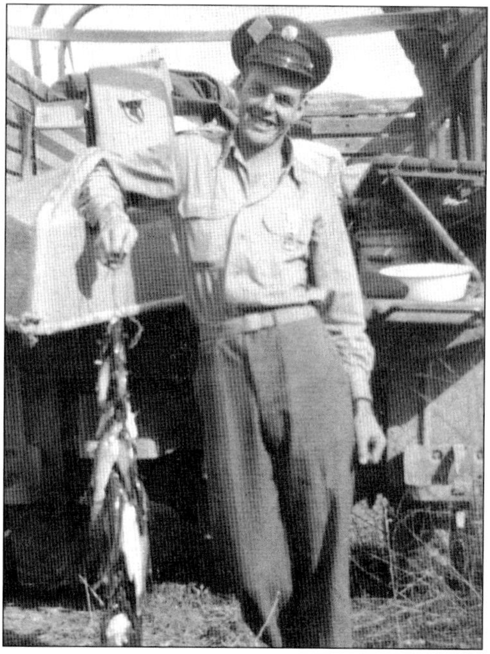

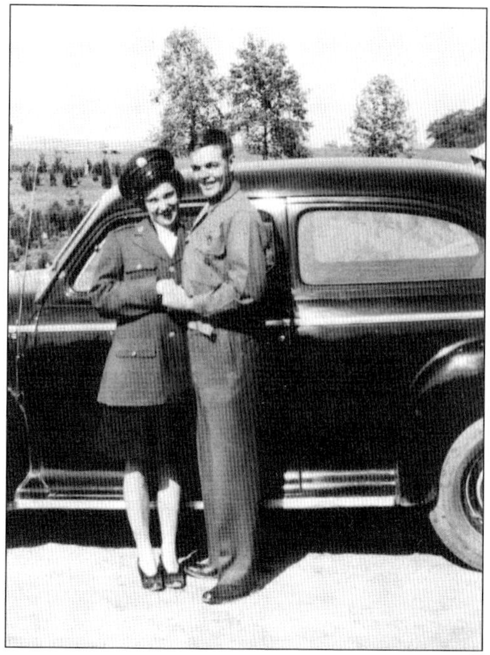

Fishing was a pastime for many Metcalfe County residents, and Pvt. Albert Richardson managed to spend a day fishing while on leave from the Army before being shipping out to the Luzon Islands in the Philippines during World War II. Here, Albert and his wife, Ollie, are shown during their last time together. (Both, courtesy of Gary Richardson.)

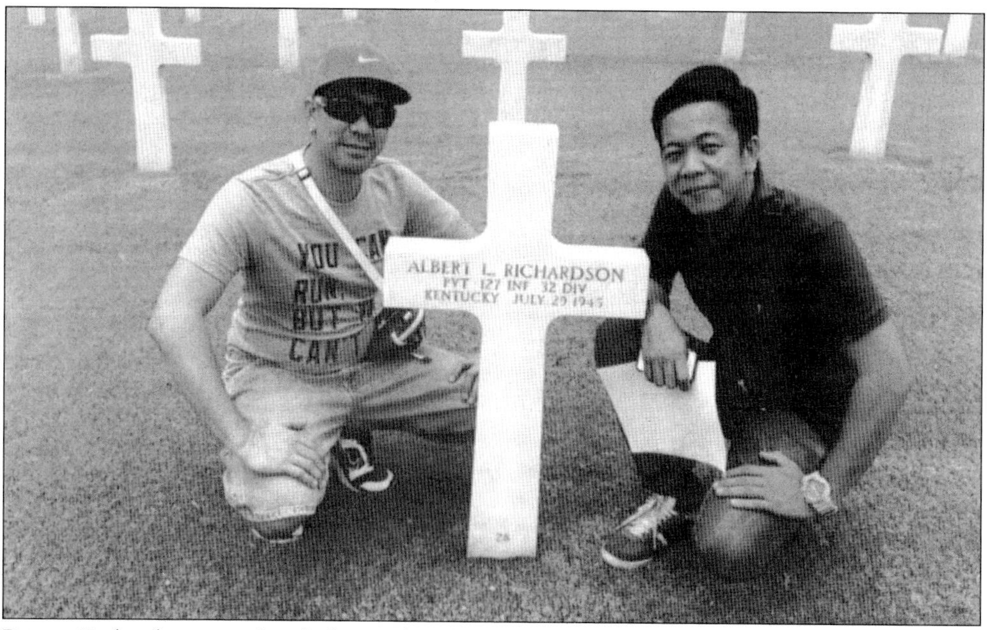

Private Richardson served with the 127th Infantry, 32nd Division in the Philippines where he was killed in action fighting against the Japanese on July 29, 1945. He is buried in the Manila American Cemetery and Memorial along with 16,859 Americans who were killed in the Philippines during World War II. His son Gary was born five months after he was killed. The graveyard is cared for every day. Shown here are caretakers of the cemetery in Manila. (Courtesy of Gary Richardson.)

Willard Parnell, pictured here, entered the US Army in 1945 and went to boot camp at Camp Atterbury in Indiana. Parnell was later sent to Germany. (Courtesy of Willard Parnell.)

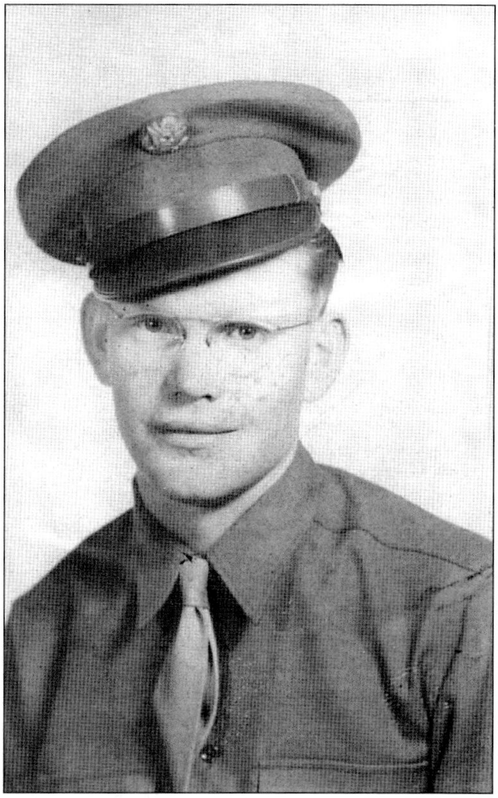

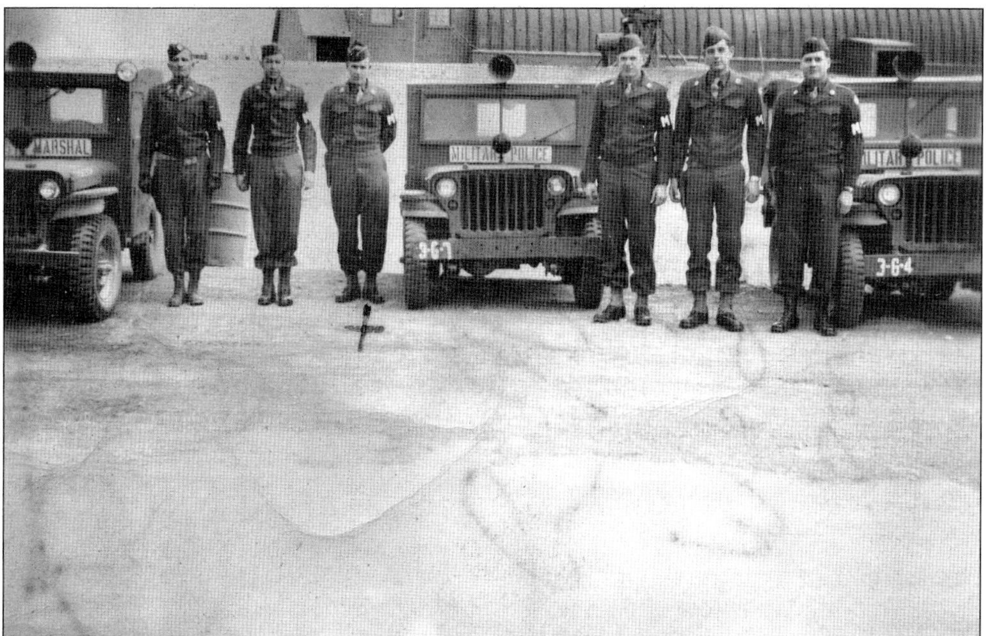

Parnell was in Regensburg, Strabin, and Dubendorf searching out and capturing Nazis immediately after the war. He is pictured here with his unit in Germany, where he was stationed from December 1945 to June 1947 as part of the occupation army. (Courtesy of Willard Parnell.)

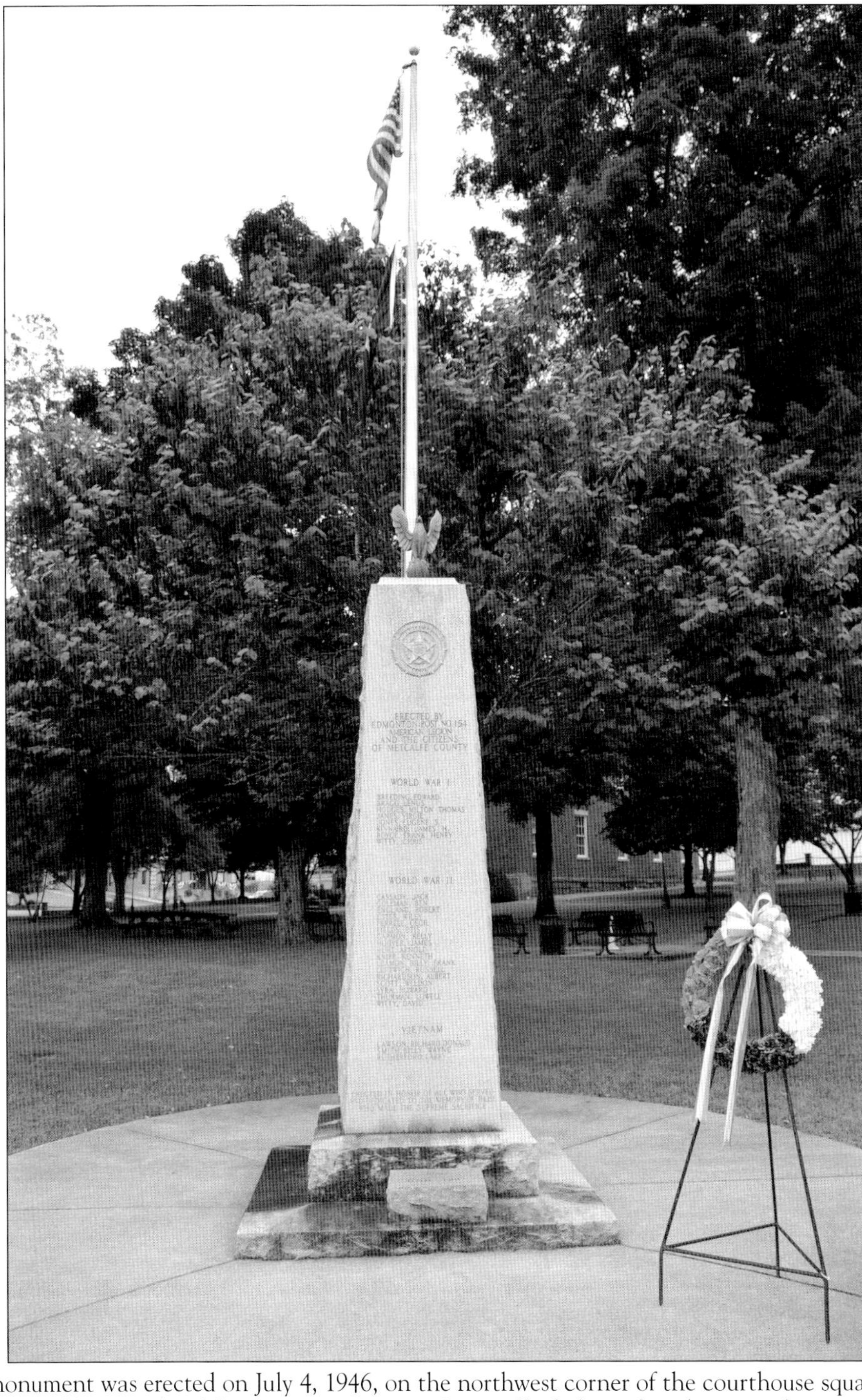

A monument was erected on July 4, 1946, on the northwest corner of the courthouse square by the Metcalfe Post 154 of the American Legion. Originally dedicated to the men who gave their lives during World War I and World War II, additional names were inscribed for those killed in Vietnam and Iraq. No Metcalfe Countians were reported killed during the Korean War. (Photograph by Richard Hines.)

Seven

Everyday Life around Metcalfe County

Everyday life in Metcalfe County runs at a different pace than in most of Kentucky's larger counties. Like a majority of Kentucky's rural counites, activities here revolve around schools, churches, and sports.

Today, Metcalfe County has only one high school, but up until the late 1950s, schools were scattered across the county in each community. A few of these schools were Possum Scratch, Savoyard, Sugarplant, and Liberty. There were many more. These small schools, many with just one room, were the center of community activities, with students making lifelong friendships.

Poor road systems made these small and isolated schools a necessity. In the early 1900s, roads were in such poor shape that one account mentioned Metcalfe County was perhaps one of the most inaccessible counties in Kentucky.

One of the most beneficial programs to arrive in Metcalfe County was the WPA. Developed by Pres. Franklin Roosevelt in 1935 during the Great Depression, the WPA provided millions of unemployed workers jobs. Hundreds in Metcalfe were employed working on buildings, bridges, and roads. This program finally began improving the county's road system, most of which was still only dirt roads.

Music is an important part of everyday life, which in many cases originated in local churches or as pastime. For some, it was the beginning of a lifelong career in the music industry. Chick Hurt and the Prairie Ramblers were some of the earliest members of the Grand Ole Opry, followed by Lonzo and Oscar, a comedy music team also popular on the Opry. In the 1980s, the award-winning Kentucky Headhunters became known for their Southern rock.

Sports have been a pastime for a majority of Metcalfe County residents, like softball leagues in the summer and high school basketball during the winter. A large segment of Metcalfe County residents enjoy hunting, fishing, and just spending time outdoors.

Many people find pleasure in rural areas, where life moves at a slower pace and people have time to enjoy the outdoors as well as their surroundings more. Numerous visitors have decided to make Metcalfe County their home.

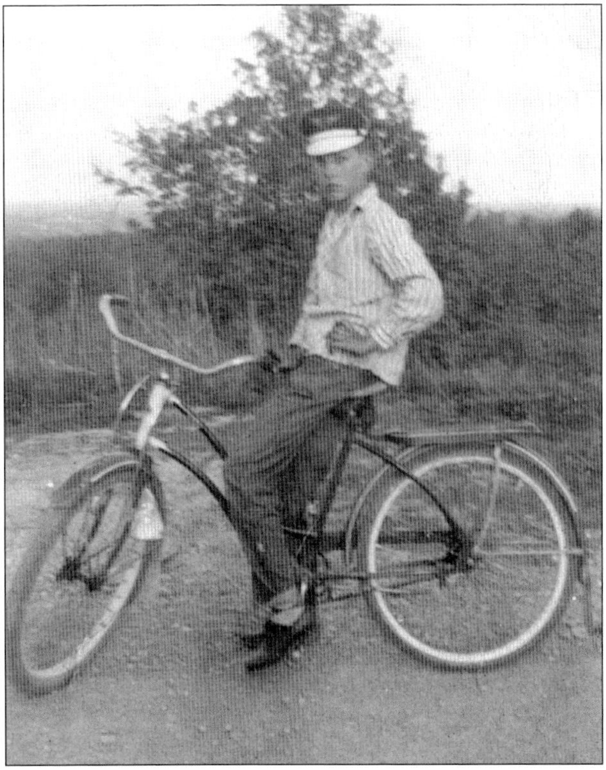

The pride of every Metcalfe County teenager was a new bike. Jody Curry shows off his bicycle and motorcycle hat. Even though it was a used girl's bike, Curry said it was all he could afford. He has operated Curry's Used Cars since 1969 and over the years has donated many new bicycles to the Metcalfe County Library for prizes in its annual reading program. (Courtesy of Jody Curry.)

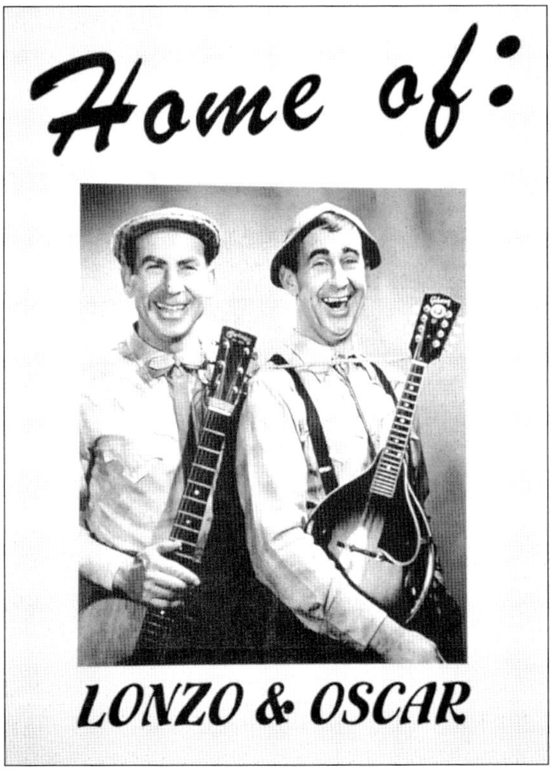

Rollin Sullivan, born in Edmonton in 1919, was part of the famous Grand Ole Opry duo Lonzo and Oscar. Sullivan toured for many years until the 1960s. He began his career playing with the Kentucky Ramblers and later with Paul Howard's Arkansas Cotton Pickers, where he played an electric mandolin. (Courtesy of the City of Edmonton.)

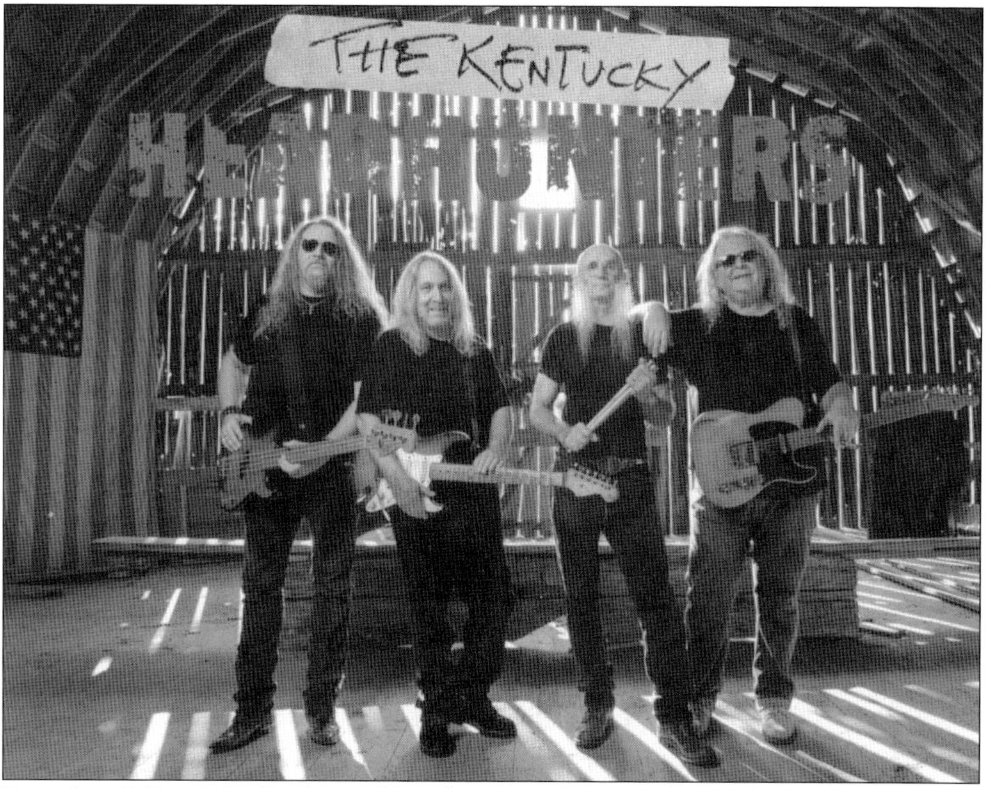

Formed in 1968 as Itchy Brother and later known as the Kentucky Headhunters, this country/Southern rock Grammy Award–winning band continues to tour across the country. Still calling Metcalfe County home, the group obtained international fame with their hit "Dumas Walker." By 1989, the Kentucky Headhunters were the top new vocal group. One of their videos features the Young-Shirley Store, shown on the front cover of this book. (Courtesy of Marla Young.)

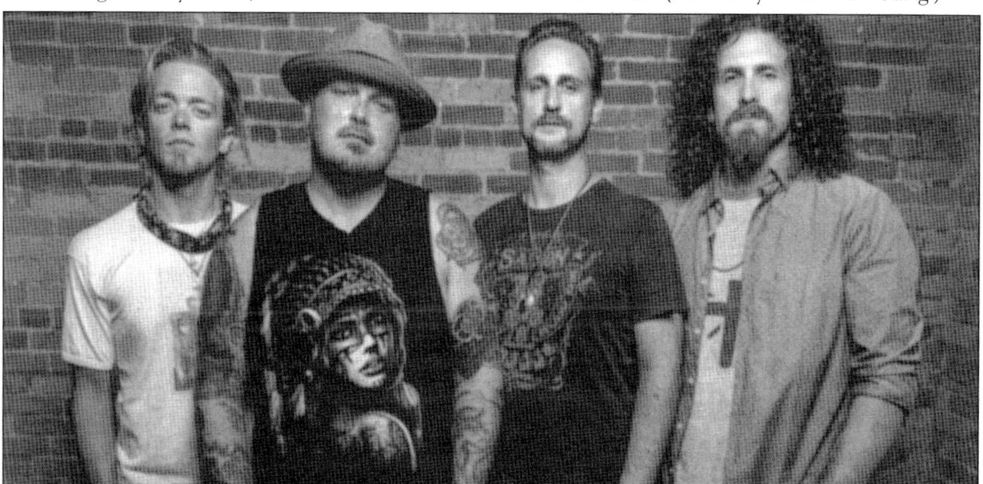

The latest rock band calling Metcalfe County home is Black Stone Cherry. Organized by a son and nephew of one of the Kentucky Headhunters, this hard rock band, which was organized in 2001, has recorded eight albums to date. The band regularly tours across the United States and Europe. (Courtesy of Marla Young.)

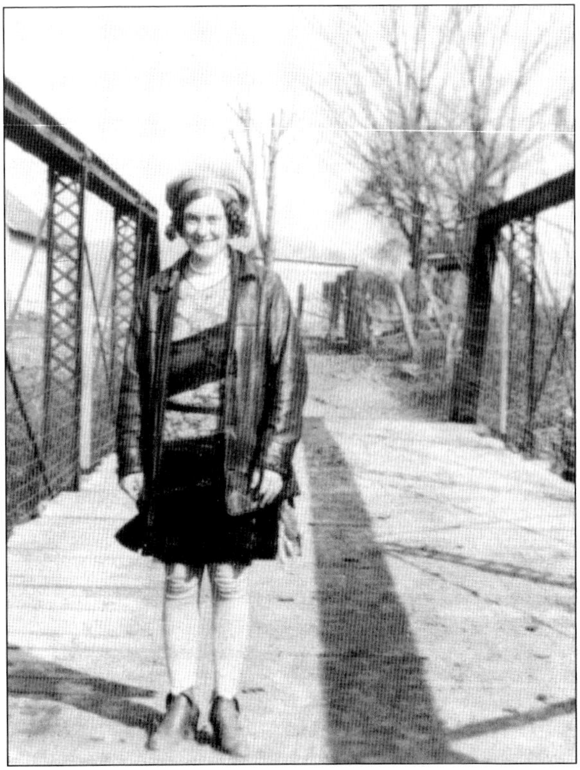

May Davis Holland is crossing the South Fork Bridge in the Bridgeport community. Bridgeport was originally named East Fork in 1853, but the name was changed because of a wooden covered bridge built prior to this metal one. Said to rival Edmonton at the time, the community was thriving, with stores, churches, and a doctor's office until the early 1900s. (Courtesy of Jeneve Holland Crenshaw.)

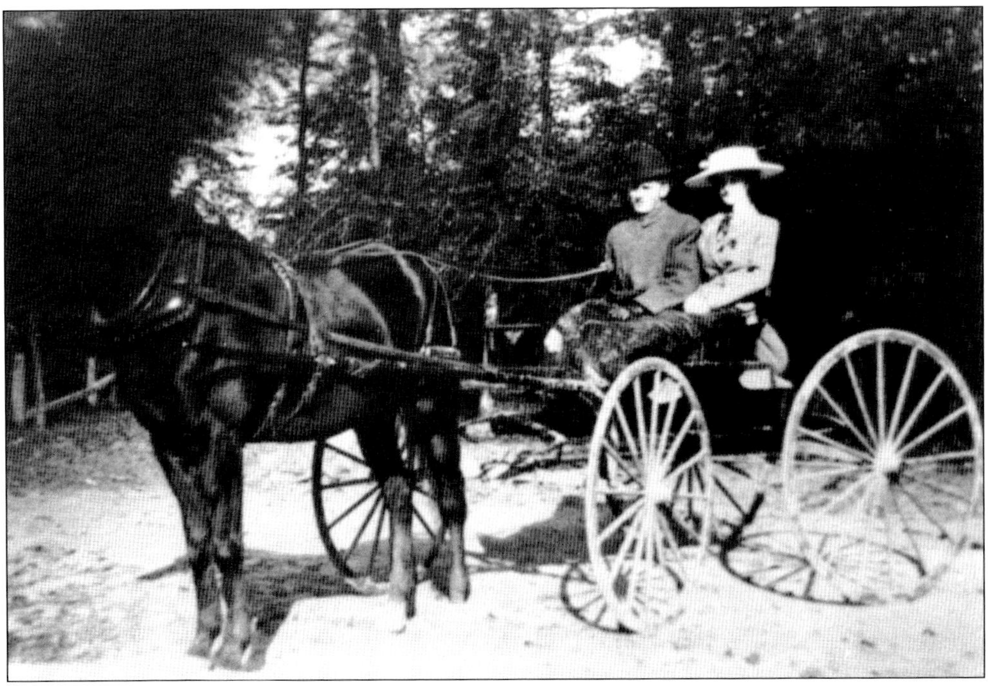

Sometime in the early 1900s, Sanford William Free and Margret Lee Hamilton, who lived in the eastern section of Metcalfe County, are shown leaving for their honeymoon. Free was born in 1885, and Hamilton was born in 1889. (Courtesy of Marion and Steve Brookshier.)

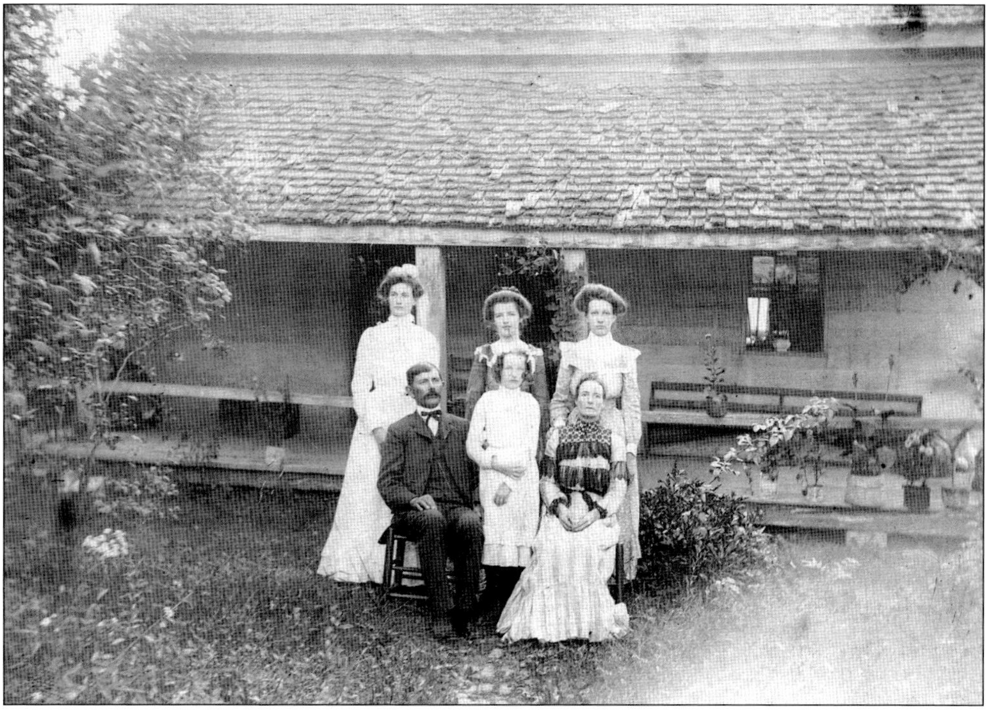

The Edward Hamilton house was built in the early 1800s near the East Fork of the Little Barren River. Hamilton studied medicine with Dr. Benjamin Taylor in Bridgeport during the winter of 1881–1882 and later attended medical lectures in Louisville in order to become a doctor. With Edward and Lula Hamilton are their daughters (from left to right) Elsie, Margaret, Clara (center), and Minnie in 1907. (Courtesy of Marion and Steve Brookshier.)

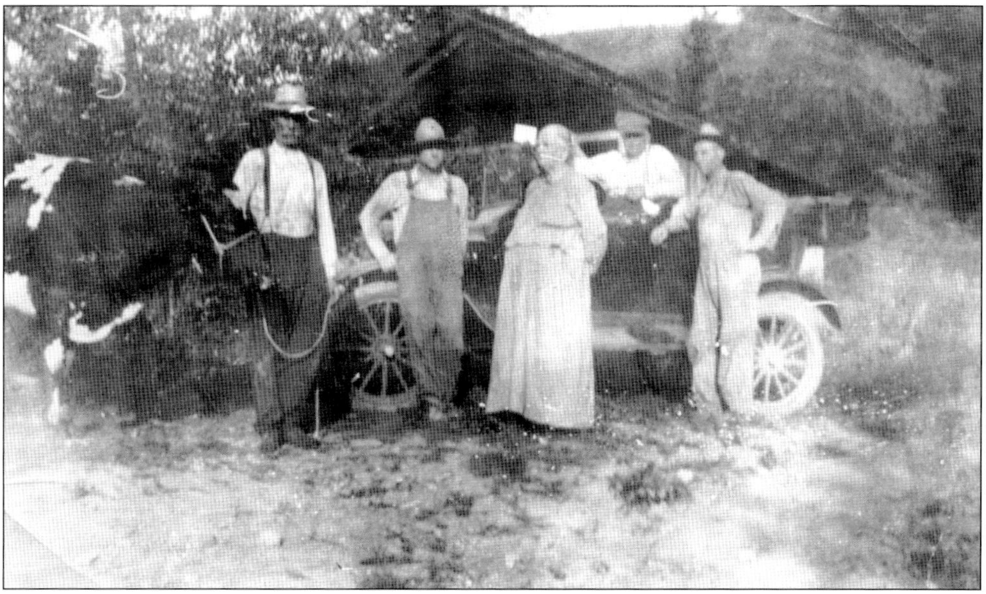

A farmer shows off his prized possessions, a cow and a car, with family members. This is the Hurt family, who lived in the Willow Shade community. (Courtesy of Carol Hurt.)

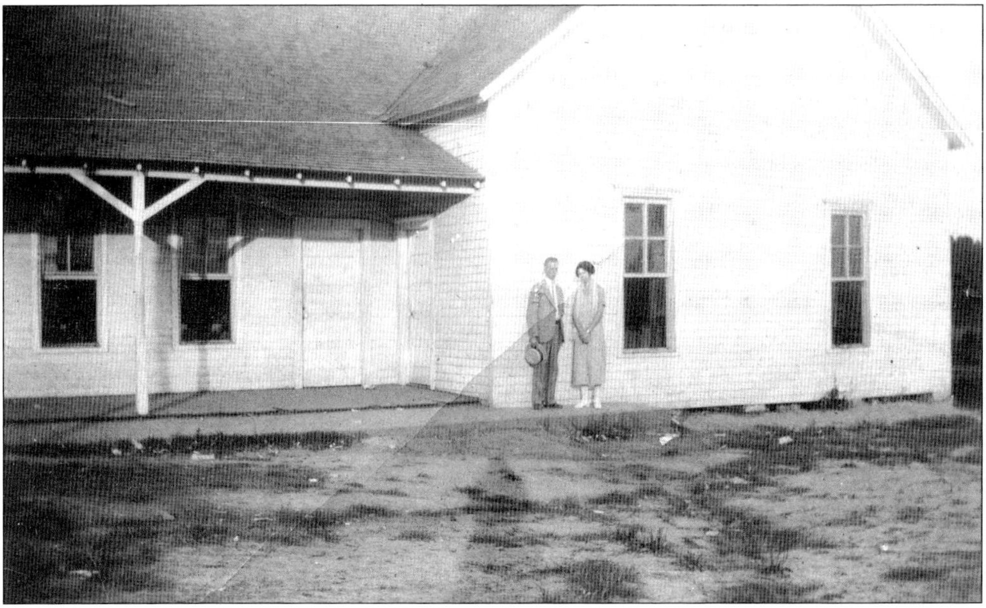

Center High School began operation in 1920 as a two-year high school. It grew into a four-year institution that was in operation from 1924 to 1956. It burned down in the 1970s. This photograph was taken around 1940. (Courtesy of Reba Gravens Norman.)

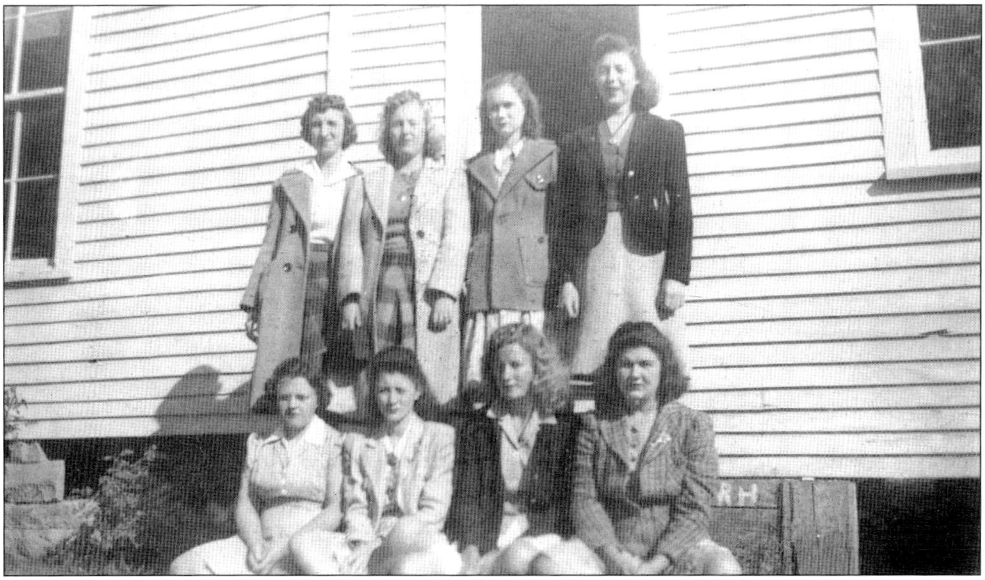

Center High School students are pictured here during the 1939–1940 school year. (Courtesy of Reba Gravens Norman.)

Although Center High School was small, principal and science teacher Angelo Fancher took field trips as far away as Florida. Here, Fancher is teaching students about birds while on one of those Florida trips. (Courtesy of Benny Lile.)

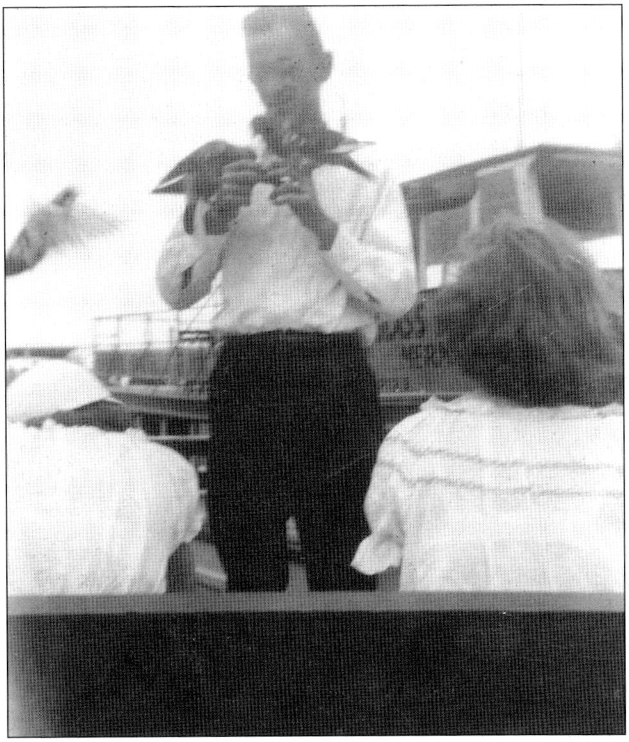

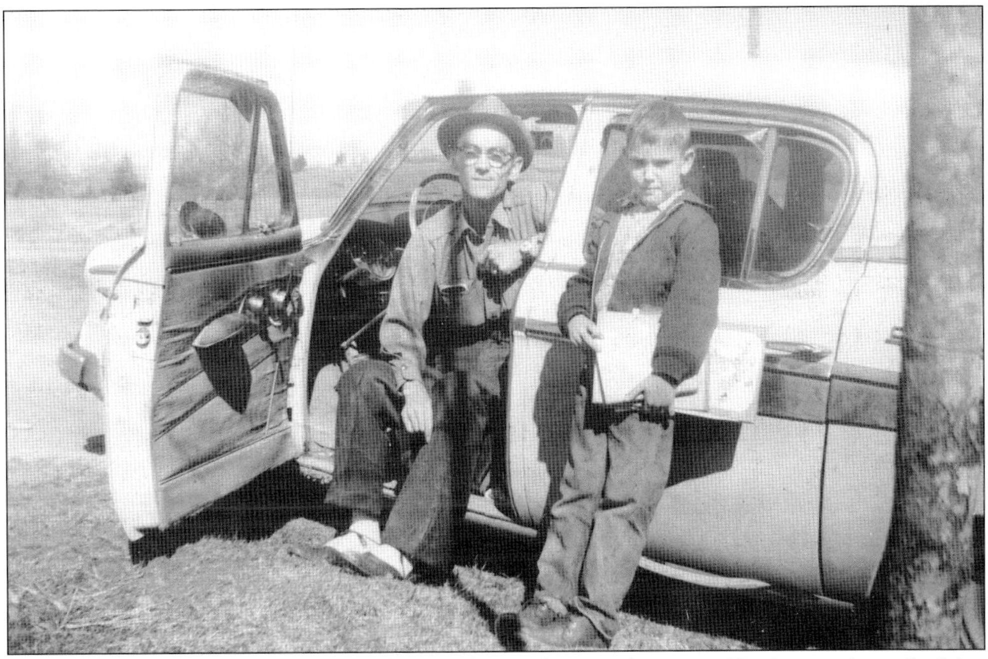

Center High School principal Angelo Fancher is showing his specially designed car. In May 1955, Fancher was injured while exploring a cave near Sulphur Well. While chipping off a piece of stalactite, the hammering jarred two rocks loose that pinned him to the cave floor. Rescue workers from Mammoth Cave National Park were called in to extract Fancher, who was paralyzed for the rest of his life but continued to teach. (Courtesy of Benny Lile.)

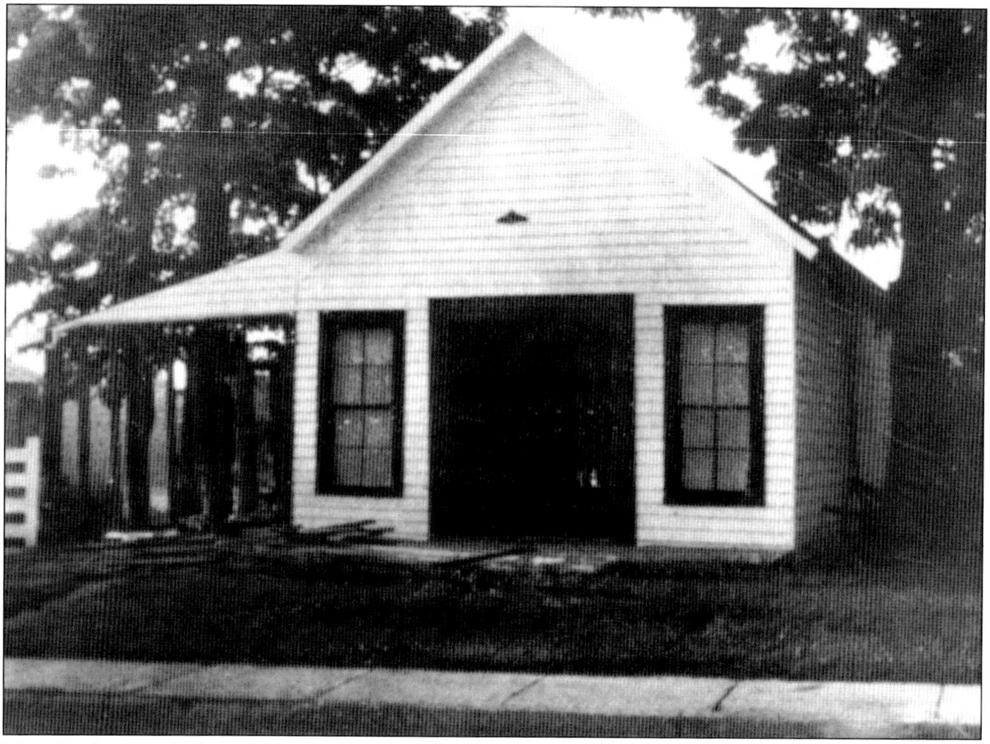

The Butler family began in the funeral business in Center. Here is the Butler Funeral Home around 1943, shortly before the building burned. The Butlers continued in the funeral business in Edmonton. (Courtesy of Donnie Butler.)

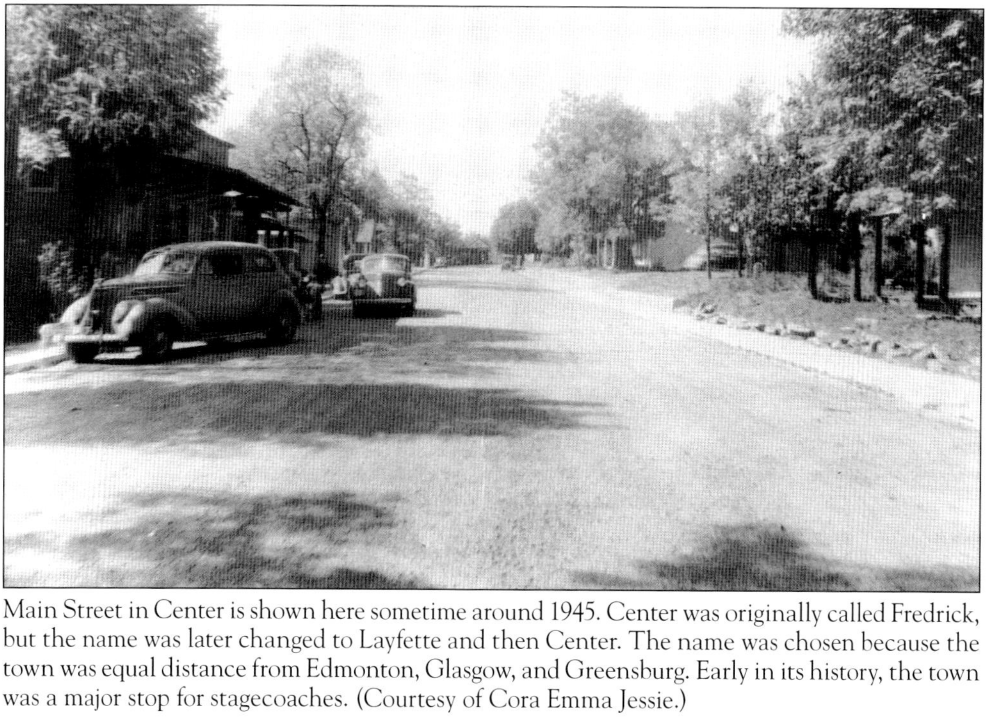

Main Street in Center is shown here sometime around 1945. Center was originally called Fredrick, but the name was later changed to Layfette and then Center. The name was chosen because the town was equal distance from Edmonton, Glasgow, and Greensburg. Early in its history, the town was a major stop for stagecoaches. (Courtesy of Cora Emma Jessie.)

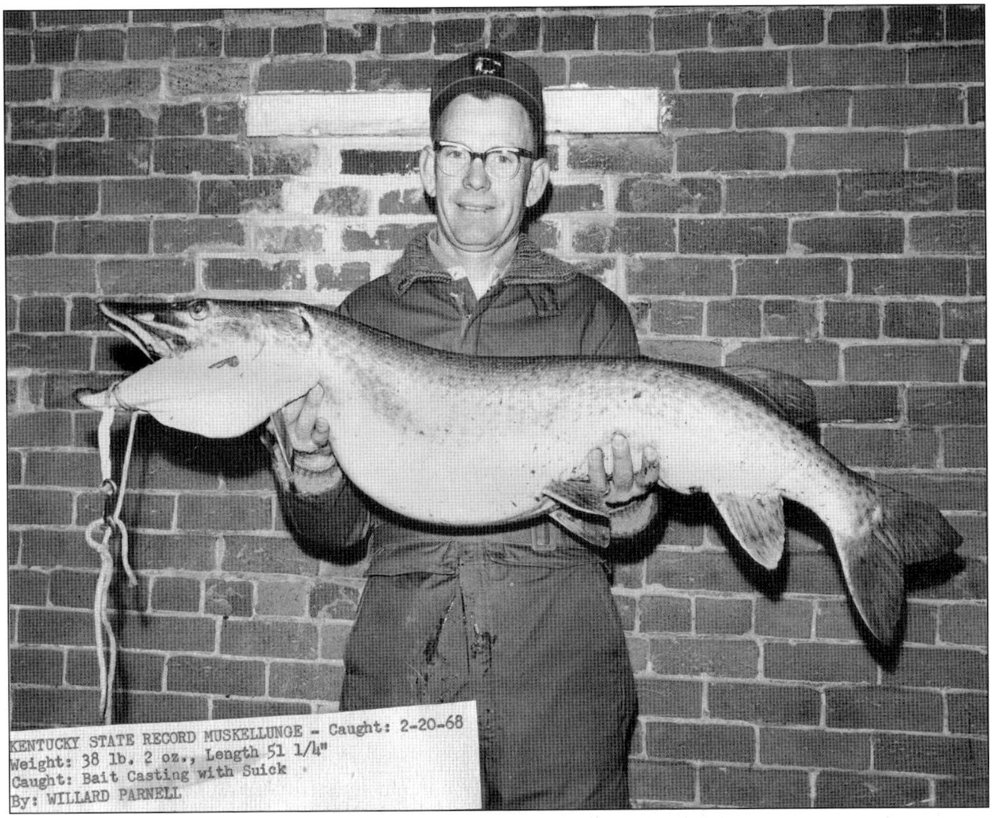

In rural areas, hunting and fishing are major pastimes, and Metcalfe County native Willard Parnell is believed to be the only angler in the United States to have caught a state record fish and then break his own record. Parnell caught his first state record muskellunge (muskie) in 1968 and then broke his record nine months later with a larger 39 pound, 14 ounce muskie. At 94 years old, Parnell continues fishing for another record muskie, one of the most difficult fish to catch. (Courtesy of Willard Parnell.)

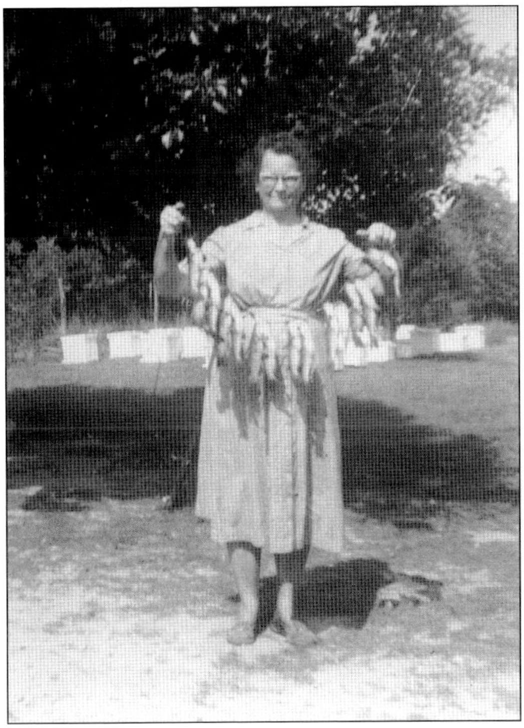

One did not have to catch a state record to be proud of one's fish. Fishing was an activity loved by all, and in 1962, this woman is showing off a nice string of fish caught for supper in one of the local streams. (Courtesy of Vicki Harris.)

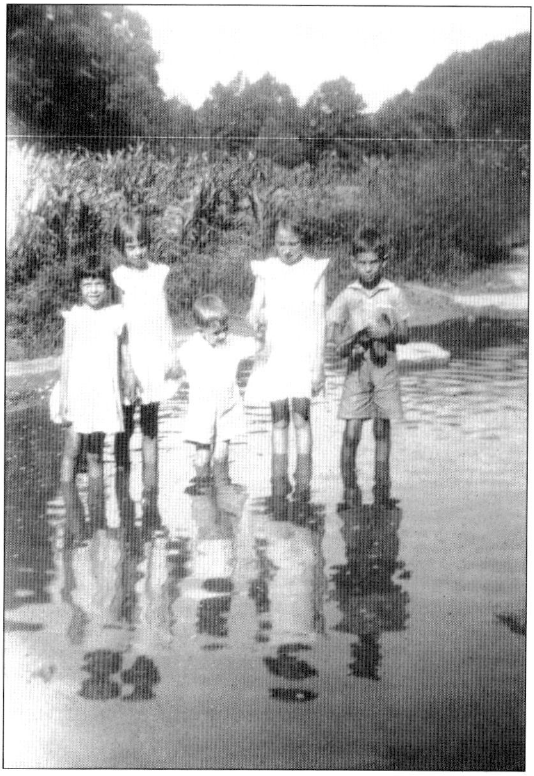

There were no swimming pools in the county in the 1930s, so the perfect place to cool off during the hot summer months was a nearby creek. Medline Coffee (second from left) and other children play in Long Creek near the Bridgeport community. (Courtesy of Willard Parnell.)

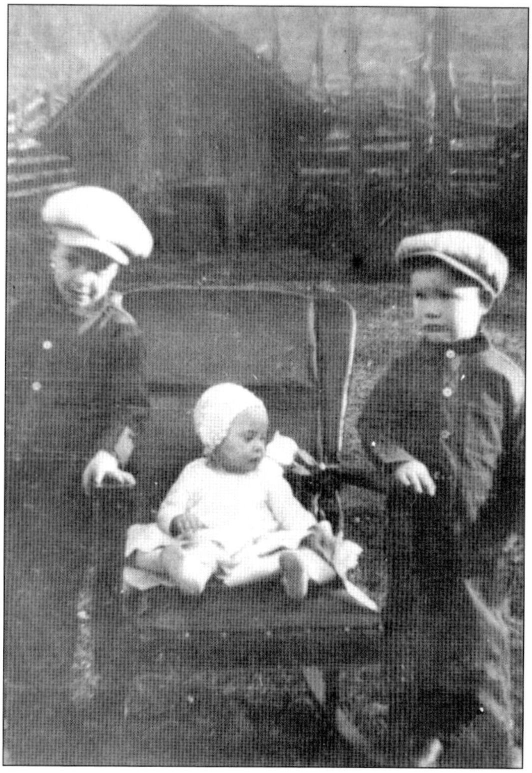

Everything a family needed could be purchased on the Edmonton Square. The Parnell children are shown after a shopping trip to town to buy new hats, clothes, and shoes for school and the coming winter. Willard Parnell is on the right. (Courtesy of Willard Parnell.)

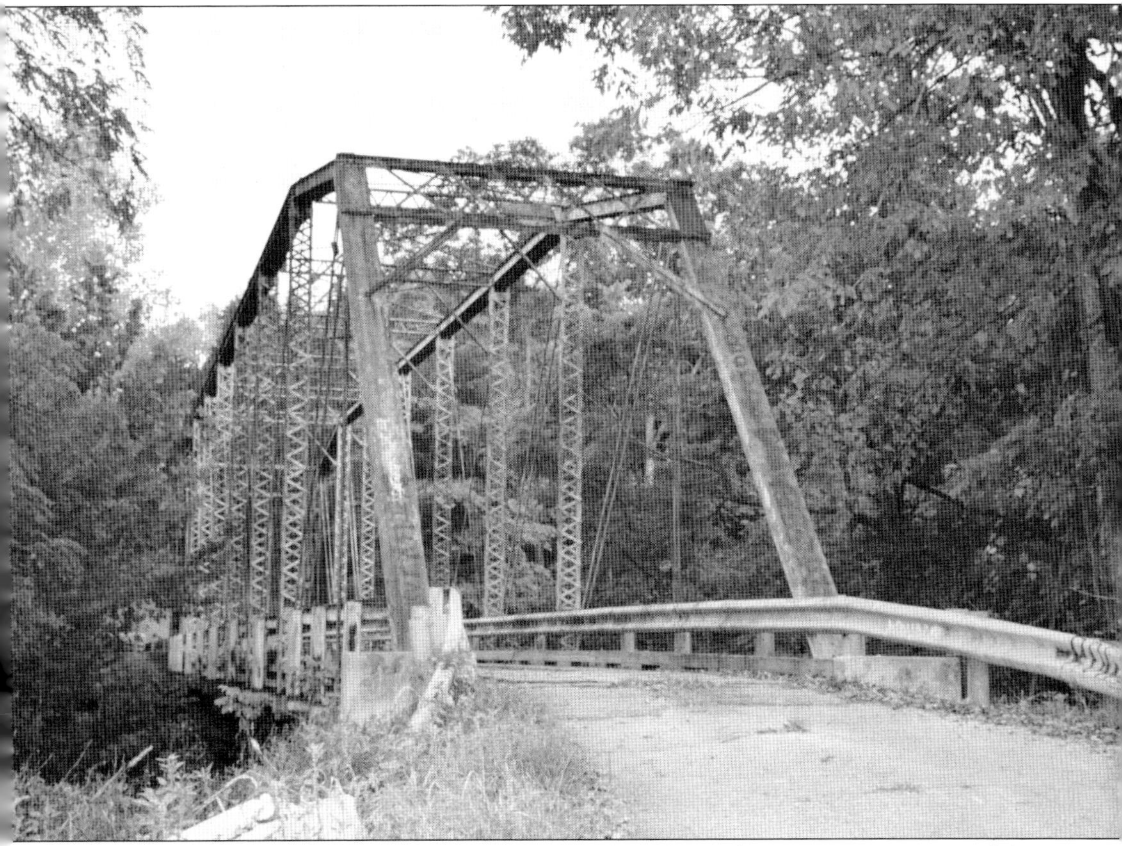

Mosby Ridge Road Bridge, which crosses the East Fork of the Little Barren River, is one of the few remaining camelback through truss bridges still in use in the United States. After being manufactured in 1911, the bridge was shipped by railroad to Campbellsville, where workers from Metcalfe County hauled it by wagon to its present location and assembled it. These truss bridges could also be disassembled and moved, which was done on many occasions. The Mosby Ridge Road Bridge is listed on several historic bridge websites. (Photograph by Richard Hines.)

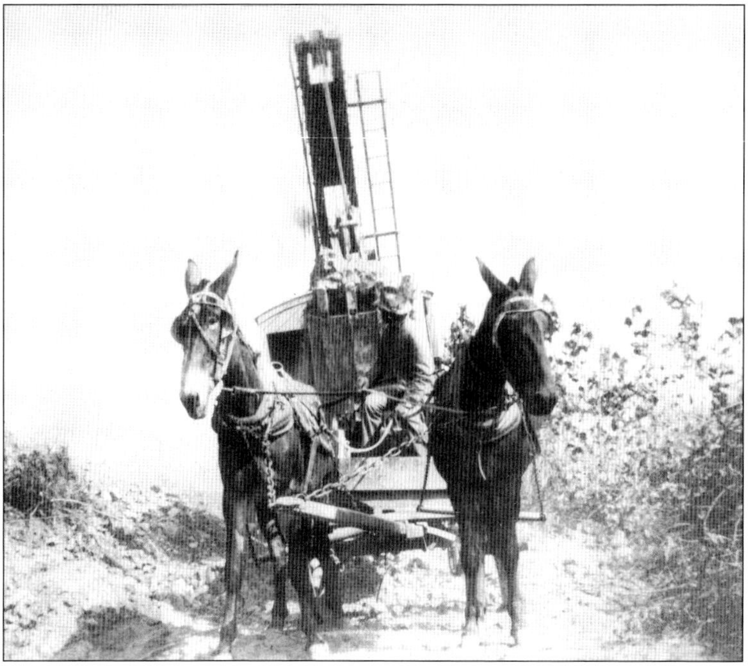

In 1923, work began on Kentucky Route 90 between Glasgow and Summer Shade, the result of obtaining needed federal funding to construct this major highway from Glasgow to Corbin. In the 1920s, road work still depended on mule-drawn equipment and hand tools. (Courtesy of Gary Richardson.)

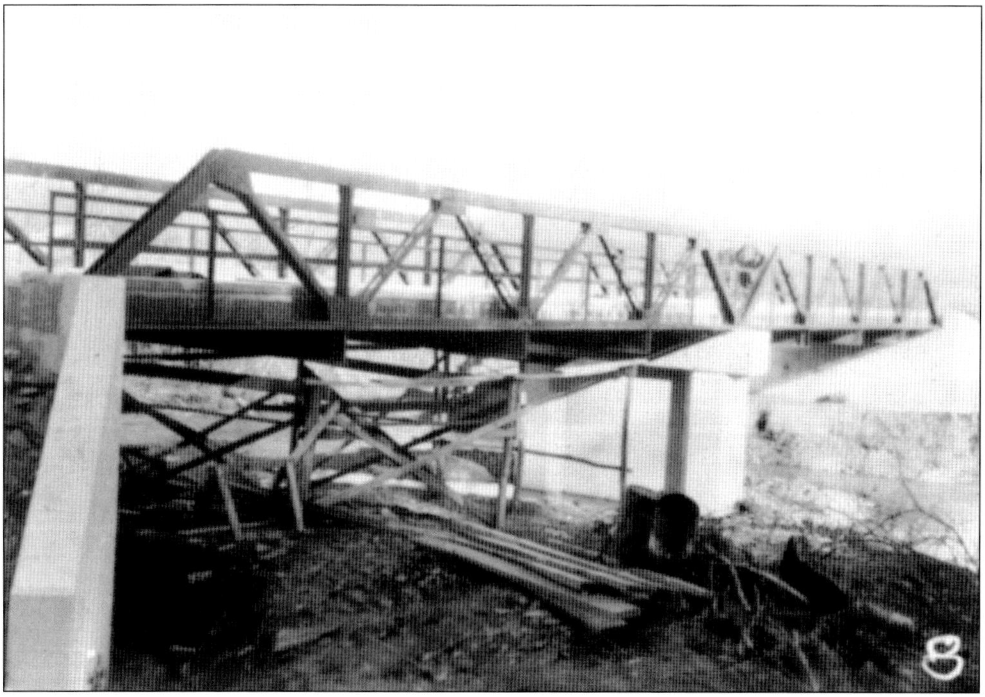

Newly completed Subtle Road Bridge was constructed by the WPA in the late 1930s. Prior to this, the county only had a few bridges crossing larger streams. Before many of these bridges were built by the WPA, local residents were forced to cross or ford streams, making travel in rainy seasons difficult and dangerous. Numerous swinging or cable bridges were used for foot travel only. (Courtesy of University of Kentucky Libraries Special Collections Research Center, Goodman-Paxton Photographic Collection.)

A WPA crew is operating a tractor pulling a road grader along the ditch line on Cave Ridge Road near the Echo community. This ditch provided a water diversion, extending the life of the roadbed. Today, graders only require one operator, but in 1935, three were required to operate this machine. (Courtesy of University of Kentucky Libraries Special Collections Research Center.)

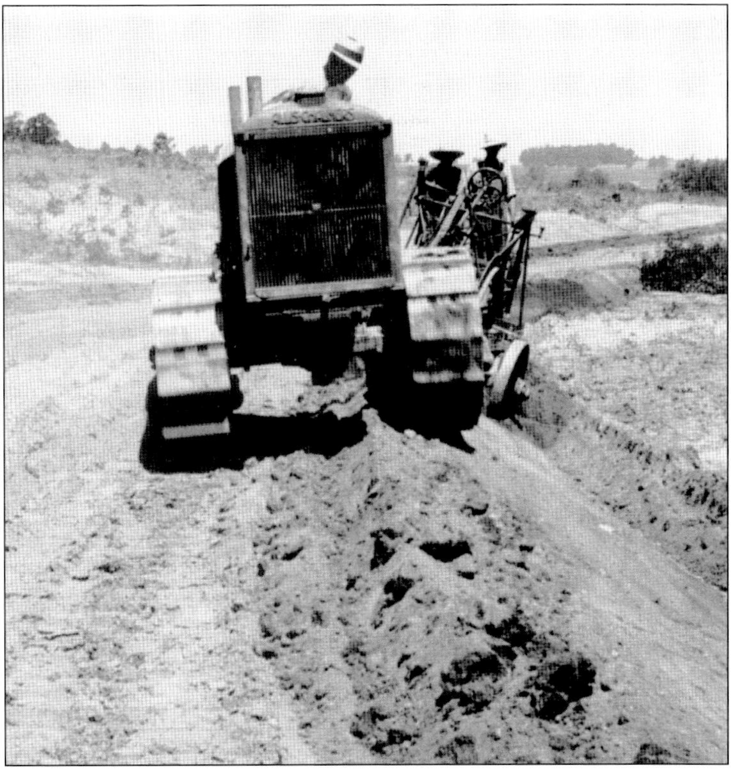

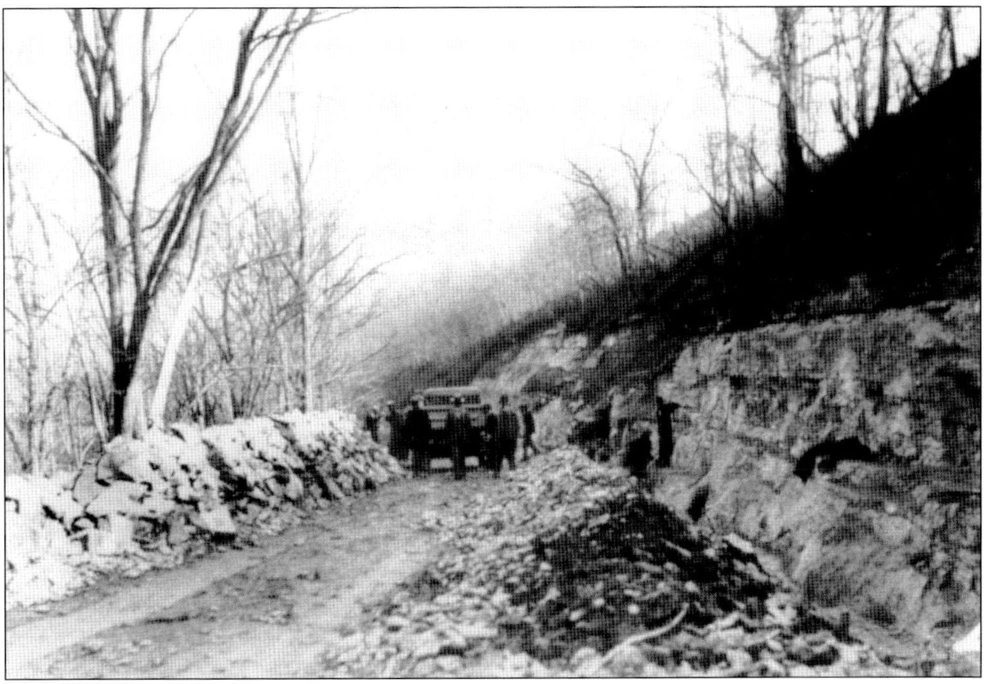

Knob Lick Road is being improved by a WPA crew, which was blasting rock, hand clearing rock rubble, and preparing the roadbed for a hard surface of gravel. This stretch of road is still in use today. (Courtesy of University of Kentucky Libraries Special Collections Research Center.)

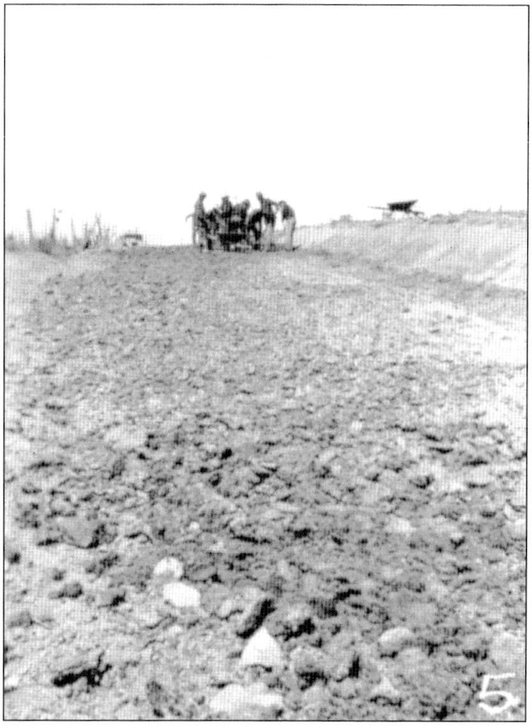

Using hand tools, a WPA crew is working on finishing a new road near the Beechville community. The WPA built and improved several new roads in Metcalfe County. Nationwide, the WPA constructed more than 620,000 miles of streets and roads between 1935 and 1943 to provide jobs to unemployed workers during the Great Depression. (Courtesy of Western Kentucky University Special Collections.)

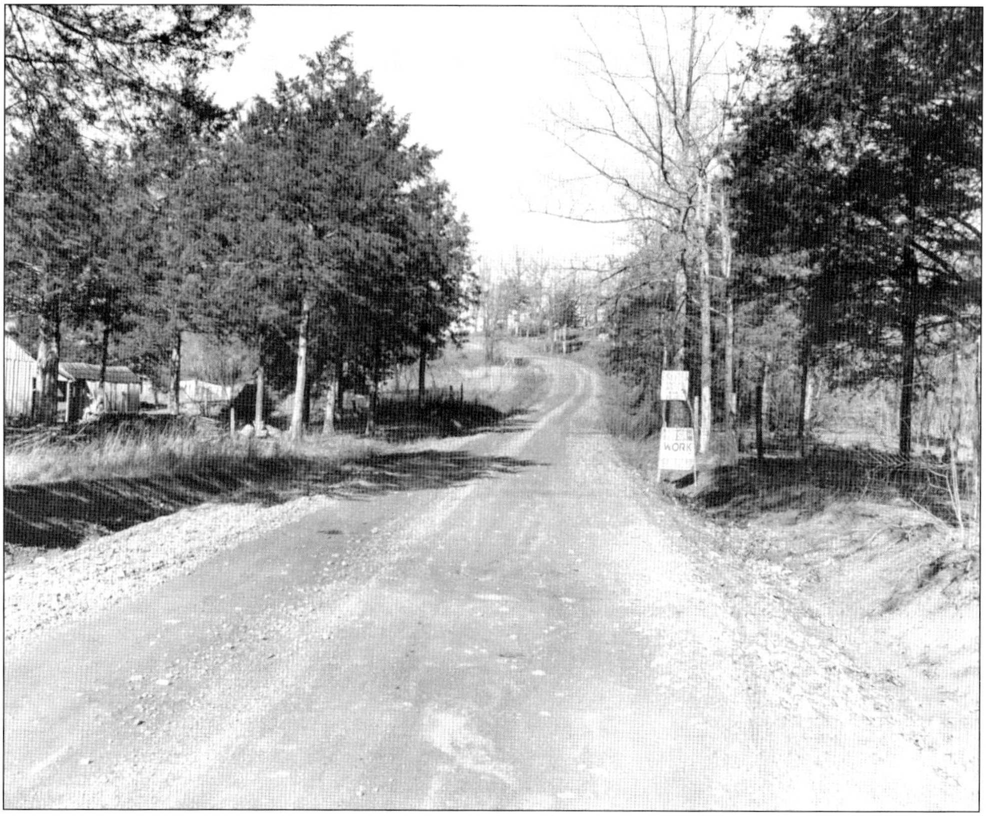

In the 1930s, the road between Center and Sulphur Well was graded and hard surfaced with gravel by the WPA. In almost all cases, final finishing of the roadbed was completed with hand tools. The sign on the side of the road was displayed at all WPA projects. Mechanized equipment was not always available, but manpower was in almost endless supply. (Courtesy of the Kentucky Museum and the Western Kentucky University Special Collections.)

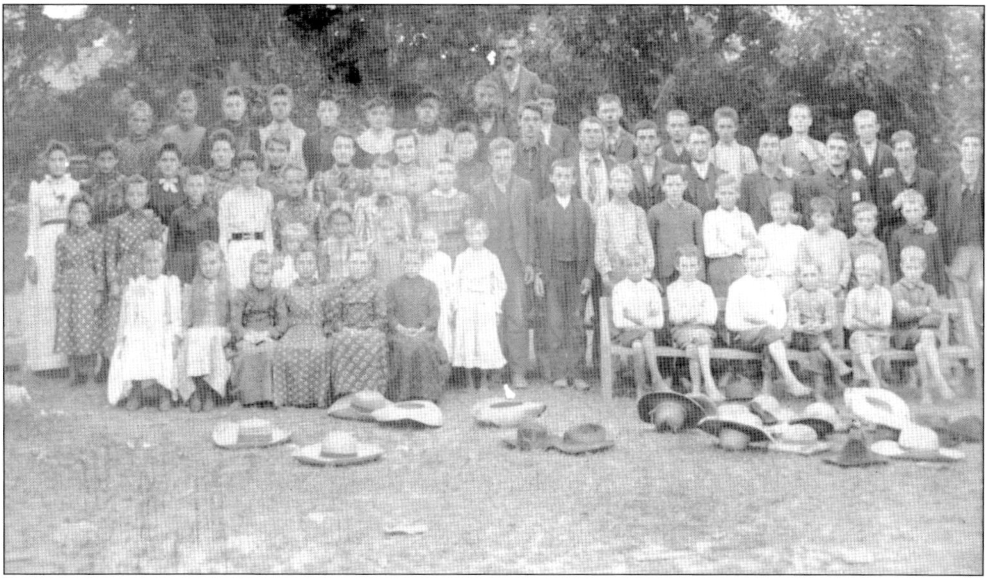

Teacher J.T. Morgan is standing at center in the back of this photograph taken at the Liberty District School. (Courtesy of Laurie Butler.)

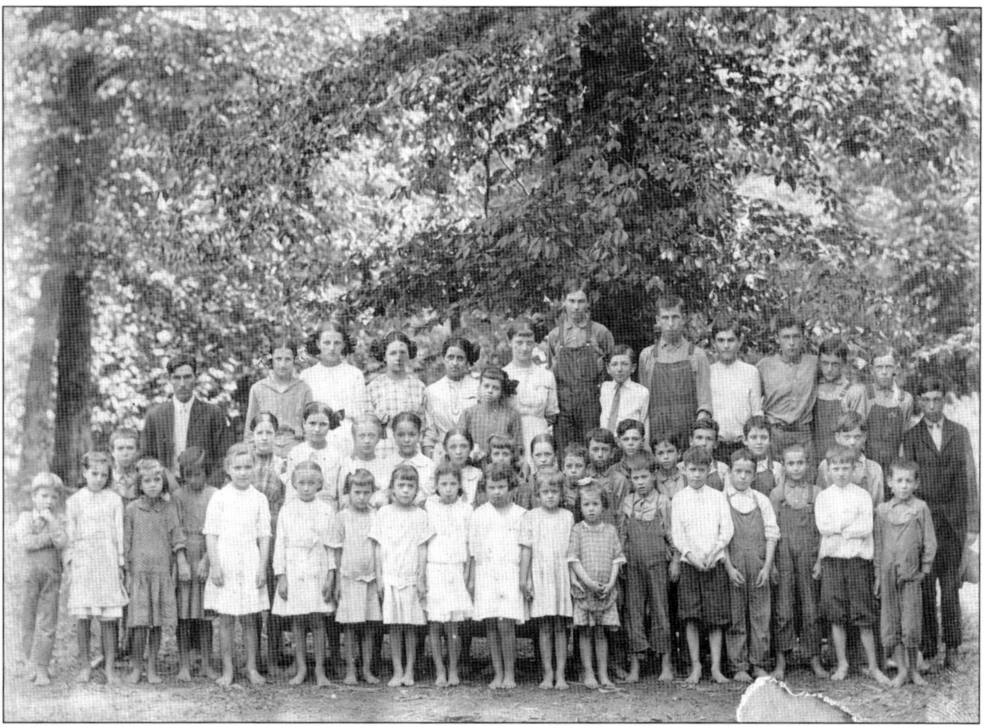

Students and teachers at the West Point School are shown around 1912. (Courtesy of Carol Hurt.)

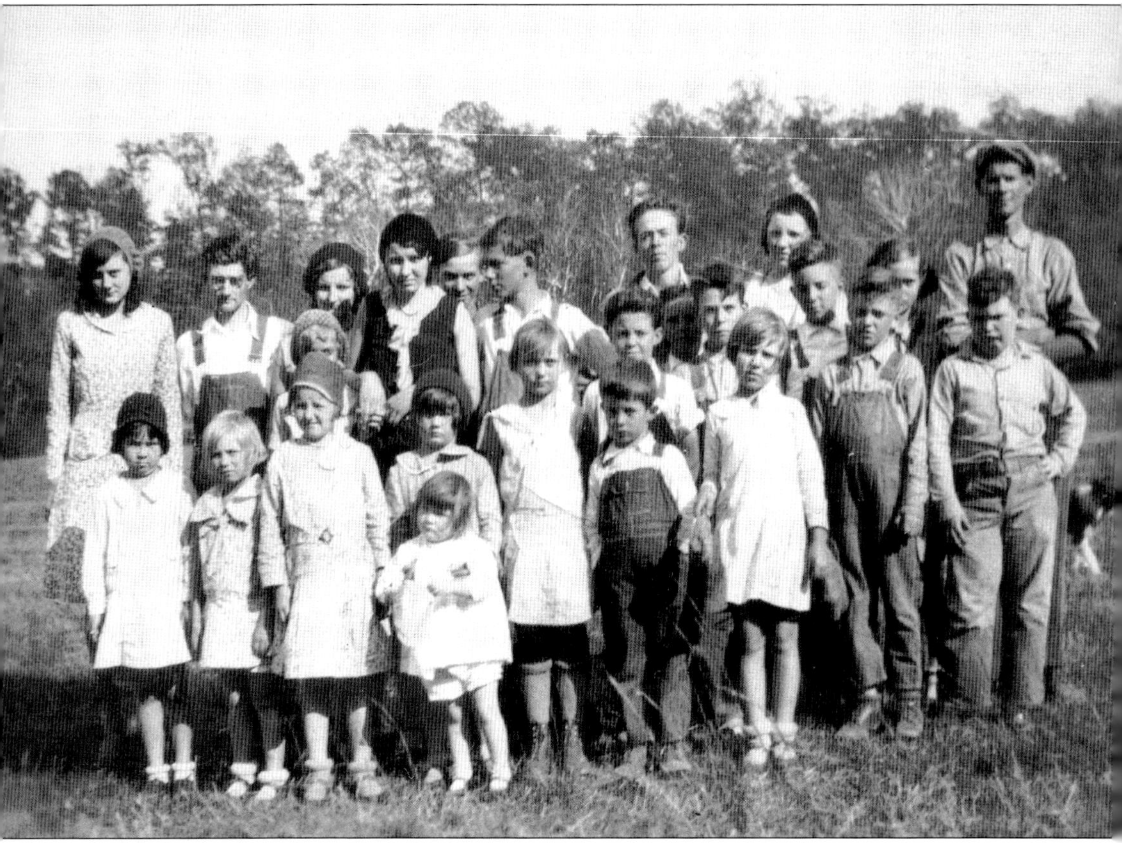

The entire assembly of students who attended Possum Scratch School is shown here. This was one of many one-room schools scattered across Metcalfe County. Possum Scratch School was near the Knob Lick community. (Courtesy of Vicki Harris.)

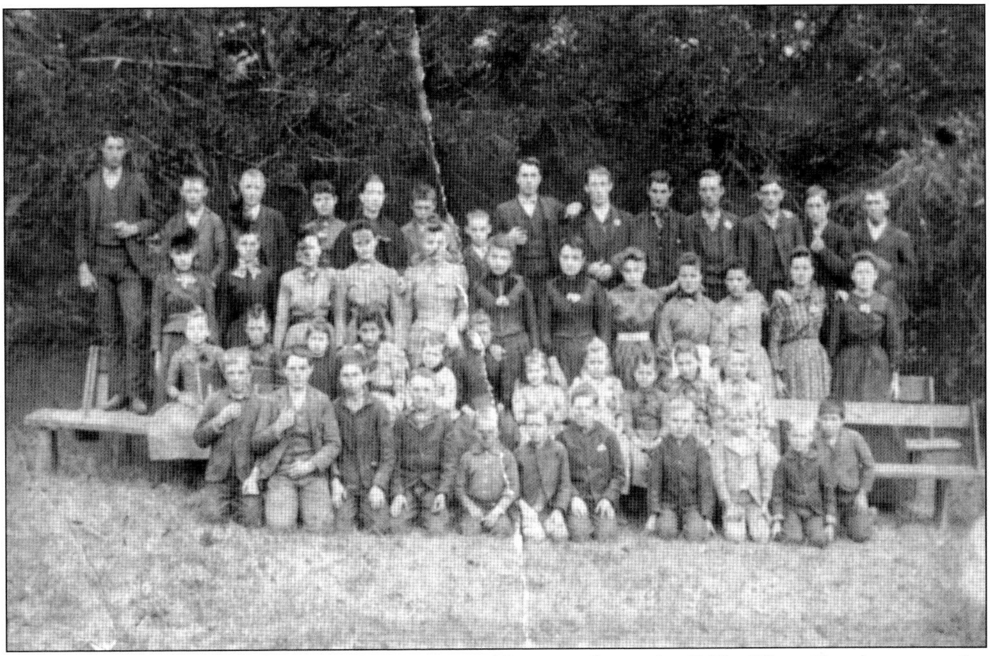

Students at the Sugar Plant School are pictured here in the early 1900s. The school was on the Obie Forrest farm and was moved in 1910 to the Helen Stark farm on Kentucky Highway 640 between Wisdom and Knob Lick. (Courtesy of Western Kentucky University Special Collections.)

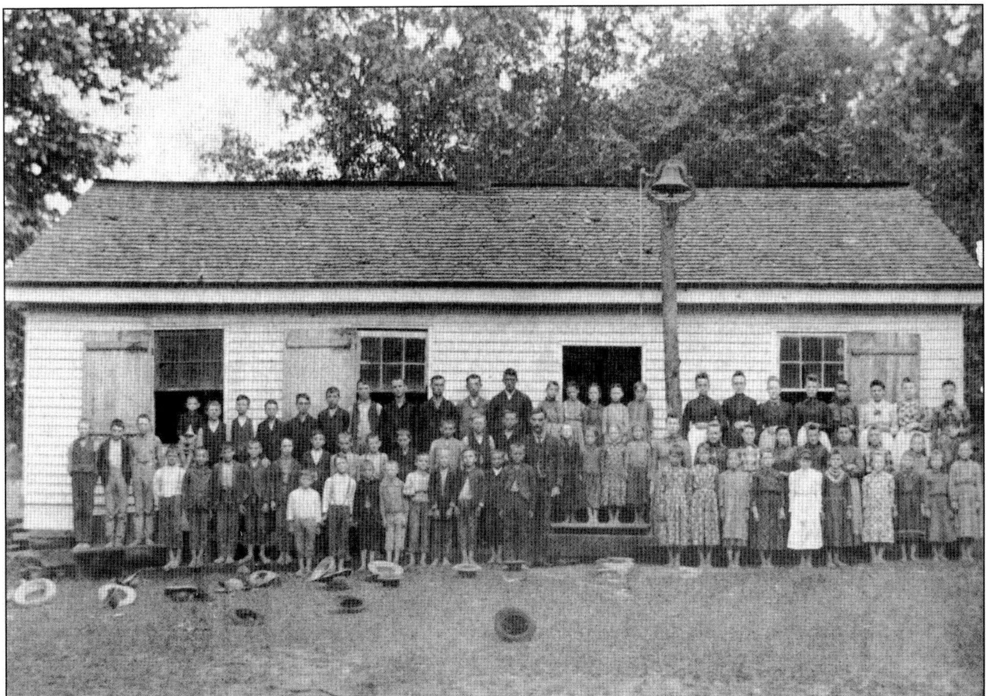

In 1891, teachers and students pose outside the Liberty District School, which was near the Cave Ridge community. (Courtesy of Laurie Butler.)

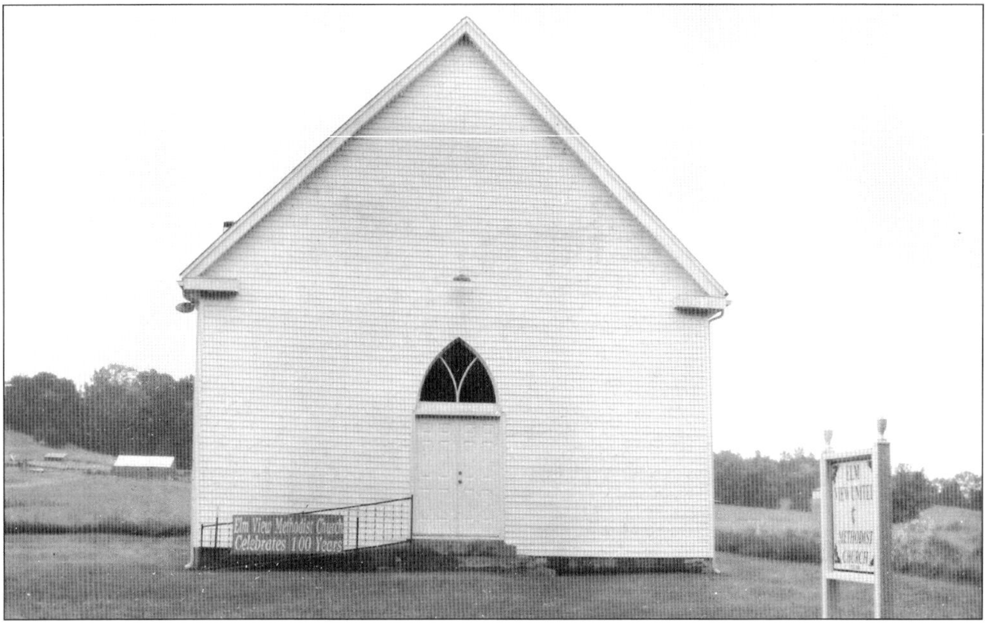

Elm View Methodist Church, on the banks of the East Fork of the Little Barren River in the Bridgeport community, was organized in 1905. The church's first pastor was Samuel Breeding, followed by J.A. Johnson and A.N. Yancey. Cecil Bragg, who lived nearby, was on the church's board of trustees. The church continues to have services each week, and since this photograph taken in 1968, has added an addition. (Courtesy of Marion Brookshier.)

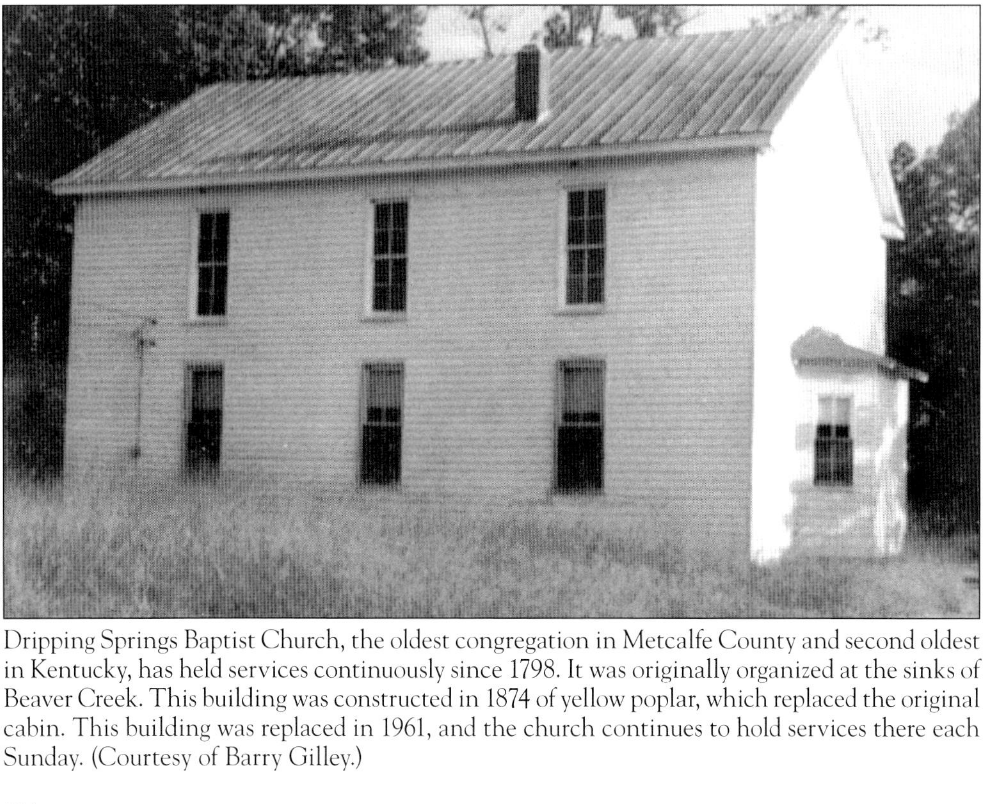

Dripping Springs Baptist Church, the oldest congregation in Metcalfe County and second oldest in Kentucky, has held services continuously since 1798. It was originally organized at the sinks of Beaver Creek. This building was constructed in 1874 of yellow poplar, which replaced the original cabin. This building was replaced in 1961, and the church continues to hold services there each Sunday. (Courtesy of Barry Gilley.)

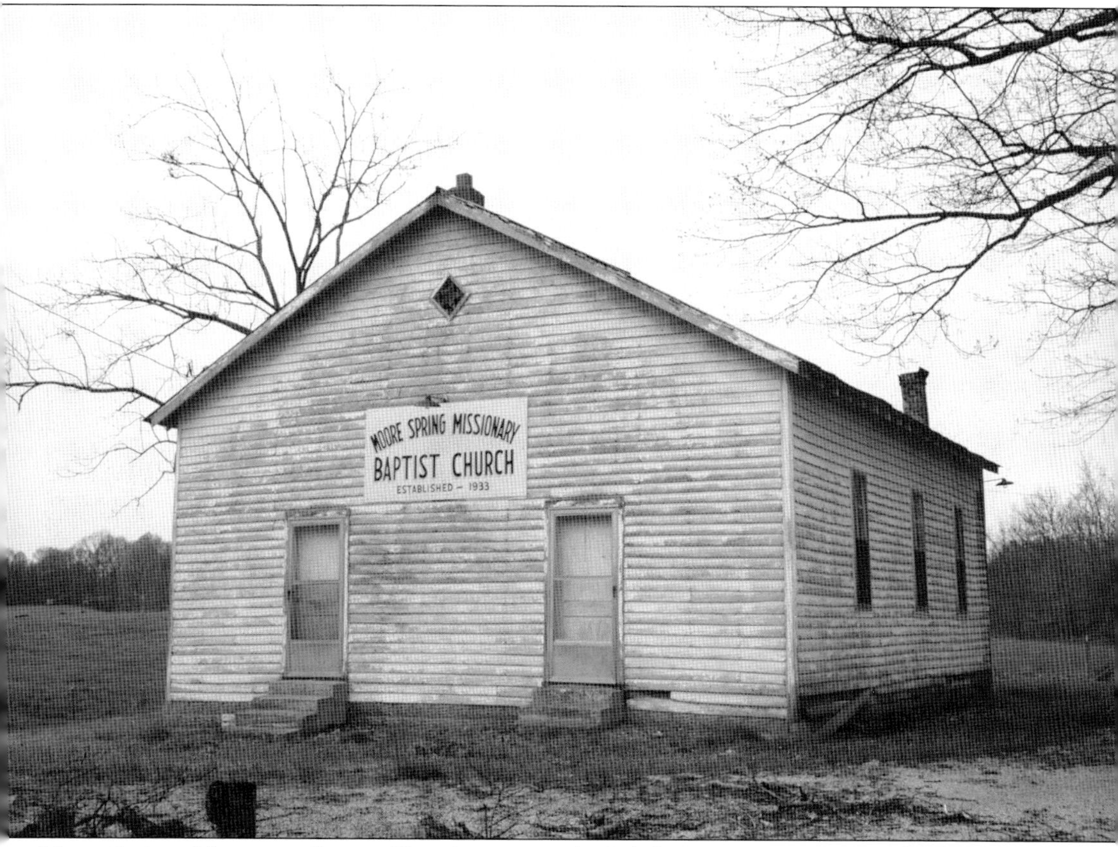

Moore Springs Missionary Baptist Church was near the Subtle community. Many early churches had two doors in front where men entered and sat on the right and women entered and sat on the left. Children and younger couples typically sat in the center section. (Courtesy of Edmonton-Metcalfe Chamber of Commerce.)

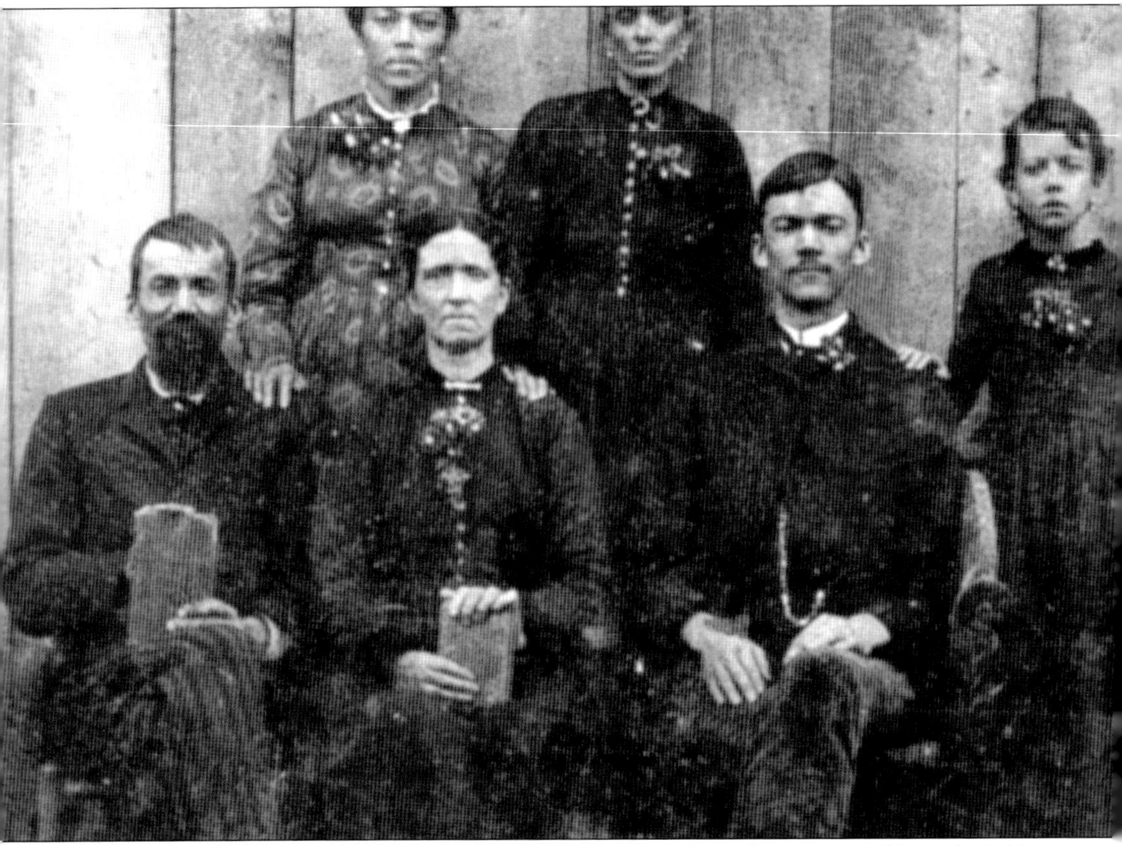

This photograph was taken at Casey Fork Baptist Church in the 1860s. Holding the bibles are Isaac and Charlotte Hurt, and one of their sons is sitting next to them. Isaac had two wives and 20 children. The women in the back were listed as maids, and although the church was listed as white, servants of members were allowed to attend. (Courtesy of Carol Hurt.)

Eight

Country Stores

If one thing demonstrates real rural America, it is a country store. Long before the development of chain and big box stores, dozens of country stores dotted Metcalfe County roadsides. These small stores were a lifeline for rural residents and supplied everything from groceries and gas to clothes and hardware.

During the winter months, many roads were only passable by horseback or jeeps. This made country stores important. Residents could not only obtain weekly supplies, but also catch up on the latest news from both the community and the outside world.

Many stores were also a post office, such as the Frontie Janes and Sons store in the Subtle community. Post offices were in numerous stores across the county. In most cases, the same family would run both the store and post office, and it was not unusual for consecutive generations to operate both. John Janes opened the Subtle Post Office in 1905 and operated it until his death in 1917. His wife then became postmaster until 1940. After her retirement, the title was handed down to her son Hyman Janes. After Hyman's death, Ivy Garmin, granddaughter of John Janes, operated the Subtle Post Office until it became a rural station of the Edmonton Post Office.

Each store had its own unique characteristic. Parnell's Store had a taxidermy business, so it was the place to find out where fish were biting. Above all, each store was judged on how big its baloney sandwiches were and which one was the cheapest, making it the lunch stop for anyone working in the area.

Most of these small stores operated on credit. Patrons charged everything from gasoline to laundry detergent. Occasionally, bills were paid at the end of the month, but in most cases, they were not paid until after the customer's tobacco crop was sold. During the winter months, some stores bought fur from local trappers and hunters, which was used in exchange for needed family supplies. During the summer months, many stores purchased wild medical roots such as ginseng, goldenseal, or mayapple.

Because of their narrow profit margin, many of the smaller stores fell by the wayside.

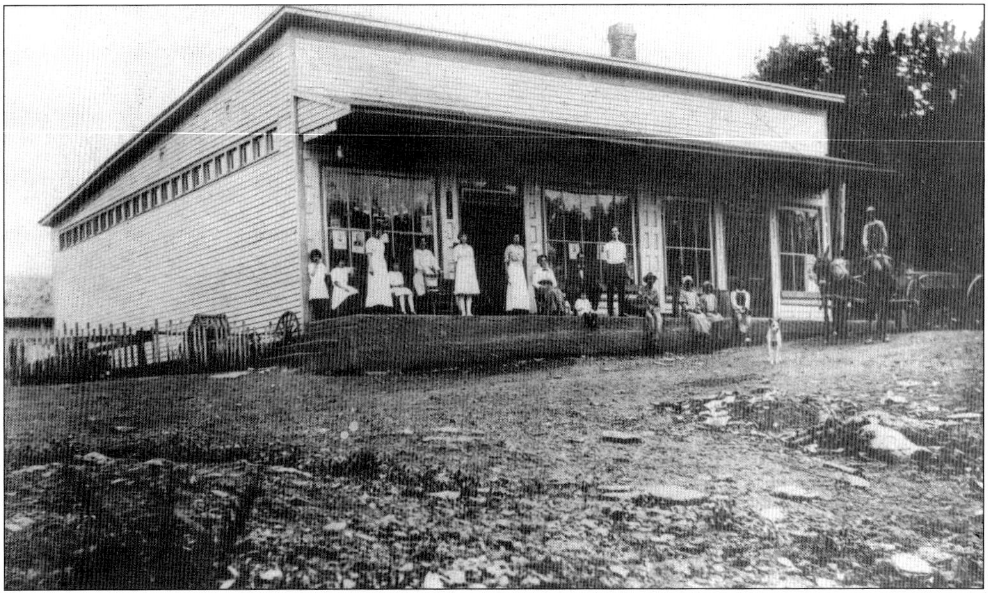

Sulphur Well store and post office is shown here in 1925. The Sulfur Well grocery store was built by Dr. Hamilton in 1880 and rebuilt in 1912. The store has been in almost continuous operation since it opened. (Courtesy of Cora Emma Jessie.)

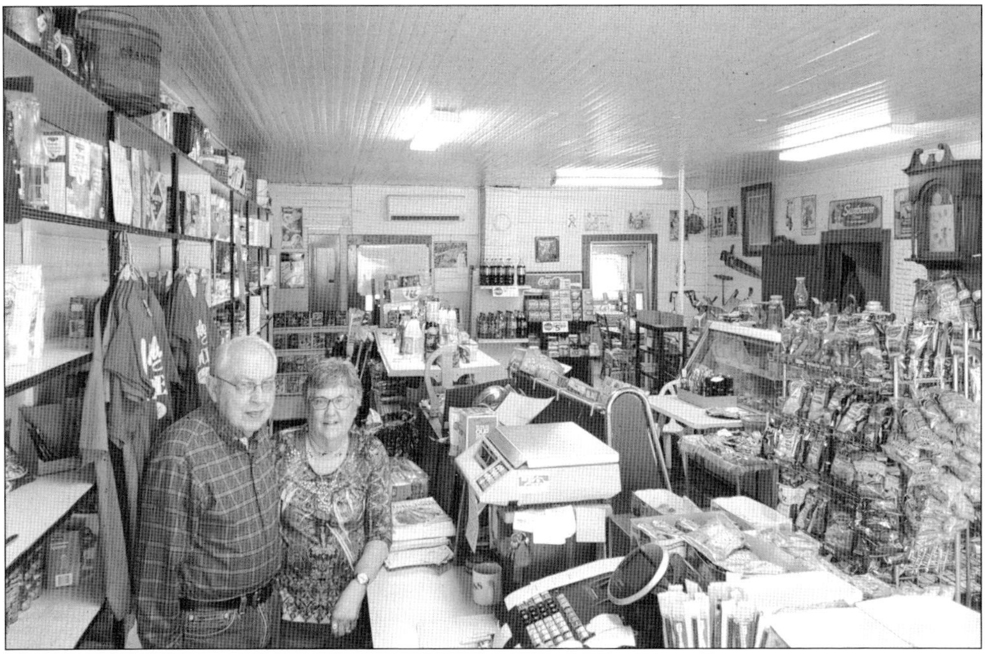

A walk into Hunley's Store is like stepping back in time. The store has changed little since it was built by Elbert and Mary Hunley in 1939. They opened the store in 1940 on US Highway 68 near Wisdom, and with the exception of one year, the store has operated continually since then. Today, their son Elbert Hunley Jr. and his wife, Martha, continue living in and operating the store where one can buy gas, groceries, and the best baloney sandwiches in Metcalfe County. (Photograph by Richard Hines.)

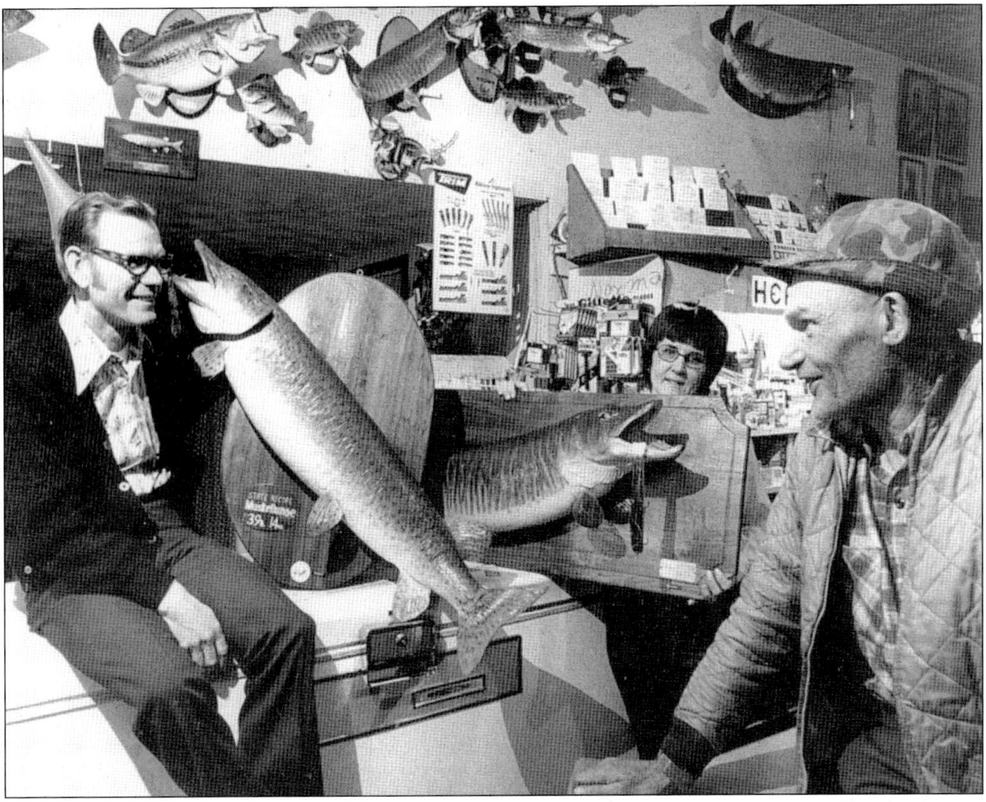

Willard Parnell (left) was the proprietor of Parnell's Store on Highway 80. Parnell also ran a taxidermy business out of his store, and as one of Kentucky's best-known muskie anglers, people would come from miles around to see the two state record fish that had made Parnell famous. Looking on is Parnell's wife, Norma, and Porter Hash, who broke Parnell's muskie record. (Courtesy of Willard Parnell.)

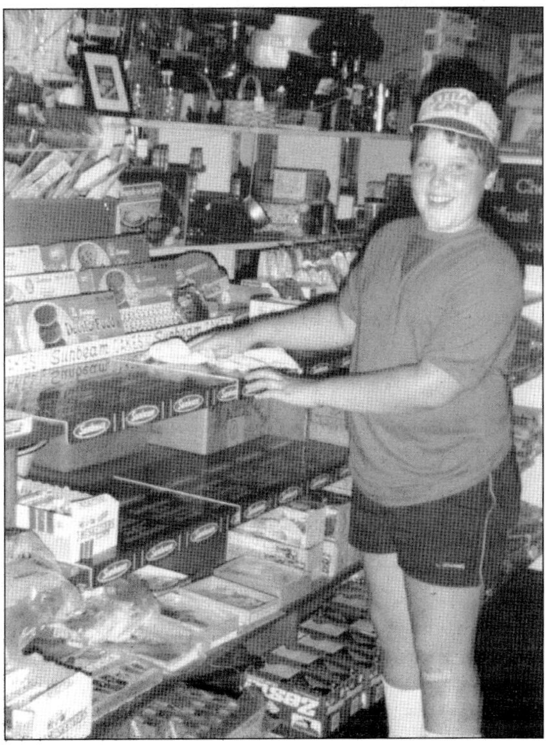

Inside Parnell's Store, which opened in the Cork-Gascon community in 1958, shelves were packed with items people could buy without making an expensive trip to town. Willard Parnell and his wife, Norma, would employ local kids to help with stocking and cleaning the store. It was difficult to keep stores supplied, and many times, Willard would have to make weekly trips to Nashville to purchase merchandise, including food, hardware, clothes, and boots. (Courtesy of Willard Parnell.)

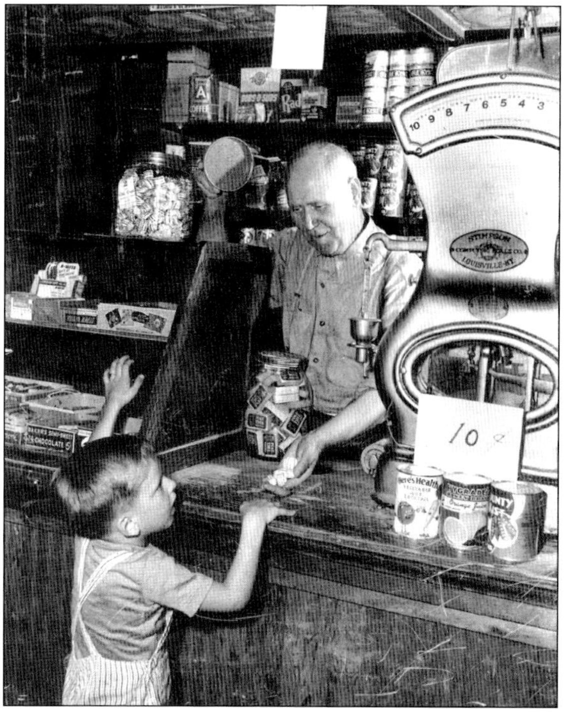

Sam Marcum is selling an item to a little boy in Marcum's Mill Grocery. The large scales were always by the cash register in most stores so the proprietor could weigh produce or meat as customers checked out. Many times, Marcum would come from the mill to take care of the store business. (Courtesy of Cora Emma Jessie.)

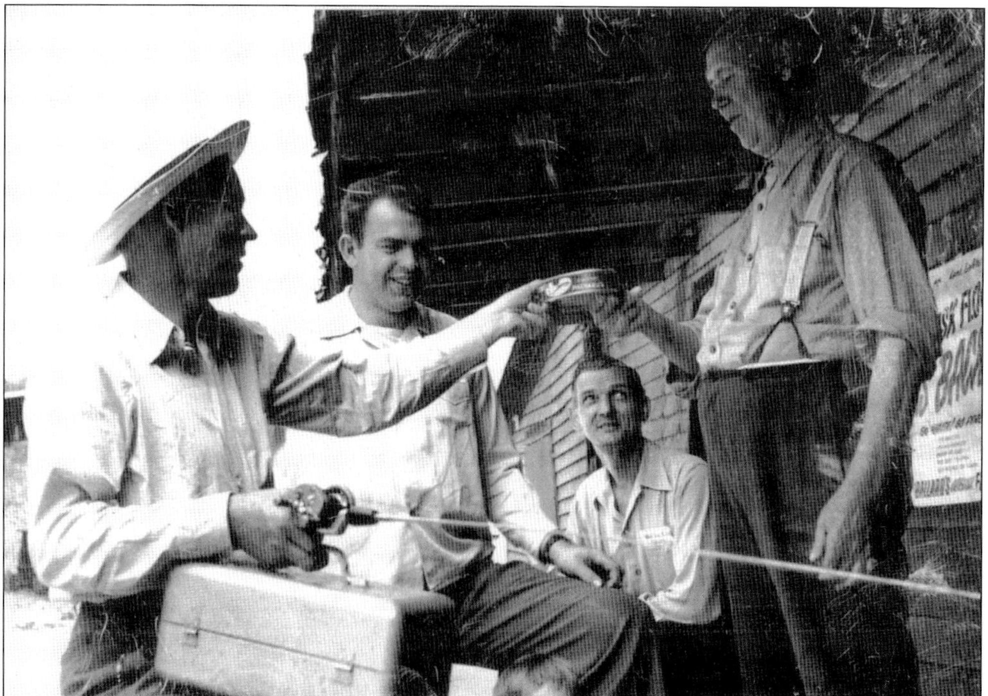

Marcum's Mill was a popular fishing area where fish would hold below the mill dam. Here, Sam Marcum is selling bait to a couple of anglers who are going to try their luck. Country stores not only sold milk, eggs, and other groceries, but also various types of fishing bait, including live minnows, night crawlers, and cut liver, which was used for catfish bait. (Courtesy of Cora Emma Jessie.)

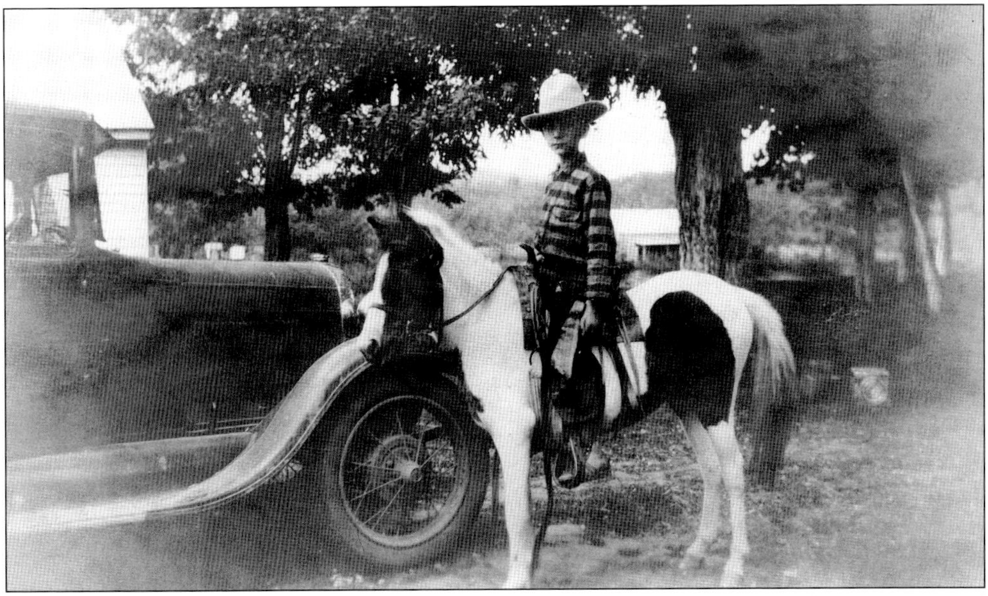

Twelve-year-old James Howard Young sits on his pony Kate. Young would later begin raising and training three-gaited and five-gaited Saddlebred horses and was instrumental in organizing the sport across Kentucky. (Courtesy of Richard Young.)

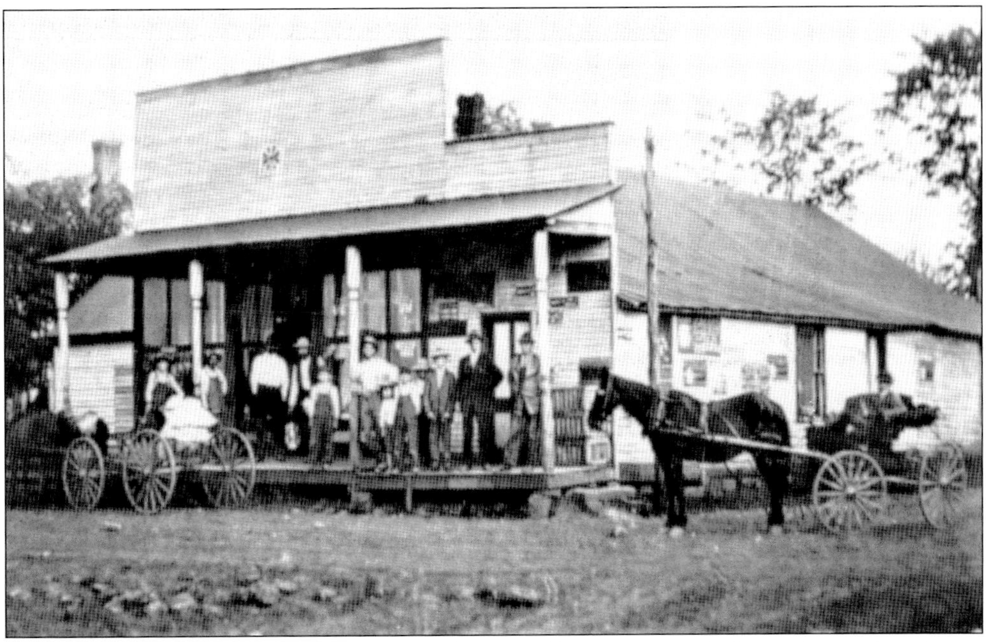

Local residents and customers pose at the Wisdom Store around 1900; it still stands today at the junction of US Highway 68 and Kentucky Highway 640. Built in 1890 by A. Neville, the store was later purchased by James Shirley and Oren and Effie Young in 1922. It served as a post office until 1958. The store sold everything from groceries to cars. It was featured in several Kentucky Headhunters music videos in the 1990s and is still owned by Richard Young. (Courtesy of Richard Young.)

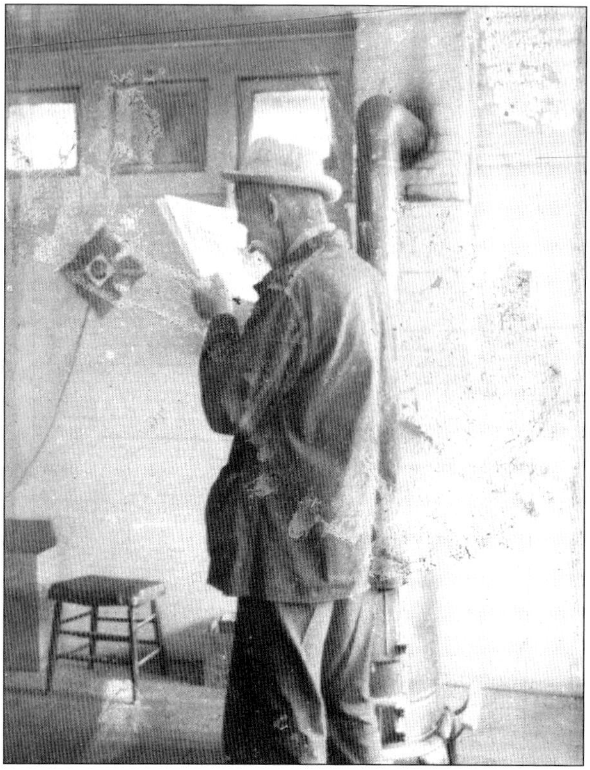

Every country store had either a wood- or coal-burning stove used for heat. It was always the gathering place on cold days. Pictured here is one of the most memorable characters from Sulphur Well, "Uncle" Matt Scroggy, who is staying warm and catching up on the latest news as he reads the *Courier Journal* newspaper. Every store got a daily newspaper, and it was shared among neighbors who stopped by every few days. (Courtesy of Cora Emma Jessie.)

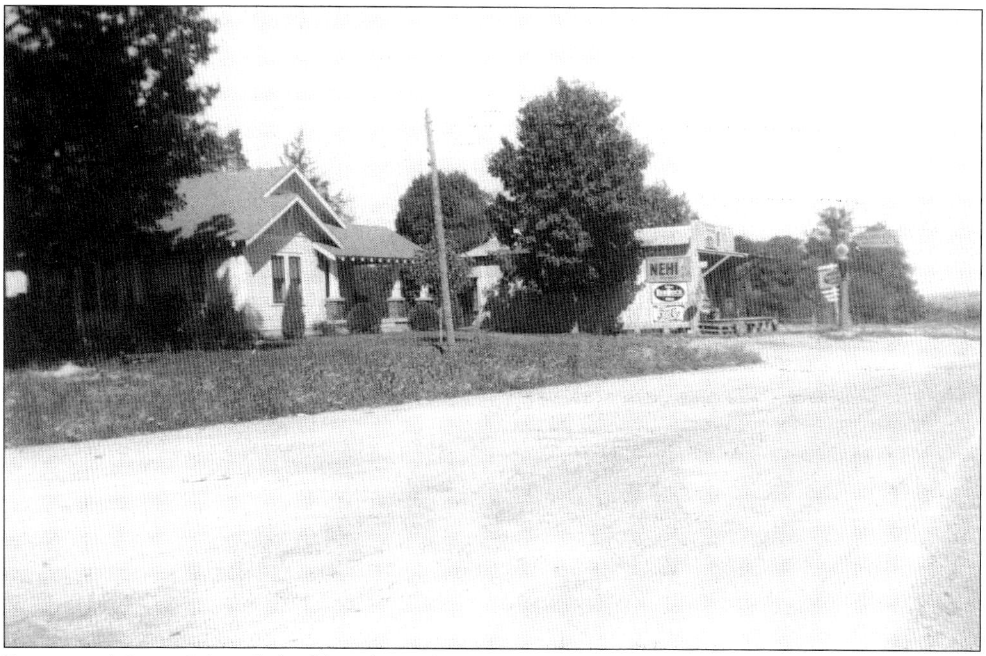

Emory and Rena Edwards had lived in a house near Pleasant Grove until they converted it to a grocery store to make extra money for the family. They sold the farm and store and moved to Cedar Flat, where they opened this larger store that was equipped with a gas pump. (Courtesy of Cebie Edwards.)

Cedar Flat Grocery Store, along the Summer Shade Road (today's Kentucky Route 163), was run by Emory and Rena Edwards for about 40 years. Proprietors of small country stores were expected to take care of every aspect of running the business, from keeping books showing daily sales and charges and stocking shelves to making sandwiches and pumping the gas. The Edwards store had a single gas pump in front, and signs advertising cold drinks were always prominent on the walls. This store closed around 1960. (Courtesy of Cebie Edwards.)

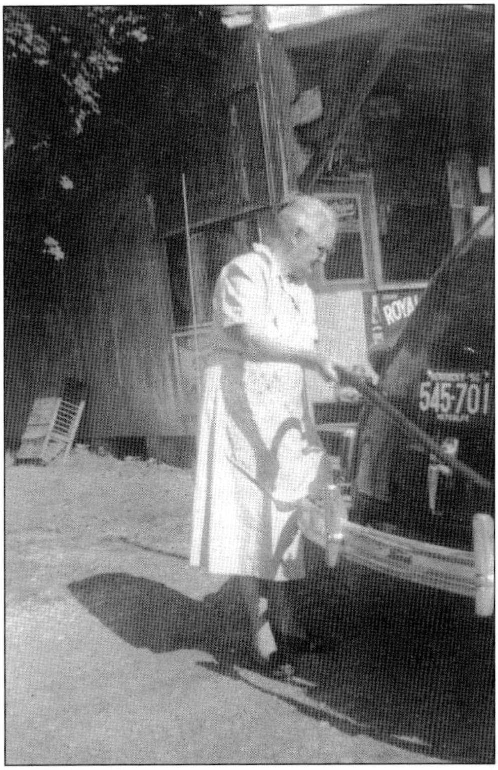

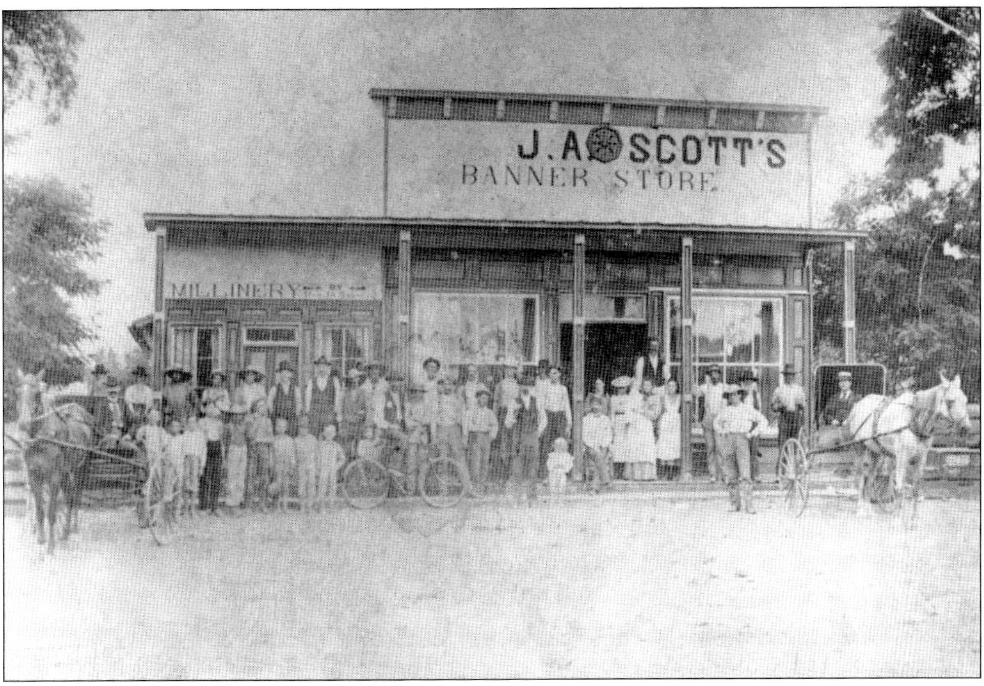

Believed to have been taken around 1905, this photograph shows J.A Scott's Banner Store, which provided all services for residents in the Center community. It looks like everyone in town stopped to have their photograph taken. (Courtesy of Lana Carroll Houk.)

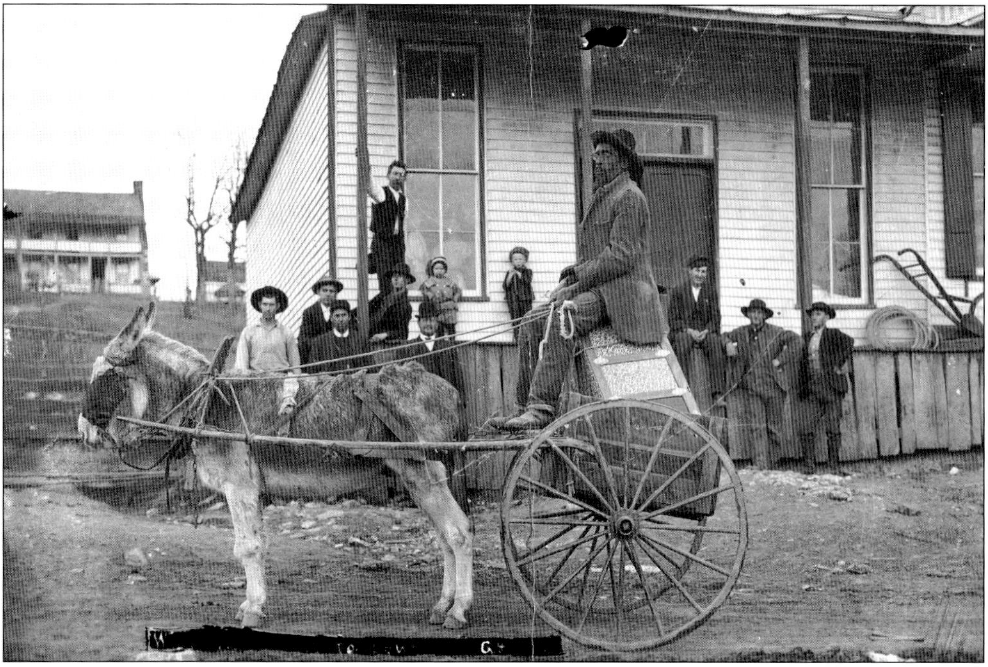

This donkey cart in front of the A.B. Mayfield Store in Summer Shade, Kentucky, is driven by George Nuckells sometime in the early 1900s. The Mayfield store was one of the larger stores in the county and supplied many residents in the south section of Metcalfe County. (Courtesy of Laurie Butler.)

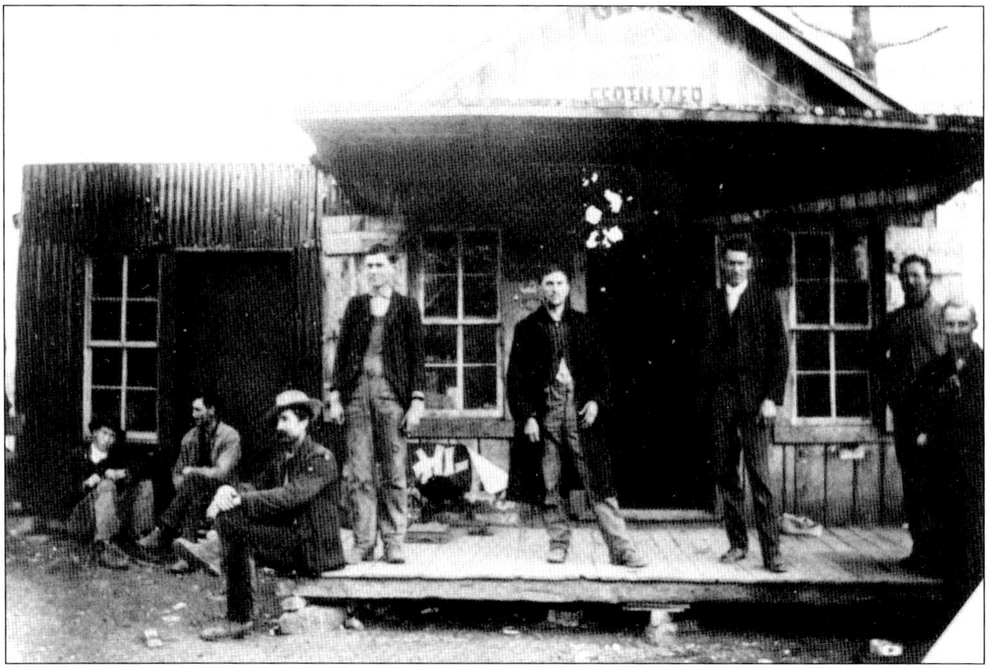

Customers gather at the Node Store around 1905. From left to right are ? Froggett, Will Lane, Will Jones, Harry Lane, Marshall Jolly, Oscar Lane, Jim Jones, and Virgil Lane. (Courtesy of Cora Emma Jessie.)

Bibliography

Campbell, Julian. "Historical Notes on the Big Barrens in Kentucky." bluegrasswoodland.com/uploads/Historical_Notes_on_the_Big_Barrens.pdf. 2012.

Gardiner, Florence Edwards. *Cyrus Edwards' Stories of Early Days and Others: In what is now Barren, Hart, and Metcalfe Counties*. Louisville, KY: Standard Printing Company, 1940.

Martin, Joseph. *A Brief History of Metcalfe County, 1860–1970*. Edmonton, KY: Statesman Heritage Series, 1970.

Newman, J.W., commissioner. *Twentieth Biennial Report of the Bureau of Agriculture, Labor, and Statistics of Kentucky for 1912–1913*. Frankfort, KY: The State Journal Company, 1914.

Perkins, Carol, and Susan Chambers. *Winter Tales: Metcalfe*. Metcalfe County, KY: self-published, 2019.

"Rogers Family." www.so-ky.com/dickinson/book/rogers.htm.

Rush, P.S. Letter to the editor. *Courier Journal*. Louisville, KY, March 25, 1865.

Works Progress Administration and Historical Records Survey. "Metcalf County – General History." scholarworks.moreheadstate.edu/kentucky_county_histories/258. 1939.

Discover Thousands of Local History Books Featuring Millions of Vintage Images

Arcadia Publishing, the leading local history publisher in the United States, is committed to making history accessible and meaningful through publishing books that celebrate and preserve the heritage of America's people and places.

Find more books like this at
www.arcadiapublishing.com

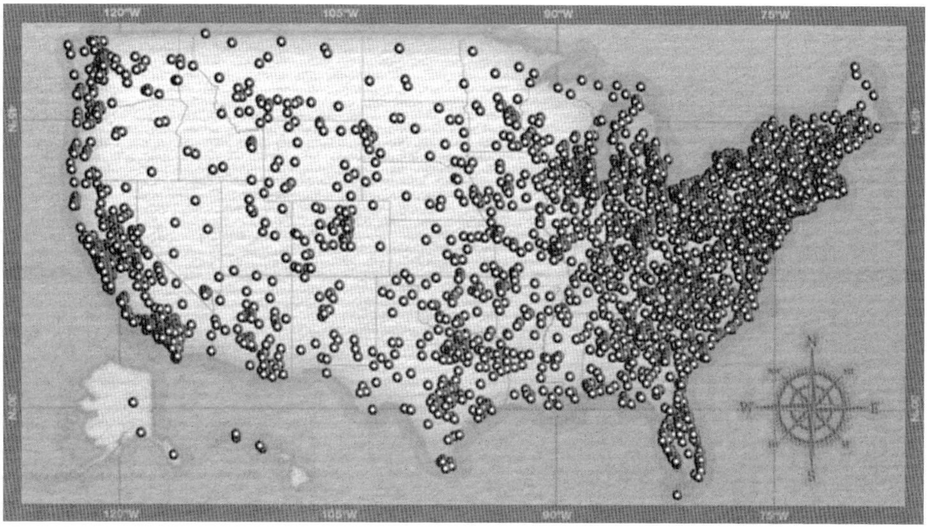

Search for your hometown history, your old stomping grounds, and even your favorite sports team.

Consistent with our mission to preserve history on a local level, this book was printed in South Carolina on American-made paper and manufactured entirely in the United States. Products carrying the accredited Forest Stewardship Council (FSC) label are printed on 100 percent FSC-certified paper.

MADE IN THE USA